DATE DUE

Mind and Brain Sciences in the 21st Century

Mind and Brain Sciences in the 21st Century

edited by Robert L. Solso

A Bradford Book
The MIT Press
Cambridge, Massachusetts
London, England

This book was set in Bembo on the Monotype "Prism Plus" PostScript Imagesetter by Asco Trade Typesetting Ltd., Hong Kong and was printed and bound in the United States of America.

Library of Congress Cataloging-in-Publication Data

Mind and Brain Sciences in the 21st Century / edited by Robert L. Solso.
    p.   cm.
"A Bradford book."
Includes bibliographical references and index.
ISBN 0-262-19385-X (hardcover : alk. paper)
 1. Psychology. 2. Twenty-first century—Forecasts. I. Solso,
Robert L., 1933–   .
BF149.T32   1997   96-43751
150'.1'12—dc20   CIP

To Carl Sagan and Roger W. Sperry
Twentieth-century scientists who led us farther and deeper into the universe
and brain

Contents

Foreword
A Personal View of 20th-Century Psychology:
With an Eye to the 21st Century

Ernest R. Hilgard

Almost a decade ago I finished writing *Psychology in America: A Historical Survey* in which I chose to concentrate on 20th-century psychology in Americas where the growth had been particularly remarkable and where I knew many of the participants and developments personally. Little did I know then that I might be asked to write a foreword to a book with the title *Mind and Brain Sciences in the 21st Century*. You will find in this book a collection of stimulating papers written by many of the people who have had a central role in the shaping of psychology as we now know it. Time, of course, will decide the validity of the prophesies.

As a historian of psychology I have been far more accustomed to writing about the past and what it means than about the future, but welcome the chance to participate in this worthy venture as, after all, "the past is (truly) prologue." We can, of course, learn much from the past as we plot the future of the science of the mind and I would like to offer a brief, personalistic commentary of where we have been, with an eye to where we might be going.

About 100 years ago, psychologists attempted to establish the field as a science among the more recognized sciences that had flourished during that remarkable century. These psychologists, perhaps more so than other scientists, sought to establish a "new psychology" as a systematic body of knowledge, independent and unified according to basic scientific principles and practices. Their ties with philosophy encouraged this desire for a systematic stance. During the early 20th century, the major competing theories in American psychology took the form of schools, each of which wanted to dominate. They had reached their height by the early 1930s, when the summarizing books appeared and contrasts between schools were sharpened. Behaviorism had gradually become ascendant by that time, primarily based on the proposed objectivity of its methods. There had, however, been little systematic development of behaviorism through detailed experimentation designed to justify the theory, rather than to serve other purposes. John B. Watson, who continued to popularize behaviorism, tied it loosely to the conditioned reflex, to extreme environmentalism, and offered proposals for child rearing that were based on a minimum of experimentation and were without careful deduction from formulated theory.

Most psychologists engaged in investigatory work during this period, even though theories of small scope had rather little to do with their day-to-day conception of what it meant to be a psychological scientist. To the typical investigator the general characteristics of science seemed well-known and familiar: careful observations, often aided by instruments; quantitative measurements; appropriate controls so that the variables under study were surely the effective ones; precisely reported procedures so that others could verify the results by repeating what was done; and so on. What was important was the new knowledge generated. Such knowledge was not a mere description of isolated facts; the search was always for some "lawfulness" in the relationships studied. If the lawfulness applied over a larger domain, then it fell in the range of "theoretical explanation." For many investigators, even today, all this seems plain and straightforward. Investigators were then, as now, problem solvers, and problems in a smaller and more accessible domain were more likely to be solved than the very large ones. Now, as we are about to enter the third millennium it would seem that even though the problems will be vastly more complicated, the matter of psychologists breaking down complex problems into manageable questions and solving them might still be an appropriate strategy in advancing knowledge.

Shortly after the midpoint of the 20th century the climate was changing in psychology as well as in the logic of science. Best known was Thomas Kuhn's viewpoint that immediately became popular in which he suggested that science does not advance primarily by accumulation but instead by revolutionary changes in the form of new ways of looking at things, described by him as "paradigm shifts." His proposal struck a very responsive chord. A social-psychological byproduct of this interpretation was that older scientists were so deeply wedded to their paradigms that the newer ones often failed to get acceptance until the older scientists had died and a younger generation took over. There is, in other words, a conservative tendency with respect to those theories that had provided a framework in which science had already advanced.

The advances of science within such an established framework were called by Kuhn "normal science." That is, some of the work of scientists in improving their instruments and methods, or in exploring new lines of investigation, require no shifts in the basic paradigms. For example, the relativity of space and time, which makes Newtonian space-time obsolete, does not make obsolete ordinary mapping of the earth's surface according to Euclidean geometry or ordinary timing of events by clocks or stopwatches, because the space-time continuum has appreciable effects only for events in space near the speed of light. Before a science has reached the stage of elegant theories of wide scope and while it still depends mostly on normal science with somewhat limited theory, it is said to be in a *preparadigmatic* stage. Most of those who tried to apply Kuhn's theory to psychology have agreed that psychology is in that stage.

My own experience in psychology came in a single course with Professor Madison Bentley at the University of Illinois in the first quarter of the 20th century, while I was majoring in chemical engineering. Naturally, I learned from him the psychology most identified with Wilhelm Wundt, by way of E. B. Titchener, who Bentley had worked with at Cornell and later succeeded. This introspective psychology, with its emphasis upon sensation, was commonly know as "structuralism" and was a very influential school of thought in the early years. It remained influential as I shifted my interest to psychology in the course of my Ph.D. studies at Yale, leading to the completion of my degree in 1930.

At Yale, the theoretical position in psychology had shifted to "functionalism," a viewpoint derived more from William James and especially from James R. Angell and John Dewey at the University of Chicago. This position was represented most strongly among my teachers by Edward S. Robinson, who had come to Yale from a faculty position at Chicago. It was a congenial environment because Angell, a former Chicago colleague of Dewey, was the President of Yale.

In the meantime, the new orientation, known as "behaviorism," had developed under Watson at The Johns Hopkins University and other universities, such as at The Ohio State University under A. P. Weiss. To some extent American psychology retained its behaviorist coloring for some 50 years between 1913 and 1963. Still, there were many who were not converted, and held a less rigid position, neither Titchnerian nor Watsonian, and described a psychology of the "middle road," as characterized by the very influential

Robert S. Woodworth. There were, of course, other systems, listed by Woodworth in his book *Contemporary Schools of Psychology* (1931) and by Edna Heidbreder in *Seven Psychologists* (1933). Much later the influential development of cognitive psychology and cognitive neuroscience occurred.

Models as theories became prominent while the psychology of learning was still the focus of American psychological theory, and new mathematical tools began to be used in dealing particularly with the changes taking place during repetitive learning, and with related problems, employing statistical concepts in the special form of stochastic models after 1950. The concept of information theory began to enter in the early 1950s, but the new cognitive psychology did not become prominent until cybernetics emerged a few years later. Then information *processing* began to be substituted for information *theory* and to supersede the prevalent SR (stimulus-response) approach. Thinking in terms of models, such as those of short-term and long-term memory, and feedback relations within them, made it possible for the new cognitive psychology to be recognized as something different from a rediscovery of old ways in psychology's history of studies of perception, memory, imagination, language, and thinking, but now there was a new orientation toward these topics, and new instrumentation, such as the high-speed computer, to give a different view to these old topics. The revitalization at the core of psychology was remarkable, and refreshed as well the many specialized areas of developmental psychology, the psychology of personality, social psychology, and clinical psychology.

In retrospect, the roots of the change can be found much earlier, but the suddenness and widespread adoption of the new standpoint shows how unpredictable such events are in the history of science. Cognitive psychology flourished around 1960 and by 1985 was 25 years old—a very long time for a popular orientation in psychology to retain its ascendancy over novel successors.

The picture of psychology at present, if it is accepted that psychology is still in a preparadigmatic stage as mentioned earlier, is that there will be a kind of pluralism for a time while theories are being tried out over somewhat limited domains of data. The procedures of refinement of the accuracy of operations of the presenting of results so that they can be replicated by others, following the generally acceptable logic of science, will continue to make some gains through accumulation. The collection of new facts will not be simply descriptive, because the smaller theoretical models will produce a selection of facts and perhaps result in significant discoveries in the special fields under investigation.

Today psychology can be conceived of as a large family of many psychologies, unified by social practice and the disciplinary structure of universities. The more typical development has been of subdisciplines interstitial between psychology and other scientific subspecialties, resulting in sensory science; cognitive science, with such subspecialties as linguistics and artificial intelligence; behavioral biology; neuroscience; and life-span development. All of the applied branches are by their very natures interdisciplinary. Why, then, should not their theories be expected to reflect the common problems with which they are involved with their associates from other disciplines?

If the growing edges of science lie in these closely related subspecialties, new disciplines may emerge, as indeed they have in such areas as biochemistry and astrophysics. For example, social psychology belongs both to psychology and to sociology—not a different social psychology for each—and neurocognition, which would be a part of neurology and cognition and brain sciences in general, would seem to be a most natural arrangement. The social organization of sciences may be maintained by tradition, loyalty, and commitment. Science as an intellectual enterprise has criteria of self-renewal and change within its very structure, and the free-market interplay of theories may prove to be the path that will be taken.

In the 100 years of modern psychology, despite many differences, psychologists have continued to have enough in common that we can all identify ourselves as part of a common tradition, distinguishable from related ones such as anthropology and sociology, even though we are interrelated in many ways.

What binds us together are agreement upon a preference for experimental approaches, the use of appropriate statistics in determining the reliability and validity of findings, and a preference for theories that integrate such findings. We have attained status as a legitimate social science and also a biological science, depending upon the subfields under consideration. While we may expect changes, our role as a legitimate member of the scientific disciplines appears to be assured.

Sections of this foreword are drawn from Hilgard, E. R. (1987). *Psychology in America: A historical survey.* New York: Harcourt, Brace, Jovanovich.

Preface

There is a strong need among people to ritualize anniversaries. In 1992, for example, we Americans commemorated Columbus's fortuitous discovery of the "New World," 500 years after he and his mates set foot on dry land in the Caribbean. Also, in 1992, American psychologists celebrated the 100th anniversary of the founding of the American Psychological Association. Traditionally, as the world is about to turn the corner on a new century, there is a palpable increase in people's curiosity about where we have been and where we might be going. When the planet is about to enter a new millennium some people seem to get overly nostalgic; a few scholars may wax philosophically; and other folks get a little giddy as they look forward to a new era. But, to put these matters into perspective, it is only a birthday based on an artificial time continuum. Nevertheless, it is a good excuse for all of us—especially those interested in the science of the mind—to reflect one our past and speculate about our future. That simple premise is the basis for the three-volume series of the future of mind sciences. The first volume, *The Science of the Mind: 2001 and Beyond*[1] appeared in 1995 (in collaboration with Dominic Massaro) and, like the present publication, contained brief essays by distinguished scholars on their visions of the future.

The 20th century has been extraordinary by all measures. Those who lived through this period, such as Ernest Hilgard (born in 1903) who wrote the foreword, and those who have been interested in its intellectual history know, certainly, that the face of science and technology (as well as other features of our lives) has changed radically over the past 100 years and, if the past is an indication of the future, changes during the next century might be even more extreme. (A contrary view is that we have changed the world in such immoderate ways that humans may feel like aliens and, as such, rebel against the artificial and return to more earthy pleasures, which include the appreciation of the natural environment, the arts, music, literature and, in general, a humanistic Renaissance.) One reason the game of predicting the future is so fascinating is the outcome is never certain. However, given an understanding of the resources available and the forces that shape our destiny, an approximation—or an "educated guess," in today's parlance—of what the world might be, is possible. Furthermore, the more serious side of guessing what the future might hold for us is that we might avoid some potentially disastrous pitfalls and maximize the chances for survival and enlightenment. Futures are created, not preordained.

In the initial letter of invitation to prospective contributors to this book I suggested that the papers should be tightly composed, well reasoned, and readable by the informed layperson, as well as stimulating to colleagues and students. When the essays began to arrive it was clear the contributors, in addition to being outstanding scientists, were also talented writers—you will find some beautifully crafted papers in this book. In a few cases the writer pleaded ignorance about the future on the basis of past histories of predictions, but then, happily for us, plunged ahead and made several predictions anyway. Others wrote fantastic papers, bordering on the whimsical or sci-fi to express their thoughts about the future, while others selected a single theme and told of their expectations for its fate. In every case, the contributors to this book worked enthusiastically and with good humor on the task. Even though some of the papers seem to picture the other side of Oz, they all have very serious implications for the type of psychology we might find on the other side of 2000. Each author has won my profound thanks, but more important, has won the appreciation of generations of people who will learn how scientists did psychology throughout the 20th century and what those scientists predicted the next century might bring.

I had an idea as to what types of essays individual authors might produce based on their previous writings. And, for the most part, those expectations were fulfilled. In a few instances however, unexpected essays were submitted, which, in every case, added richness to the book. Each chapter was edited for content, aptness, and style and returned for revision. Thus, the eventual organization of the book was fashioned around the chapters submitted rather than forcing chapters to conform to a preconceived taxonomy. Three major categories emerged: Consciousness and the 21st Century has chapters by Bernard Baars, Carl Sagan and Ann Druyan, Richard Thompson, and Endel Tulving. The second section, Brain and Mind in the 21st Century, contains chapters by Edward Smith, Michael Posner and Dan Levitin, Alan Gevins, Karl Pribram, and Michael Gazzaniga. The third major category is called Psychology

(Memory, Theory, and Cognition) in the 21st Century and has chapters by Henry Roediger, Gay Snodgrass, Jerome Kagan, George Sperling, Neal Miller, and Hans Eysenck. The final section, called The Science of the Mind, has an overview chapter by Robert Solso.

Many people contributed to this book who are gratefully acknowledged here. Each of the authors is recognized for writing an interesting and prophetic chapter. In addition, Jerry Weinstein of The MIT Press gave support, encouragement, and moved the manuscript through what to an outsider seems like a labyrinthine editorial process. Betty Stanton, senior editor of The MIT Press/ Bradford Books, a most sagacious editor indeed, has offered her wise editorial advice and counsel. I am grateful to my graduate students at the University of Nevada, Reno, who read and discussed most of the manuscripts and gave interesting perspectives on the contents. Finally, I wish to acknowledge Kim Beal, who has served as a resident editor who made cogent remarks on most of the chapters, including my own, and to Alan Rees, who not only read and commented on the chapters but also drafted a copy of the biographical sketches.

The assembling of talented psychologists and brain scientists for this volume was not done (entirely) for intellectual amusement but to give insight into the types of worlds which might emerge. These eminent scholars have given you their visions of a world that might be, not what is determined to be. Fortunately, with knowledge of the existing resources, the forces of society and politics, and comprehension of nature, it is possible to plan future societies in which the community of humans may achieve greater understanding of who we are and where we are going. A major goal of The Science of the Mind project is to encourage contemporary scientists and scholars to consider alternative worlds, to make choices about the allocation of resources (both human and physical), and to develop plans to maximize the actualization of favorable conditions and avoid many of the problems we endured during the 20th century.

R.L.S
May 1996
Lake Tahoe, Nevada

Note

1. Solso, R. L., & Massaro, D. W. (Eds.) (1995). *The science of the mind: 2001 and beyond.* New York: Oxford University Press.

I   CONSCIOUSNESS AND THE 21ST CENTURY

1 Psychology in a World of Sentient, Self-Knowing Beings: A Modest Utopian Fantasy

Bernard J. Baars

There is no more important quest in the whole of science probably than the attempt to understand those very particular events in evolution by which brains worked out that special trick that enabled them to add to the cosmic scheme of things: colour, sound, pain, pleasure, and all the other facets of mental experience.

—Roger Sperry

Suppose that in the 21st century, psychology—or more likely biopsychology—actually began to work? And suppose that it began to deal with the reality of our personal experience? What might that world be like?

Western thought began with the Socratic injunction "Know thyself" and Asian philosophies have pursued a similar aim throughout history. Science has allowed us to know the world with stunning depth and accuracy, changing the conditions of life for humans more than any other development since the invention of agriculture, 10 millenia ago. But it has been extraordinarily difficult to turn the powerful lens of science inward, toward ourselves, so much so that for most of this century psychology and the brain sciences have tended to evade the very existence of our own experience. That denial is now on the way out, and we are beginning to gain a firmer understanding of consciousness, voluntary control, and even self.

Many scientific students of consciousness believe that the necessary evidence and theory have begun to build in a sustained way in the last 10 years or so, and that this process is now accelerating. In a decade or so we may have an early biopsychology of consciousness. Not an ultimate understanding (if such a thing exists), and certainly not one that is immune to further shifts, but some genuine scientific knowledge nevertheless. If that prediction is anywhere near accurate, humans will be confronted with something entirely new, because the only sciences we know are sciences of *otherness*, of things outside of ourselves. What would this unprecedented event mean for everyday life?

Is It a Clearly Defined Phenomenon?

For many decades it was customary in psychology to dismiss personal experience, because there seemed to be no way to obtain solid evidence about it, and theory was simply inconceivable. Many of us now believe that that was a self-fulfilling prophecy, a sort of avoidant confirmation bias. If you think a subject is impossible to study, you won't study it, thereby "proving" that it is impossible to study. Avoidant thinking is not unusual in the history of science, but like any unreasonable fear, we must eventually confront the things we have been avoiding, or give up the whole enterprise.

Table 1.1 shows 25 polarities that have been found useful in the last decade or two in studies of human cognition. They range from "attended vs. unattended information" and "explicit vs. implicit memory," all the way to "waking EEG compared to deep sleep and coma." Each polar pair of terms is fundamental for a considerable scientific literature. To a considerable extent, all 25 polarities can be captured under two major headings: conscious and unconscious phenomena. The realization that we have been "speaking consciousness" all of our lives has been coming home to many of us, and the consensus seems to be that we might as well call the thing by its proper name. That is not to say that we have a well-established grasp of the problem today, but we seem to be making incremental progress, just as we have been able to make progress on other formidable topics such as attention, perception, and language.

Evidence

In its major features consciousness is not a subtle thing. When humans are not conscious, our bodies wilt, our eyes roll up in their orbits, our brain waves become large, slow, and regular, and we cannot read a sentence like this one.

While the outer signs of consciousness are pretty clear, it is our inner life that counts for most of us. At this instant you and I are surely conscious of some aspects of the act of reading—the shape of *these letters* against the white texture of *this page*, and the inner sound of *these words*. But we are probably not

Table 1.1
Polar pairs of terms used in contemporary psychology

Associated with Consciousness	Associated with Unconsciousness
1. Explicit cognition	1. Implicit cognition
2. Immediate memory	2. Long-term memory
3. Controlled processes	3. Automatic processes
4. Novel, informative, and significant information	4. Old, predictable, or insignificant information
5. Attended stimulation	5. Nonattended stimulation
6. Declarative memory (beliefs)	6. Procedural memory (skills)
7. Autobiographical memory	7. Semantic memory
8. Supraliminal stimulus processing	8. Subliminal stimulus processing
9. Recalled memories	9. Stored memories
10. Explicit goals, decisions, problem-solving	10. Implicit goals, decisions, incubation
11. Available memories	11. Unavailable memories
12. Stimuli in implicit learning	12. Learned pattern in implicit learning
14. Rehearsed item in working memory	14. Unrehearsed items in working memory
15. Current images	15. Images in memory, or which are automatic
17. Wakefulness and dreams (rapid EEG)	17. Deep sleep and coma (slow EEG)
18. Wide access to mental functions	18. Local access to mental routines
19. Voluntary control	19. Automatisms used by voluntary system
20. Explicit reasoning	20. Unconscious inferences
21. Focal contents	21. Fringe experiences (feelings of familiarity, etc.)
23. Autonoetic (E. Tulving)	23. Noetic memory
24. Intact reticular formation and intralaminar nuclei	24. Lesioned reticular formation and intralaminar nuclei
25. Explicit ideas, beliefs, etc.	25. Presupposed or implicit ideas

aware of the touch of the chair, of a certain background taste, the subtle balancing of our body against gravity, a flow of conversation in the background, or the syntax of *this phrase*; nor are we aware of the fleeting present of only a few seconds ago, of our affection for a friend, or the multiple meanings of words, as in *this case*. There is nevertheless good evidence that such unconscious events are actively processed in our brains, every waking moment of the day.

The contents of consciousness include the immediate perceptual world; inner speech and visual imagery; the fleeting present and its fast-fading traces in immediate memory; bodily feelings like pleasure, pain and excitement; surges of emotional feelings; autobiographical memories; clear and immediate intentions, expectations, and actions; explicit beliefs about oneself and the world; and concepts that are abstract but focal. In spite of decades of behavioristic avoidance, few would quarrel with this list today.

These examples illustrate the meaning of the word "consciousness" we are trying to understand: that is, focal consciousness of easily described events, like "I see a printed page," or "I am imagining my mother's face." A great body of objective evidence shows that conscious contents like these can be reported *as conscious* with great accuracy under the right conditions. These conditions include immediate report, freedom from distraction, and some means for corroborating the report. These are standard laboratory conditions in thousands of experiments in perception, memory, language, attention, and imagery. In all these conditions subjects will tell us they are conscious of certain events, and it is always a good idea as a psychologist to listen to your subjects.

The Rebirth of Consciousness in Science

Outside of psychology the greatest impetus to consciousness research has come from prominent researchers in biology and brain science, notably Francis Crick, Gerald Edelman, Rodolfo Llinás, Michael Gazzaniga, and many others. Crick, Edelman, and Gazzaniga in particular have been influential in encouraging brain researchers to work on the empirically accessible parts of the problem, of which there are now quite a few.

In psychology the renewal of consciousness studies has its roots in the cognitive revolution of the 1970s, which set the framework for much of contemporary psychology. After a long series of very careful experiments on what we now call "working memory" and "selective attention," psychologists found themselves making careful *inferences* to explain the observations. Making inferences about explanatory entities is a standard gambit in science, of course. "Atoms" were entirely inferential to Dalton, though today we can observe atomic lattices with electron micrographs. The existence of the planet Pluto was first inferred from perturbations in the orbit of the more visible outer planets. The vast depth of geological time was inferred from the fossil record, the layering of rock on an exposed mountain side, and the decay of carbon 14. The list of inferential constructs simply goes on and on. Science simply cannot grow without making inferences, "going beyond the information given," as Jerome Bruner has phrased it. There is no reason for psychology to be different.

George Miller's famous paper on the "magical number seven, plus or minus two" provides a nice illustration. It appeared in 1956, at the start of the "cognitive revolution" in psychology. Alfred Binet, the French pioneer psychologist, already knew that people cannot keep in mind more than five to nine unrelated numbers. It seemed to be a more-or-less random fact, a little like the observation that many people, when asked to choose a number between 1 and 10, will choose 7. Miller was smart enough to notice that we are actually "persecuted by an integer"—that the magic number reappears over and over again in our evidence, whenever we study the way human beings deal with unrelated sets of words, numbers, colors, short phrases, tones, and rating categories. Of course, we can always "chunk" sets of unrelated numbers by learning predictable number sequences, chunks like 1900, 1914, and 1776. But then the immediate memory limit turns into seven plus or minus two *chunks*. The magic number simply pops out in a different form.

A vast outpouring of research followed Miller's 1956 paper, by and large confirming a powerful and unexpected pattern of results that stayed solid across many different kinds of items and conditions. Eventually that solid behavioral pattern came to be understood to reflect the operation of a "buffer memory," an interface between the timing of events in the outer world and in memory. *A sentence like this one cannot be understood unless somehow we can store the underlined words for several seconds, while we wait for the rest of the sentence to arrive, with the information needed to complete a coherent thought*. The words *a coherent thought* in the last sentence came perhaps 5 to 10 seconds after the subject, *a sentence like this one*. Yet the later words must be integrated with the earlier ones in a way that makes sense. We can even switch the beginning and ending of the sentence by writing a paraphrase: *The information needed to* *complete **a coherent thought** may arrive several seconds after the subject of **a sentence** **like this one has** been introduced.* Our brains are constructed so that the order of subject and object does not matter very much. But that seems to imply the existence of a short-term memory for sentences, one that allows words arriving at different times to be organized in a meaningful structure, regardless of which arrived first.

Now we can do many other things with immediate memory. We can easily interfere with our ability to understand the italicized sentence above, by reading it again while keeping in mind a few arbitrary numbers, let's say 31, 15, and 11. Try it—you'll see that it now becomes quite difficult to understand. But that suggests that short-term memory for language and for numbers is the same thing, or at least that they make use of overlapping mental resources. Dozens of other manipulations are possible, and they create a robust and broadly understandable pattern of results.

Constructs like "short-term memory" were soon followed by many others: "semantic networks," "imagery," "implicit knowledge," "mental grammars," and the like. Today we routinely use our data to index underlying explanatory entities. It must be done carefully, to avoid circularity. But once we have found a vast array of evidence indicating there is such a thing as immediate memory, or elemental oxygen, we can use the construct to explain new observations, to tie all of the evidence together into a cohesive story.

Making inferences about psychological constructs is a crucial step for understanding consciousness. Once psychologists developed the habit of postulating inferred constructs to explain and simplify a solid pattern of observations, there was no more *principled* objection to thinking of consciousness in just the same way, as a theoretical construct based on reliable, public evidence.

The cognitive approach to consciousness can be understood strictly in terms of public evidence, the things we can all agree upon. But consciousness is special, of course. Each of us has some useful access to our own experience that is not shared by others. Some things, especially perceptual events, can be accessed consciously with extraordinary precision—witness 150 years of solid scientific work in sensory psychophysics. Mental images can be reported quite accurately, as shown by Stephen Kosslyn and others. Inner speech has been found to be quite reliable in studies of mental problem solving and spontaneous thought.

Other aspects of mental functioning are very hard to operationalize with private reports. Long-term intentions are notoriously difficult to report accurately; witness the self-deception we all engage in annually with New Year's resolutions. We can feel utterly convinced that we intend to drop those 15 pounds, but apparently it is difficult to distinguish between long-term goals that will be carried out and those that are destined to fade in a few weeks.

From a scientific point of view we cannot share our personal experience directly with one another, so that we deal publicly only with *descriptions* of experiences. But for many well-studied phenomena the subjective and objective evidence converges so well that the distinction has little practical meaning. We can all understand perceptual events, like the reader's experience of *this page*, from a subjective or an objective point of view. Indeed, perception researchers tacitly recognize the close mapping between subjective and objective descriptions of experimental stimuli, when they routinely "run themselves" in any new experiment. We could pretend that perceptual events do not apply to our own experience, and that we are only exploring the objective behavioral and brain processes of an utterly unknown species infesting the surface of the fourth planet of Sol. But that pretense is not necessary, because in most experimental situations the inside and outside perspectives dovetail so well. This pattern of convergence persuades me at least that in practice, the famous gap between mind and body is a bit of a myth.

Contrastive Analysis; Treating Consciousness as a Variable

Earth gravity is so constant in our experience that its very existence goes unnoticed. Historically, it took a great effort of imagination to understand that gravitational attraction could be different elsewhere in the universe than on earth. Newton's ability to take that imaginative leap made it possible to solve the ancient mystery of planetary motion. In the same way, 19th-century naturalists had to *learn* to think of species as changeable—animals and plants appear to be immutable, after all. Prior to Darwin few naturalists believed in the gradual evolution of species, but seeing species as varying over time made it possible to understand the living world.

William James, along with most educated people in the 19th century, could not imagine consciousness as a variable, because he believed it was the *only* proper topic for psychology. Nothing was in any way commensurate with it. Yet he knew about the principle of comparison. In discussing the functions of consciousness he wrote:

> The study ... of *the distribution* of consciousness shows it to be exactly such as we might expect in an organ added for the sake of steering a nervous system grown too complex to regulate itself. (Emphasis added)

That is the essence of the experimental method, but it was not conceptually possible to apply it to conscious experience until surprisingly recently, perhaps as recent as the last 20 years. James could not apply the standard scientific strategy of comparison to consciousness as such, because he believed that it was the sole instance of mentality, while *un*conscious events were "only physical." Most people in the 19th century could not imagine that conscious and unconscious events could be compared. "Unconscious intelligence" was a bizarre oxymoron to our greatgrandparents. Consciousness was the crown of human reason; unconsciousness was a different metaphysical substance.

We know something about the reader's experience of *this word*, and we have some evidence about its unconscious representation when the same word is provided subliminally, or in an unattended channel, or when it has become automatic through repetition. Indeed, we now have robust evidence that for many conscious events, we can find unconscious analogues. We know that unattended speech is processed at least up to the meaning of individual words, that subliminal words can stimulate mental processes related to the meaning of those words, and that the reader's mind even now is computing the syntax of *this sentence*, quite unconsciously. That is, we can find comparison conditions in which the content of input is held constant, while consciousness can be varied. Thus we can treat consciousness as a variable across a great variety of cases.

When we run these comparisons in detail, we obtain the pattern of results shown in table 1.2. The left column shows that conscious processes tend to be computationally inefficient, which is to say that a conscious symbolic computation, like mental arithmetic, seems to be slow and vulnerable to error and interference. Of course the range of conscious contents is vast: imagine all the sensory contents, all the mental images, the memories, ideas, and so on. Conscious events are always internally consistent, they occur serially, one after the next, and have limited capacity. In the right-hand column are unconscious comparison conditions. If we compare automatic computation, like analyzing the syntax of a sentence, with conscious computation, it is clear that automatic processes tend to be highly efficient, fast, and robust. There is much evidence

Table 1.2
Capabilities of conscious and unconscious processes

Conscious processes	Unconscious processes
1. Computationally inefficient: e.g., mental arithmetic.	1. Very efficient in routine tasks: e.g., syntax.
Many errors, relatively low speed, and mutual interference between conscious processes.	Few errors, high speed, and little mutual interference.
2. Great range of contents.	2. Each routine process has a limited range of contents.
3. High internal consistency at any single moment, seriality over time, and limited processing capacity.	3. The set of routine, unconscious processes is diverse, can sometimes operate in parallel, and together has great processing capacity.

that each unconscious patch of neural tissue is specialized in just a single function, but that all the specialized patches operate in parallel, all at the same time. Taking the unconscious specialized tissues of the brain together, they have vast processing capacity.

This pattern of evidence has been interpreted in a framework called Global Workspace (GW) theory (Baars, 1988). GW theory presents a "theater model" in which consciousness requires a central workspace, much like the stage of a theater. The theory is based on the belief that, like the cells of the human body, the detailed workings of the brain are widely distributed. There is no centralized command that tells neurons what to do. Just as each cell in the body is controlled by its own molecular code, the adaptive networks of the brain are controlled by their own aims and contexts. To organize this vast distributed domain, there is a network of neural patches that work together to display conscious events. Today the best candidates for these loci of conscious experience may be the sensory projection areas of the cortex, where the great neural radiations coming from the eyes, the ears, and the body first reach the surface of the brain. A few small structures of the core brain stem and midbrain are essential to consciousness, but great quantities of tissue elsewhere in the brain can be lost without causing a loss of conscious experience. Conscious contents appear to be disseminated globally to a great multitude of networks throughout the brain that are unconscious but that have observable conscious consequences downstream.

As it happens, all unified theories of cognition today are theater models. GW theory derives from the integrative modeling tradition of Allan Newell,

Herbert A. Simon, John Anderson, and others in cognitive science. It is consistent with models of working memory by Alan Baddeley, of the mind's eye by Stephen Kosslyn, of explicit knowledge after brain damage by Daniel Schacter and Morris Moscovitch, the thalamocortical searchlight elaborated by Francis Crick, and society models outlined by Michael Gazzaniga and Marvin Minsky. The brain implications of GW theory have been explored by James Newman and myself. British mathematician John G. Taylor and others are working to apply modern "neural net" models to the problem. The convergence of ideas today is simply astonishing.

It seems now that the failure of 19th-century psychology was not primarily a matter of *empirical* difficulties in dealing with questions like "imageless thought." Rather, it seems now that it was a *conceptual* inability to understand the very idea of an intelligent unconscious. I believe that James's often desperate inner struggles with mind-body issues stem largely from this single conceptual block: his inability, and that of his entire generation, to deal with consciousness as a variable with a natural comparison condition. Such conceptual blocks are of course utterly routine historically. One can see the history of science as a process of grappling with, yielding to, and finally overcoming conceptual blocks much like this one.

Behaviorists after James's death in 1910 rejected the whole topic because it seemed rife with endless, useless perplexities. They made little progress on it because they avoided *both* conscious *and* unconscious processes. They, too, were unable to see consciousness as a variable. Neither James nor Skinner could apply the experimental method to the most humanly important topic of all.

If we live at an historic time for the study of human experience, it is not just that we have more facts but because we can treat consciousness as something that exists to a greater or lesser degree, something with a comparison condition. When we repeat a single word to the point where its meaning fades from consciousness, consciousness is a *dependent* variable. When we observe the effects of an anesthetic on learning, consciousness is an *independent* variable. Most theoretical constructs in science can be explored either as dependent or independent variables, and consciousness is no exception. In a slightly different vocabulary, conscious experience is both a cause and an effect. It participates in a network of inferred and observable relationships with the rest of reality.

Today, spectacular new imaging techniques are giving us remarkable insight into the living brain. Experimental methods have been honed to great precision, so that we routinely measure the time course of mental processes, down to a few tens of milliseconds. We have much improved ways of modeling neural nets and cognitive architectures. But even the best technical tools do not help if we cannot *think* about our topic with clarity. That is why the notion of contrastive analysis, of "treating consciousness as a variable," is crucial.

What's Different About Psychological Knowledge

There is something different in learning about oneself compared to learning about the external world. Scientific knowledge about stars and atoms and species has had the most astonishing impact on our view of the world. But scientific knowledge about *ourselves* may be different. It seems to me that knowledge about ourselves has immediate implications, even about our values and ethics. It isn't that we now have a scientific basis for values, but rather that facts about ourselves tend to raise compelling value implications.

Take an example. Suppose you enjoy smoking cigarettes, but some believable person tells you of the health risks. In one sense those risks are just another fact. Yet the facts present to smokers a frightening threat of a painful and premature death. That sort of connection seems to exist often when we learn facts about ourselves. In these cases, scientific findings do not need to carry any value implications, because we fill those in ourselves. If we hear someone yell "Fire!" we seldom simply take that as a statement of fact, although we certainly want to know whether it is true or not. Facts about ourselves are motivationally powerful, not because science has suddenly gained the ability to legislate true values (I don't think it can), but because most humans understandably fear death and pain. In that sense, a deeper understanding of conscious experience may carry value implications in the minds of many people, even though strictly speaking scientific findings are value neutral.

Consider the following example.

Consciousness is Humanizing: The Example of Inner Speech

Inner speech is one of the basic facts of human nature, one that takes only a few minutes to demonstrate. Try, for example, to *stop* the flow of your own inner speech a few times, just to see how predictable the urge to talk really is. I cannot do it for more than 5 seconds, and that seems to be roughly true for most people. Self-talk seems to be an uncontrollable compulsion, something pretty basic in the human condition. Indeed, most people seem to spend more hours talking to themselves than to anyone else. Social psychologists like Jerome Singer and John Antrobus have been especially productive in exploring spontaneous inner speech. Inner speech also corresponds to the verbal component of "working memory."

Yet earlier in this century positivist philosophers denounced the whole idea as meaningless. Ludwig Wittgenstein inveighed against "mentalistic language"—the reality of such things as the inner monologue—as "a general disease of thinking," and later took a strong stand against the possibility of any "private language."

Given how easy it is to demonstrate the inner monologue, and how reliable the results can be, you might expect introductory psychology textbooks to begin by describing the easily accessible evidence for inner speech. It is rarely even mentioned. Self-talk was not studied during the seven decades of behaviorism because it could not be observed directly, and even today most psychologists don't give it much thought. (They don't talk much to themselves about inner speech!) Yet the data are reliable, and there are many ways to corroborate them (Newell & Simon 1972; Ericsson & Simon, 1994; Baddeley, 1992).

In respect of reliability there is little difference between inner speech and color perception, which has been studied very successfully since the time of Newton and Goethe. We have two centuries of careful scientific thought about color, and very little about the running narrative of our lives. It is a great historical anomaly.

For psychologists it is interesting just to imagine the inner monologue that people around us are carrying on, in the privacy of their minds. What could our family members and colleagues be saying to themselves at this moment? Our students? That elderly man in the park, or those bored-looking children? We do not need to pry. Just acknowledging the experiences others may be having tends to humanize them in our minds. It changes them from animated bodies into private worlds.

What has happened to a psychology that ignores the inner voice? It is obviously missing a major modality of experience. Has it not become inadvertently depersonalized? For many people, psychology is a major source of knowledge about themselves. But in colleges throughout the industrialized world we teach a psychology without personal consciousness—without inner speech, mental imagery, in fact, absent the entire rich stream of thought. That is something to worry about. Are we inadvertently depersonalizing our students' lives?

We tend to think of the sciences as directed outward, discovering things about the world. But science also shapes our framework for looking at the world. Ideas have consequences, and mistaken ideas about ourselves surely have self-alienating consequences. I would suggest that *consciousness is humanizing*. As we become more surefooted in this new territory, I believe a new kind of science may arise, that will on the evidence alone encourage a richer sense of self and other. This kind of self-understanding will grow, not by evading objectivity but rather by cultivating it. That is one reason why our return to human experience has implications far beyond the laboratory.

Psychology in a World of Sentient, Self-Knowing Beings

To return to the title of this chapter, what would it be like to live in a world of sentient, self-knowing beings? The utopian temptation has long been part of psychology, from the recruitment of Pavlovian conditioning to help create the New Soviet Man in the 1930s, to Skinner's Walden Two. It is out of fashion today, but what if human consciousness becomes as unavoidable a fact as the law of practice or the psychophysical curve? We might then have to acknowledge the reality of one another's experience much more than we do today.

Not that such a development would bring about a utopian world. But there is a sort of complementarity between human beings—a golden rule, if you like—that proclaims that if I step on your toe, your experience resembles the one I would have if you stepped on mine. Scientifically, that complementarity has not been recognized as a major fact, because we have avoided the issue for so long. But once we can see sensorimotor cortex "lighting up" on a brain scan when your toe is stepped on, just at the very moment you say "Ouch!"—well, then denying the other's experience becomes pretty tenuous.

How would that knowledge change the world? It is a science fiction question, of course, one that we cannot answer today with any certainty. But it seems increasingly likely that the premise will come true relatively soon. The scientific evidence about conscious experience is mounting steadily, and perhaps even more important, we are trying out new ideas for thinking about it.

Ready or Not, Here Comes the New Millenium

As I write this chapter it is 4 years before the third millenium. For the past century or so, scientists and philosophers have been hotly debating personal experience—not its nature, but whether we are even *allowed to think about it.* All too often we engage in preliminary arguments that never touch on the issue itself, thereby shutting out any discussion of consciousness as such. Yet personal experience can be treated much like other psychological constructs, like immediate memory, selective attention, grammar, semantic networks, and all the others. We only need to view consciousness as a variable, comparing closely matched instances of conscious and unconscious events.

As we are drawn inexorably, day by day, toward January 1, 2001, the debate is finally evolving into a genuine scientific question: not whether, but *how* to tackle this wonderful and humbling topic. I believe the time for "whether" is long gone. After a century of preliminary debates, we may now be able to make some solid progress toward understanding.

Bibliography

Baars, B. J. (1986). *The cognitive revolution in psychology.* New York: Guilford Press.

Baars, B. J. (1988). *A cognitive theory of consciousness.* New York: Cambridge University Press.

Baars, B. J. (1993). Why volition is a foundation issue for psychology. *Consciousness & Cognition, 2*(4), 281–309.

Baars, B. J., & McGovern, K. A. (1994). Consciousness. In V. S. Ramachandran (Ed.), *Encyclopedia of behavior,* New York: Academic Press.

Baars, B. J. (1996). *Consciousness discovered: A walk through the theater of mind.* New York: Oxford University Press.

Baars, B. J. (in press) Treating consciousness as an empirical variable: The contrastive analysis approach. In N. Block, O. Flanagan, & G. Guzeldere (Eds.), *Consciousness in philosophy and science.* Cambridge, MA: MIT Press.

Baddeley, A. (1992). Working memory and conscious awareness. In A. F. Collins, S. E. Gathercole, M. A. Conway, and P. E. Morris (Eds.) *Theories of memory,* pp. 11–20. Hove: Lawrence Erlbaum Assoc.

Crick, F., & Koch, C. (1992). The problem of consciousness. *Scientific American, 267,* 152–159.

Ericsson, K. A., & Simon, H. A. (1994). *Protocol analysis: Verbal reports as data.* (2nd ed.) Cambridge, MA: MIT Press.

James, W. (1890/1983). *The principles of psychology.* Cambridge, MA: Harvard University Press.

Newell, A., & Simon, H. A. (1972). *Human problem solving.* Englewood Cliffs, NJ: Prentice-Hall.

Newman, J., & Baars, B. J. (1993). A neural attentional model for access to consciousness: A Global Workspace perspective. *Concepts in Neuroscience, 4*(2), 255–290.

2   **What Thin Partitions . . .**

CARL SAGAN AND ANN DRUYAN

How instinct varies in the grovelling swine,
Compar'd, half-reasoning elephant, with thine!
'Twixt that, and reason, what a nice barrier,
Forever sep'rate, yet forever near!
Remembrance and reflection how ally'd!
What thin partitions sense from thought divide!

—Alexander Pope, *Essay on Man*

Is there an unbridgeable gap between the consciousness of humans and other animals? Or is there a continuum between them, perhaps going all the way back to the micro-organisms of the primeval seas? In this chapter, we argue that the partition that divides the cognitive lives of the beings on Earth is very thin. Clearly, much can be learned on the nature of human consciousness by studying congenor processes in other beings— whether of biological or technological origin. Light has been progressively shed on this matter in each of the last four centuries. Conceivably, the issue will be largely settled in the next.

Most people would rather be alive than dead. But why? It's hard to give a coherent answer. An enigmatic "will to live" or "life force" is often cited. But what does that explain? Even victims of atrocious brutality and intractable pain may retain a longing, sometimes even a zest, for life. Why, in the cosmic scheme of things, one individual should be alive and not another is a difficult question, an impossible question, perhaps even a meaningless question. Life is a gift that, of the immense number of possible but unrealized beings, only the tiniest fraction are privileged to experience. Except in the most hopeless of circumstances, hardly anyone is willing to give it up voluntarily—at least until very old age is reached.

A similar puzzlement attaches to sex. Very few, at least today, have sex for the conscious purpose of propagating the species or even their own personal DNA; and such a decision for such a purpose, coolly and rationally entered into, is exceedingly rare in adolescents. (For most of the tenure of humans on Earth, the average person did not live much beyond adolescence.) Sex is its own reward.

Passions for life and sex are built into us, hard-wired, preprogrammed. Between them, they go a long way toward arranging for many offspring with slightly differing genetic characteristics, the essential first step for natural selection to do its work. So we are the mostly unconscious tools of natural selection, indeed its willing instruments. As deeply as we can go in assessing our own feelings, we do not recognize any underlying purpose. All that is added later. All the social and political and theological justifications are attempts to rationalize, after the fact, human feelings that are at the same time utterly obvious and profoundly mysterious.

Now imagine us with no interest at all in "explaining" such matters, no weakness for reason and contemplation. Suppose you unquestioningly accepted these predispositions for surviving and reproducing, and spent your time solely in fulfilling them. Might that be something like the state of mind of most beings? Every one of us can recognize these two modes coexisting within us. A moment of introspection is often all it takes. Religious writers have described them as our animal and spiritual states. In everyday speech, the distinction is between feeling and thought. Inside our heads there seem to be two different ways of dealing with the world, the second, in the sweep of evolutionary time, arisen in earnest only lately.

Consider the world of the tick. Plumbing aside, what must it do to reproduce its kind? Ticks often have no eyes. Males and females find each other by aroma, olfactory cues called sex pheromones. For many ticks the pheromone is a molecule called 2,6-dichlorophenol. If C stands for a carbon atom, H for hydrogen, O for oxygen, and Cl for chlorine, this ring-shaped molecule can be written $C_6H_3OHCl_2$. A little 2,6-dichlorophenol in the air and ticks go wild with passion.

After mating, the female climbs up a bush or shrub and out onto a twig or leaf. How does she know which way is up? Her skin can sense the direction from which light is coming, even if she cannot generate an optical image of her surroundings. Poised out on the leaf or twig, exposed to the elements, she waits. Conception has not yet occurred The sperm cells within her are neatly encapsulated; they've been put in long-term storage. She may wait for months or even years without eating. She is very patient.

What she's waiting for is a smell, a whiff of another specific molecule, perhaps butyric acid, which can be written C_3H_7COOH. Many mammals, including humans, give off butyric acid from their skin and sexual parts. A small cloud of the stuff follows them around like cheap perfume. It's a sex attractant for mammals. But ticks use it to find food for prospective mothers. Smelling the butyric acid wafting up from below, the tick lets go. She drops from her perch and falls through the air, legs akimbo. If she's lucky, she lands on the passing mammal. (If not, she falls to the ground, shakes herself off, and tries to find another bush to climb.)

Clinging to the fur of her unsuspecting host, she works her way through the thicket to find a less hairy spot, a patch of nice warm bare skin. There, she punctures the epidermis and drinks her fill of blood.[1]

The mammal may feel a sting and rub the tick off, or intently comb through its hair and pick it off. Rats may spend as much as one-third their waking hours grooming themselves. Ticks can draw a great deal of blood, they secrete neurotoxins, they carry disease microbes. They're dangerous. Too many of them on a mammal at the same time can lead to anemia, loss of appetite, and death. Monkeys and apes meticulously search through each other's fur; this is one of their principal cultural idioms. When they find a tick, they remove it with their precision grip and eat it. As a result, they are remarkably free from such parasites in the wild.

If the tick has avoided the hazards of grooming, and has become engorged with blood, she drops heavily to the ground. Thus fortified, she unseals the chamber with the stored sperm cells, lays the fertilized eggs in the soil (perhaps ten thousand of them) and dies—her descendants left to continue the cycle.

Note how simple are the sensory abilities required of the tick. They may have been feeding on reptile blood before the first dinosaurs evolved, but their repertoire of essential skills remains fairly meager. The tick must be crudely responsive to sunlight so she knows which way is up; she must be able to smell butyric acid so she knows when to fall animalward; she must be able to sense warmth; she must know how to inch her way around obstacles. This is not asking much. Today we have very small photocells easily able to find the sun on a cloudless day. We have many chemical analytic instruments that can detect small amounts of butyric acid. We have miniaturized infrared sensors that sense heat. Indeed, all three such devices have been flown on spacecraft to explore other worlds—the Viking missions to Mars, for example. A new generation of mobile robots being developed for planetary exploration is now able to amble over and around large obstacles. Some progress in miniaturization would be needed, but we are not very far from being able to build a little machine that could duplicate—indeed far surpass—the central abilities of the tick to sense the outside world. And we certainly could equip it with a hypodermic syringe. (Harder for us to duplicate just yet would be its digestive tract and reproductive system. We are very far from being able to simulate from scratch the biochemistry of a tick.)

What would it be like inside the tick's brain? You would know about light, butyric acid, 2,6-dichlorophenol, the warmth of a mammal's skin, and obstacles to clamber around or over. You have no image, no picture, no vision of your surroundings; you are blind. You are also deaf. Your ability to smell is limited. You are certainly not doing much in the way of thinking. You have a very limited view of the world outside. But what you know is sufficient for your purpose.

There's a thump on the window and you look up. A moth has careened headlong into the transparent glass. It had no idea the glass was there: There have been things like moths for hundreds of millions of years, and glass windows only for thousands. Having bumped its head against the window, what does the moth do next? It bumps its head against the window again. You can see insects repeatedly throwing themselves against windows, even leaving little bits of themselves on the glass, and never learning a thing from the experience.

Clearly there's a simple flying program in their brains, and nothing that allows them to take notice of collisions with invisible walls. There's no subroutine in that program that says, "If I keep bumping into something, even if I can't see it, I should try to fly around it." But developing such a subroutine carries with it an evolutionary cost, and until lately there were no penalties levied on moths without it. They also lack a general-purpose problem-solving ability equal to this challenge. Moths are unprepared for a world with windows.

If we have here an insight into the mind of the moth, we might be for-given for concluding that there isn't much mind there. And yet can't we rec-ognize in ourselves—and not just in those of us gripped by a pathological repetition-compulsion syndrome—circumstances in which we keep on doing the same stupid thing, despite irrefutable evidence it's getting us into trouble?

We don't always do better than moths. Even heads of state have been known to walk into glass doors. Hotels and public buildings now affix large red circles or other warning signs on these nearly invisible barriers. We too evolved in a world without plate glass. The difference between the moths and us is that only rarely do we shake ourselves off and then walk straight into the glass door again.

Like many other insects, caterpillars follow scent trails left by their fel-lows. Paint the ground with an invisible circle of scent molecule and put a few caterpillars down on it. Like locomotives on a circular track, they'll go around and around forever—or at least until they drop from exhaustion. What, if anything, is the caterpillar thinking? "The guy in front of me seems to know where he's going, so I'll follow him to the ends of the Earth"? Almost always, following the scent trail gets you to another caterpillar of your species, which is where you want to be. Circular trails almost never occur in Nature—unless some wiseacre scientist shows up. And so this weakness in their program almost never gets caterpillars into trouble. Again we detect a simple algorithm and no hint of an executive intelligence evaluating discordant data.

When a honeybee dies it releases a death pheromone, a characteristic odor that signals the survivors to remove it from the hive. This might seem a supreme final act of social responsibility. The corpse is promptly pushed and tugged out of the hive. The death pheromone is oleic acid [a fairly complex molecule, $CH_3(CH_2)_7CH=CH(CH_2)_7COOH$, where = stands for a double chemical bond]. What happens if a live bee is dabbed with a drop of oleic acid? Then, no matter how strapping and vigorous it might be, it is carried "kicking and screaming" out of the hive. Even the queen bee, if she's painted with invisible amounts of oleic acid, will be subjected to this indignity.

Do the bees understand the danger of corpses decomposing in the hive? Are they aware of the connection between death and oleic acid? Do they have any idea what death is? Do they think to check the oleic acid signal against other information, such as healthy, spontaneous movement? The answer to all these questions is, almost certainly, no. In the life of the hive there's no way that a bee can give off a detectable whiff of oleic acid other than by dying. Elaborate contemplative machinery is unnecessary. Their perceptions are adequate for their needs.

Does the dying insect make a special last effort to generate oleic acid, to benefit the hive? More likely, the oleic acid derives from a malfunction of fatty acid metabolism around the time of death, which is recognized by the highly sensitive chemical receptors in the survivors. A strain of bees that had a slight tendency to manufacture a death pheromone would do better than one in which decomposing, disease-ridden dead bodies were littering the hive. And this would be true even if no other bee in the hive were a close relative of the recently departed. On the other hand, since they are all close relatives, special manufacture of a death pheromone can be understood perfectly well in terms of kin selection.

So here's a bejeweled insect, elegantly architectured, prancing among the dust grains in the noonday sun. Does it have any emotions, any consciousness? Or is it only a subtle robot made of organic matter, a carbon-based automaton packed with sensors and actuators, programs and subroutines, all ultimately manufactured according to the DNA instructions? (Later, we will want to look more closely at what "only" means.) We might be willing to grant the proposition that insects are robots; there's no evidence, so far as we know, that compellingly argues the contrary; and most of us have no deep emotional attachments to insects.

In the first half of the 17th century, René Descartes, the "father" of modern philosophy, drew just such a conclusion. Living in an age when clocks were at the cutting edge of technology, he imagined insects and other creatures as elegant, miniaturized bits of clockwork—"a superior race of marionettes," as Huxley described it, "which eat without pleasure, cry without pain, desire nothing, know nothing, and only simulate intelligence as a bee simulates a mathematician" (in the geometry of its hexagonal honeycombs). Ants do not have souls, Descartes argued; automatons are owed no special moral obligations.

What then are we to conclude when we find similar very simple behavioral programs, unsupervised by any apparent central executive control, in much "higher" animals? When a goose egg rolls out of the nest, the mother goose will carefully nudge it back in. The value of this behavior for goose genes is clear. Does the mother goose who has been incubating her eggs for weeks understand the importance of retrieving one that has rolled away? Can she tell if one is missing? In fact, she will retrieve almost anything placed near the nest, including ping-pong balls and beer bottles. She understands something, but, we might say, not enough.

> If a chick is tied to a peg by one leg, it peeps loudly. This distress call makes the mother hen run immediately in the direction of the sound with ruffled plumage, even if the chick is invisible. As soon as she catches sight of the chick, she begins to peck furiously at an imaginary antagonist. But if the fettered chick is set before the mother hen's eyes under a glass bell, so that she can see it but not hear its distress call, she is not in the least disturbed by the sight of him.
>
> ... The perceptual cue of peeping normally comes indirectly from an enemy who is attacking the chick. According to plan, this sensory cue is extinguished by the effector cue of beak thrusts, which chase the foe away. The struggling, but not-peeping chick is not a sensory cue that would release a specific activity.

Male tropical fish show fighting readiness when they see the red markings of other males of their species. They also get agitated when they glimpse a red truck out the window. Humans find themselves sexually aroused by looking at certain arrangements of very small dots on paper or celluloid or magnetic tape. They pay money to look at these patterns.

So now where are we? Descartes was prepared to grant that fish and poultry are also subtle automatons, also soulless. But then what about humans?

Descartes was here treading on dangerous ground. He had before him the chastening example of the aged Galileo, threatened with torture by the self-styled "Holy Inquisition" for maintaining that the Earth turns once each day, rather than the view, clearly expressed in the Bible, that the Earth is stationary and the heavens race around us once each day. The Roman Catholic Church was quite prepared to coerce conformity—to intimidate, torture, and murder to force people to think as it did. At the very beginning of Descartes' century, the Church had burned the philosopher Giordano Bruno alive because he thought for himself, spoke out, and would not recant. And here, the proposal that animals are clockwork automatons was a far riskier and theologically more sensitive matter than whether the Earth turns—touching not peripheral but central dogmas: free will, the existence of the soul. As on other issues, Descartes walked a fine line.

We "know" we are more than just a set of extremely complex computer programs. Introspection tells us that. That's the way it feels. And so Descartes, who attempted a thorough, skeptical examination of why he should believe anything, who made famous the proposition *cogito ergo sum* ("I think, therefore I am"), granted immortal souls to humans, and to no one else on Earth.

But we, who live in a more enlightened time, when the penalties for disquieting ideas are less severe, not only may, but have an obligation to, inquire further—as many since Darwin have done. What, if anything, do the other animals think? What might they have to say if properly interrogated? When we examine some of them carefully, do we not find evidence of executive controls weighing alternatives, of branched contingency trees? When we consider the kinship of all life on Earth, is it plausible that humans have immortal souls and all other animals do not?

The moth doesn't need to know how to fly around the pane of glass, or the goose to retrieve eggs but not beer bottles—again because glass windows and beer bottles have not been around long enough to have been a significant factor in the natural selection of insects and birds. The programs, circuits, and behavioral repertoires are simple when no benefit accrues from their being complex. Complex mechanisms evolve when the simple ones will not do.

In Nature, the goose's egg-retrieval program is adequate. But when the goslings hatch, and especially just before they're ready to leave the nest, the mother is delicately attuned to the nuances of their sounds looks, and (perhaps) smells. She has learned about her chicks. Now, she knows her own very well, and would not confuse them with someone else's goslings, however similar they may seem to a human observer.

In species of birds where mix-ups are likely, where the young may fledge and mistakenly land in a neighboring nest, the machinery for maternal recognition and discrimination is even more elaborate. The goose's behavior is flexible and complex when rigid and simple behavior is too dangerous, too likely to lead to error; otherwise it *is* rigid and simple. The programs are parsimonious, no more complex than they need be—if only the world does not produce too much novelty, too many windows and beer bottles.

Consider our prancing insect again. It can see, walk, run, smell, taste, fly, mate, eat, excrete, lay eggs, metamorphose. It has internal programs for accomplishing these functions—contained in a brain of mass, perhaps, only a milligram—and specialized, dedicated organs for carrying the programs out. But is that all? Is there anyone in charge, anyone inside, anyone controlling all these functions? What do we mean by "anyone"? Or is the insect just the sum of its functions, land nothing else, with no executive authority, no director of the organs, no insect soul?

You get down on your hands and knees, look at the insect closely, and you see it cock its head, triangulating you, trying to get a sense of this immense, looming, three-dimensional monster before it. The fly strides unconcernedly; you lift the rolled-up newspaper and it quickly buzzes off. You turn on the light and the cockroach stops dead in its tracks, regarding you keenly. Move toward it and it scampers into the woodwork. We "know" such behavior is due to simple neuronal subroutines. Many scientists get nervous if you ask about the consciousness of a housefly or a roach. But sometimes you get an eerie feeling that the partitions separating programs from awareness may be not just thin, but porous.

We know the insect decides who to eat, who to run away from, who to find sexually attractive. On the inside, within its tiny brain, does it have no perception of making choices, no awareness of its own existence? Not a milligram's worth of self-consciousness? Not a hint of a hope for the future? Not even a little satisfaction at a day's work well done? If its brain is one-millionth the mass of ours, shall we deny it one-millionth of our feelings and our consciousness? And if, after carefully weighing such matters, we insist it is still "only" a robot, how sure are we that this judgment does not apply as well to us?

We can recognize the existence of such subroutines precisely because of their unbending simplicity. But if instead we had before us an animal brimming over with complex judgments, branched contingency trees, unpredictable decisions, and a strong executive program, would it seem to us that there is more here than just an elaborate, exquisitely miniaturized computer?

The honeybee scout returns to the hive from a foraging expedition and "dances," rapidly crawling in a particular, fairly complex pattern over the honeycomb. Pollen or nectar may adhere to her body, and she may regurgitate some of her stomach contents for her eager sisters. All this is done in complete darkness, her motions monitored by the spectators through their sense of touch. Given only this information, a swarm of bees then flies out of the hive in the proper direction to the proper distance to a food supply they've never visited as effort-lessly as if this was their daily, familiar commute from home to work.

They partake of the meal described to them. All this occurs more often when food is scarce or the nectar especially sweet. How to encode the location of a field of flowers into the language of dance, and how to decode the choreography is knowledge present in the hereditary information stored inside the insect. Maybe they are "only" robots, but if so these robots have formidable capabilities.

When we characterize such beings as only robots, we are also in danger of losing sight of the possibilities in robotics and artificial intelligence over the next few decades. Already, there are robots that read sheet music and play it on a keyboard, robots that translate pretty well between two very different languages, robots that learn from their own experiences—codifying rules of thumb never taught to them by their programmers. (In chess, for example, they might learn that it is generally better to position bishops near the center than near the periphery of the board, and then teach themselves circumstances in which an exception to this rule is warranted.) Some open-loop chess-playing robots can defeat all but a handful of human chess masters. Their moves surprise their programmers. Their completed games are routinely analyzed by experts who speculate about what the robot's "strategy," "goals," and "intentions" must have been. If you have a large enough preprogrammed behavioral repertoire and if you are able to learn enough from experience, don't you begin to appear to an outside observer *as if* you're a conscious being making voluntary choices—whatever may or may not be going on inside your head (or wherever you keep your neurons)?

And when you have a massive collection of mutually integrated programs, capability for learned behavior, data-processing prowess, and means of ranking competing programs, might it not start feeling, on the inside, a little bit like thinking? Might our penchant for imagining someone inside pulling the strings of the animal marionette be a peculiarly human way of viewing the world?[2] Could our sense of executive control over ourselves, of pulling our own strings, be likewise illusory—at least most of the time, for most of what we do? How much are we really in charge of ourselves? And how much of our actual everyday behavior is on automatic pilot?

Among the many human feelings that, although culturally mediated, may be fundamentally preprogrammed, we might list sexual attraction, falling in love, jealousy, hunger and thirst, horror at the sight of blood, fear of snakes and heights and "monsters," shyness and suspicion of strangers, obedience to those in authority, hero worship, dominance of the meek, pain and weeping, laughter, the incest taboo, the infant's smiling delight at seeing members of its family, separation anxiety, and maternal love. There is a complex of emotions attached to each, and thinking has very little to do with any of them. Surely, we can imagine a being whose internal life is nearly wholly composed of such feelings, and nearly devoid of thought.

The spider builds her web near our porch light. The fine, tough thread reels out from her spinneret. We first notice the web glistening with tiny droplets after a rainstorm, the proprietor repairing a damaged circumferential strut. The elegant, concentric, polygonal pattern is carefully stabilized with a single guy thread extending to the cowl of the lamp itself, and another to a nearby railing. She repairs the web even in darkness and foul weather. At night, when the light is on, she sits at the very center of her construction, awaiting the hapless insect who is attracted by the light and whose eyesight is so poor that the web is quite invisible. The moment one becomes entangled, news of this event travels to her in waves along the threads. She rushes down a radial strut, stings it, quickly wraps it in a white cocoon, packaging it for future use, and rushes back to her command center—composed, a marvel of efficiency, not even, as far as we can see, a little out of breath.

How does she know to design, construct, stabilize, repair, and utilize this elegant web? How does she know to build it near the lamp, to which the insects are attracted? Did she scamper all over the house tallying the abundance of insects in various potential campsites? How could her behavior be pre-programmed, since artificial lights have been invented much too recently to be taken account of in the evolution of spiders?

When spiders are given LSD or other consciousness-altering drugs, their webs become less symmetrical, more erratic, or, we might say, less obsessive, more freeform—but also less effective in catching insects. What has a tripping spider forgotten?

Maybe its behavior is entirely preprogrammed in its ACGT code. But then, couldn't much more complex information be locked away in a much longer, much more elaborate code? Or maybe some of this information is learned from past adventures in spinning and repairing webs, immobilizing and eating prey. But then look how small that spider's brain is. How much more sophisticated behavior might emerge out of the experience of a much larger brain?

The web is anchored opportunistically to a local geometry of lamp cowling, metal railing, and wood siding. That could not per se have been preprogrammed. There must have been some element of choice, of decision making, of connecting a hereditary predisposition to an environmental circumstance never before encountered.

Is she "only" an automaton, unquestioningly performing actions that seem to her the most natural thing in the world—and being rewarded, her behavior reinforced by an ample supply of food? Or might there be a component of learning, decision making, and self-consciousness?

Adopting high standards of engineering precision, she spins her web now. She reaps the reward later, maybe much later. She patiently waits. Does she know what she's waiting for? Does she dream of succulent moths and foolish mayflies? Or does she wait with her mind a blank, idling, thinking of nothing at all—until the telltale tug sends her scurrying down one of the radial struts to sting the struggling insect before it frees itself and escapes? Are we really sure she doesn't have even a faint and intermittent spark of consciousness?

We would guess that some rudimentary awareness flickers in the most humble creatures, and that with increasing neuronal architecture and brain complexity, consciousness grows. "When a dog runs," said the naturalist Jakob von Uexküll, "the dog moves his legs; when a sea urchin runs, the legs move the sea urchin." But even in humans, thinking is often a subsidiary state of consciousness.

If it were possible to peer into the psyche of a spider or a goose, we might detect a kaleidoscopic progression of inclinations—and maybe some premonitions of conscious choice, actions selected from a menu of possible alternatives. What individual nonhuman organisms may perceive as their motivations, what they feel is happening inside their bodies, is for us one of the nearly inaudible counterpoints to the music of life.

When an animal goes out to seek food, it often does so according to a definite pattern. A random search is inefficient, because the path would turn back on itself many times; the same places would then be examined again and again. Instead, while the animal may dart off to left and right, the general search pattern is almost always progressive forward motion. The animal finds itself on new ground. The search for food becomes an exercise in exploration. A passion for discovery is hard-wired. It's something we like to do for its own sake, but it brings rewards, aids survival, and increases the number of offspring.

Perhaps animals are almost pure automatons—with urges, instincts, hormonal rushes, driving them toward behavior which in turn is carefully honed and selected to aid the propagation of a particular genetic sequence. Perhaps states of consciousness, no matter how vivid, are as Huxley suggested, "immediately caused by molecular, changes in the brain substance." But from the point of view of the animal, it must seem—as it does with us—natural, passionate, and occasionally even thought out. Perhaps a flurry of impulses and intersecting subroutines at times feels something like the exercise of free will. Certainly the animal cannot much have an impression of being impelled *against* its will. It voluntarily chooses to behave in the manner dictated by its contending programs. Mainly, it's just following orders.

So when the days become long enough, it feels an unfocused restlessness, something like spring fever. It hasn't thought through conception, gestation, the optimum season for the birth of the young and the continuance of its genetic sequences; all that is far beyond its abilities. But from the inside it may well feel as though the weather is intoxicating, life is tempestuous, and moonlight becomes you.

We do not mean to be patronizing. The depth of understanding exhibited by our fellow creatures is of course limited. So is ours. We also are at the mercy of our feelings. We too are profoundly ignorant about what motivates us. Some of those beings have, as familiar aspects of their everyday lives, sensibilities wholly absent in humans. Other beings have different tastes and appreciations of the outside world—"To a worm in horseradish, the horseradish seems sweet," as an old Yiddish folk adage has it. Beyond that, the horseradish worm lives in a world of smells, tastes, textures, and other sensations unknown to us.

Bumblebees detect the polarization of sunlight, invisible to uninstrumented humans; pit vipers sense infrared radiation and detect temperature differences of $0.01\,°C$ at a distance of half a meter; many insects can see ultraviolet light; some African freshwater fish generate a static electric field around themselves and sense intruders by slight perturbations induced in the held; dogs, sharks, and cicadas detect sounds wholly inaudible to humans; ordinary scorpions have microseismometers on their legs so they can detect in pitch darkness the footsteps of a small insect a meter away; water scorpions sense their depth by measuring the hydrostatic pressure; a nubile female silkworm moth releases ten billionths of a gram of sex attractant per second, and draws to her every male for miles around; dolphins, whales, and bats use a kind of sonar for precision echo-location.

The direction, range, amplitude, and frequency of sounds reflected back to echo-locating bats are systematically mapped onto adjacent areas of the bat brain. How does the bat perceive its echo-world? Carp and catfish have taste buds distributed over most of their bodies, as well as in their mouths; the nerves from all these sensors converge on massive sensory processing lobes in their brains, lobes unknown in other animals. How does a catfish view the world? What does it feel like to be inside its brain? There are reported cases in which a dog wags its tail and greets with joy a man it has never met before; he turns out to be the long-lost identical twin of the dog's "master," recognizable by his odor. What is the smell-world of a dog like? Magnetotactic bacteria contain within them tiny crystals of magnetite—an iron mineral known to early sailing ship navigators as lodestone. The bacteria literally have internal compasses that align them along the Earth's magnetic field. The great churning dynamo of molten iron in the Earth's core—as far as we know, entirely unknown to uninstrumented humans—is a guiding reality for these microscopic beings. How does the Earth's magnetism feel to them? All these creatures may be automatons, or nearly so, but what astounding special powers they have, never granted to humans, or even to comic book superheroes. How different their view of the world must be, perceiving so much that we miss.

Each species has a different model of reality mapped into its brain. No model is complete. Every model misses some aspects of the world. Because of this incompleteness, sooner or later there will be surprises—perceived, perhaps, as something like magic or miracles. There are different sensory modalities, different detection sensitivities, different ways the various sensations are integrated into a dynamic mental map of ... a snake, say, in full hunting slither.

But Descartes was unimpressed. He wrote to the Marquis of Newcastle:

> I know, indeed, that brutes do many things better than we do, but I am not surprised at it; for that, also, goes to prove that they act by force of nature and by springs, like a clock, which tells better what the hour is than our judgment can inform us.

As life evolved, the repertoire of feelings expanded. Aristotle thought that "in a number of animals we observe gentleness or fierceness, mildness or cross temper, courage or timidity, fear or confidence, high spirit or low cunning, and, with regard to intelligence, something equivalent to sagacity." Emotions that Darwin argued are manifested by at least some mammals other than humans—chiefly dogs, horses, and monkeys—include pleasure, pain, happiness, misery, terror, suspicion, deceit, courage, timidity, sulkiness, good temper, revenge, selfless love, jealousy, hunger for affection and praise, pride, shame, modesty, magnanimity, and a sense of humor.

And at some point, probably long before the first humans, a new set of emotions—curiosity, insight, the pleasures of learning and teaching—also slowly emerged. Neuron by neuron, the partitions began to go up.

Notes

1. It's not the taste of the blood that attracts her, but the warmth. If she drops onto a butyric acid–scented toy balloon filled with warm water, she will readily puncture it and, an inept Dracula, gorge herself on tap water.

2. One promising finding in artificial intelligence is the discovery that distributed data processing—many small computers working in parallel without much of a central processing unit—does very well, by some standards better than the largest and fastest lone computer. Many little minds working in tandem may be superior to one big mind working alone.

Are Animals Machines? Four Views

A 17th-Century View: Descartes

[A]s you may have seen in the grottoes and the fountains in royal gardens, the force with which the water issues from its reservoir is sufficient to move various machines, and even to make them play instruments, or pronounce words according to the different disposition of the pipes which lead the water . . .

The external objects which, by their mere presence, act upon the organs of the senses; and which, by this means, determine the corporal machine to move in many different ways, according as the parts of the brain are arranged, are like the strangers who, entering into some of the grottoes of these waterworks, unconsciously cause the movements which take place in their presence. For they cannot enter without treading upon certain planks so arranged that, for example, if they approach a bathing Diana, they cause her to hide among the reeds; and if they attempt to follow her, they see approaching a Neptune, who threatens them with his trident; or if they try some other way, they cause some other monster, who vomits water into their faces, to dart out; or like contrivances, according to the fancy of the engineers who have made them. And lastly, when the *rational soul* is lodged in this machine, it will have its principal seat in the brain, and will take the place of the engineer, who ought to be in that part of the works with which all the pipes are connected, when he wishes to increase, or to slacken, or in some way to alter their movements . . .

All the functions which I have attributed to this machine (the body), as the digestion of food, the pulsation of the heart and of the arteries; the nutrition and the growth of the limbs; respiration, wakefulness, and sleep; the reception of light, sounds, odours, flavours, heat, and such like qualities, in the organs of the external senses; the impression of the ideas of these in the organ of common sense and in the imagination; the retention, or the impression, of these ideas on the memory; the internal movements of the appetites and the passions; and lastly, the external movements of all the limbs, which follow so aptly, as well as the action of the objects which are presented to the senses, as the impressions which meet in the memory, that they imitate as nearly as possible those of a real man: I desire, I say, that you should consider that these functions in the machine naturally proceed from the mere arrangement of its organs, neither more nor less than do the movements of a clock, or other automaton, from that of its weights and its wheels; so that, so far as these are concerned, it is not necessary to conceive any other vegetative or sensitive soul, nor any other principle of motion, or of life.

AN 18TH-CENTURY VIEW: VOLTAIRE

What a pitiful, what a sorry thing to have said that animals are machines bereft of understanding and feeling, which perform their operations always in the same way, which learn nothing, perfect nothing, etc.!

What! that bird which makes its nest in a semi-circle when it is attaching it to a wall, which builds it in a quarter circle when it is in an angle, and in a circle upon a tree; that bird acts always in the same way? That hunting-dog which you have disciplined for three months, does it not know more at the end of this time than it knew before your lessons? Does the canary to which you teach a tune repeat it at once? Do you not have to spend a considerable time in teaching it? Have you not seen that it has made a mistake and that it corrects itself?

Is it because I speak to you, that you judge that I have feeling, memory, ideas? Well, I do not speak to you; you see me going home looking disconsolate, seeking a paper anxiously, opening the desk where I remember having shut it, finding it, reading it joyfully. You judge that I have experienced the feeling of distress and that of pleasure, that I have memory and understanding.

Bring the same judgment to bear on this dog which has lost its master, which has sought him on every road with sorrowful cries, which enters the house agitated, uneasy, which goes down the stairs, up the stairs, from room to room, which at last finds in his study the master it loves, and which shows him its joy by its cries of delight, by its leaps, by its caresses.

A 19th-Century View: Huxley

Consider what happens when a blow is aimed at the eye. Instantly, and without our knowledge or will, and even against the will, the eyelids close. What is it that happens? A picture of the rapidly-advancing fist is made upon the retina at the back of the eye. The retina changes this picture into an affection of a number of the fibres of the optic nerve; the fibres of the optic nerve affect certain parts of the brain; the brain, in consequence, affects those particular fibres of the seventh nerve which go to the orbicular muscle of the eyelids; the change in these nerve-fibres causes the muscular fibres to alter their dimensions, so as to become shorter and broader; and the result is the closing of the slit between the two lids, round which these fibres are disposed. Here is a pure mechanism, giving rise to a purposive action, and strictly comparable to that by which Descartes supposes his waterwork Diana to be moved. But we may go further, and inquire whether our volition, in what we term voluntary action, ever plays any other part than that of Descartes' engineer, sitting in his office, and turning this tap or the other, as he wishes to set one or another machine in motion, but exercising no direct influence upon the movements of the whole . . .

Descartes pretends that he does not apply his views to the human body, but only to an imaginary machine which, if it could be constructed, would do all that the human body does; throwing a sop to Cerberus unworthily; and uselessly, because Cerberus was by no means stupid enough to swallow it . . .

. . . [W]hat living man, if he had unlimited control over all the nerves supplying the mouth and larynx of another person, could make him pronounce a sentence? Yet, if one has anything to say, what is easier than to say it? We desire the utterance of certain words: we touch the spring of the word-machine, and they are spoken. Just as Descartes' engineer, when he wanted a particular hydraulic machine to play, had only to turn a tap, and what he wished was done. It is because the body is a machine that education is possible. Education is the formation of habits, a superinducing of an artificial organisation upon the natural organisation of the body; so that acts, which at first required a conscious effort, eventually became unconscious and mechanical. If the act which primarily requires a distinct consciousness and volition of its details, always needed the same effort, education would be an impossibility.

According to Descartes, then, all the functions which are common to man and animals are performed by the body as a mere mechanism, and he looks upon consciousness as the peculiar distinction of the "*chose pensante*," of the "rational soul," which in man (and in man only, in Descartes' opinion) is superadded to the body. This rational soul he conceived to be lodged in the pineal gland, as in a sort of central office; and here, by the intermediation of the animal spirits, it became aware of what was going on in the body, or influenced the operations of the body. Modern physiologists do not ascribe so exalted a function to the little pineal gland, but, in a vague sort of way, they adopt Descartes' principle, and suppose that the soul is lodged in the cortical part of the brain—at least this is commonly regarded as the seat and instrument of consciousness.

... [T]hough we may see reason to disagree with Descartes' hypothesis that brutes are unconscious machines, it does not follow that he was wrong in regarding them as automata. They may be more or less conscious, sensitive, automata; and the view that they are such conscious machines is that which is implicitly, or explicitly, adopted by most persons. When we speak of the actions of the lower animals being guided by instinct and not by reason, what we really mean is that, though they feel as we do, yet their actions are the results of their physical organisation. We believe, in short, that they are machines, one part of which (the nervous system) not only sets the rest in motion, and co-ordinates its movements in relation with changes in surrounding bodies, but is provided with special apparatus, the function of which is the calling into existence of those states of consciousness which are termed sensations, emotions, and ideas. I believe that this generally accepted view is the best expression of the facts at present known.

... It is quite true that, to the best of my judgment, the argumentation which applies to brutes holds equally good of men; and, therefore, that all states of consciousness in us, as in them, are immediately caused by molecular changes of the brain-substance. It seems to me that in men, as in brutes, there is no proof that any state of consciousness is the cause of change in the motion of the matter of the organism. If these positions are well based, it follows that our mental conditions are simply the symbols in consciousness of the changes which take place automatically in the organism; and that, to take an extreme illustration, the feeling we call volition is not the cause of a voluntary act, but the symbol of that state of the brain which is the immediate cause of that act. We are conscious automata ...

A 20th-Century View: James L. and Carol G. Gould

In considering the issue of mental experiences in animals, we have begun to wonder if the implicit assumption that humans are almost wholly conscious and aware (and hence fully competent to evaluate our cognitively less sophisticated animal brethren) is correct. Could it be that the degree to which conscious thinking is involved in the everyday lives of most people is greatly overestimated? We know already that much of our learned behavior becomes hardwired: despite the painfully difficult process of learning the task originally, who has to concentrate consciously as an adult on how to walk or swim, tie a shoe, write words, or even drive a car along a familiar route? Certain linguistic behavior, too, falls into such patterns. Michael Gazzaniga, for instance, tells the story of a former physician who suffered from a left (linguistic) hemisphere lesion so serious that he could not form even simple three-word sentences. And yet, when a certain highly touted but ineffective patent medicine was mentioned, he would launch into a well-worn and perfectly grammatical five-minute tirade on its evils. This set piece had been stored on the undamaged right side (along with the usual collection of songs, poetry, and epigrams) as a motor tape requiring no conscious linguistic manipulation to deliver.

... Indeed, what evidence is there that those sublime intellectual events known as "inspiration" involve any conscious thought? Most often our best ideas are served up to us out of our unconscious while we are thinking or doing something perfectly irrelevant. Inspiration probably depends on some sort of repetitive and time-consuming pattern-matching program which runs imperceptibly below the level of consciousness searching for plausible matches.

It strikes us that a skeptical and dispassionate extraterrestrial ethologist studying our unendearing species might reasonably conclude that *Homo sapiens* are, for the most part, automatons with overactive and highly verbal public relations departments to apologize for and cover up our foibles.

From Sagan C., & Druyan, A. (1992). Shadows of forgotten ancestors: A search for who we are. New York: Random House.

3   Will the Mind Become the Brain in the 21st Century?

RICHARD F. THOMPSON

If any one feature characterizes the modern "cognitive revolution" in psychology it is the profusion of loose writing and thinking about the "mind," what Skinner (1990) referred to as the "ghost in the machine." To me, the current situation is somewhat reminiscent of the state of introspectionism in psychology at the time when John B. Watson was required to describe the sensations, feelings, and thoughts of his rats as they learned to traverse a maze for his Ph.D. thesis (see Boring, 1929; Kimble, 1994). My field is behavioral neuroscience, the attempt to understand the neurobiological substrates of behavior. I was trained in a thoroughly behavioristic tradition in the psychology department at the University of Wisconsin in the 1950s, the heyday of such distinguished behavioral scientists as Harry Harlow, Wulf Brogden, and David Grant. At that time the department was known far and wide as the "dustbowl of empiricism," a description that pleased Harlow so much he had a chamber pot so inscribed displayed prominently in his office.

I begin my discussion of brain and mind with my favorite quotation from John Watson's "Psychology as the Behaviorist Views It" (1913). After stressing that measurable behavior is the proper object of study in psychology, he says:

> Will there be left over in psychology a world of pure psychics, to use Yerkes' term? I confess I do not know. The plans which I most favor for psychology lead practically to the ignoring of consciousness in the sense that that term is used by psychologists today. I have virtually denied that this realm of psychics is open to experimental investigation. I don't wish to go further into the problem at present because it leads inevitably over into metaphysics. If you will grant the behaviorist the right to use consciousness in the same way that other natural scientists employ

it—that is, without making consciousness a special object of observation—you have granted all that my thesis requires. (Watson, 1913, p. 175)

Watson's statement can hardly be called doctrinaire and must come as a surprise to those ardent cognitive scientists who decry behaviorism. The basic point he makes, and it is the thesis of my chapter, is that terms like "consciousness" and "mind" do not refer to phenomena that are in principle unmeasurable. At present, they can only be studied indirectly by measuring behavior, verbal and otherwise. By "a special object of observation" I believe Watson had in mind the method of introspection and the view then prevalent in psychology that mind/consciousness was somehow nonphysical, the traditional mind-body dualism. As Watson notes, this "leads inevitably over into metaphysics." The view of mind as nonphysical cannot of course be entertained in science.

My editor and colleague in the field, Robert Solso, is of the opinion that there is more to consciousness than meets the eye, that is, than is measurable: "this more difficult form of consciousness deals with 'inner thoughts' which are jealously concealed from observation. Such things as what a boy (or girl) might be thinking while on a date or a student may be thinking while talking with his professor. It is the private world of consciousness that poses the major issue in contemporary psychology, not the one that can be measured by implicit memory experiments and priming ... " Solso (personal communication, 1 February 1996).

Watson actually provided the solution to this issue of private thought many years ago with his motor theory of thought. Again, to quote Watson: "The hypothesis that all of the so called 'higher thought' processes go on in terms of faint reinstatements of the original muscular act (including speech here) and that these are interpreted into systems which respond in serial order (associative mechanisms) is I believe, a tenable one." (Watson, 1913, p. 174).

It is indeed the case that thinking in normal adult humans is accompanied by movements of the vocal apparatus: subvocal speech. Jacobson recorded electromyographic activity from the tongue and was able to determine from this measure whether the subject was thinking of the word "one" or "two" or "three." (Jacobson, 1931).

The more extreme Watsonian view that these movements, per se, *are* thought is probably not correct (see Thompson, 1994). But to return to Solso's point, so-called secret thoughts can indeed be measured by recording the electrical/mechanical activity of the vocal apparatus, activated in turn by the neuronal processes that "are" the thoughts. Again, my thesis is that there is nothing more to thoughts than neural activity and its outward expressions in behavior.

Perhaps the most remarkable work in this field has been done by Roger Sperry and his associates in their classic studies of patients with disconnection of the corpus callosum, the large band of fibers connecting the two hemispheres (done to treat severe epileptic conditions) (Sperry, 1968). Most readers are familiar with the basic experiment. The subject looks at a fixation point on a screen. A word or object is flashed to the right or left of the fixation point. If to the right, the information is projected only to the visual areas on the left side of the brain, and vice versa (because of the way the visual system is wired and because the connections between the two sides of the forebrain have been severed).

If a word or picture of an object was presented to the left hemisphere, the patient would immediately say the correct word. However, if a picture of an object, for example, a pencil, was presented to the right hemisphere, the patient could not identify it verbally. But if he could reach behind the screen with his left hand (controlled by the right hemisphere) and feel objects he would immediately hold up the pencil, but he still could not say it. In fact, the right hemisphere could also identify words for simple objects, but could not say them.

So the left hemisphere can say the words when it sees them or the objects referenced but the right hemisphere cannot. On the other hand, the right hemisphere can understand simple words and objects and identify them correctly by another kind of behavior, namely by touch with the left hand that projects information to and is controlled by the right hemisphere. Which hemisphere has consciousness? The left hemisphere is clearly far more verbal but both can identify words and objects. It is important to stress that all of the measures in these experiments are of verbal or manual behaviors. In general, the important advances made in cognitive psychology are all due entirely to careful measures of behavior, for example, the nature, latency, and timing of verbal or manual behaviors (Posner, 1989, Posner & Shulman, 1979). The other kinds of measures are of brain activity. Neither of these types of measures measure the mind.

Verbal behavior (or other motor behavior) can be extremely precise, or perhaps more accurately, extremely reliable, as in psychophysical experiments. Measurement of absolute auditory threshold in a given experienced listener will generate highly reliable measures of absolute threshold for a given auditory stimulus, judgments with very low variance. The fields of sensory psychophysics are replete with such examples. Is this a part of the proper definition of consciousness, that is, reliable behavioral judgments about stimuli? Fechner and Titchner would certainly agree. Other measurable and verifiable aspects would include accurate reports of previously learned material ("memories"). William James and many others identified consciousness loosely with short-term or working memory, what you can *report* at any given moment—stimuli, thoughts, feelings, memories, etc. Again, a perfectly respectable behavioral definition. Mind of course includes consciousness plus all the vast repository of knowledge, experience, feelings, and skills stored in long-term memory that you are not aware of at any given moment but that can in some manner or another be "called up" and *expressed*. These are basically the definitions given in introductory psychology texts.

For those of us in behavioral neuroscience, these definitions are quite acceptable—they reference behaviors that can be measured. But do terms like "mind" or "consciousness" refer to anything more than this? I return to the phenomena of psychophysical judgments. One of my students trained rabbits in an absolute auditory threshold detection task, using classical conditioning of the eye blink response as the behavioral measure, the rabbit equivalent of a verbal report. Our rabbits exhibited absolute auditory thresholds (white noise stimulus) that were slightly better than those of human subjects but more striking was the fact that the within-subject variance was lower for the rabbits than for humans (Kettner et al., 1980; Kettner & Thompson, 1982, 1985). So by this definition rabbits are just as conscious as we.

If "consciousness" does have any reality or meaning, it seems most unlikely to be limited to humans. Evolution proceeds in small steps to change the physical characteristics of animals. Hence it cannot have appeared de novo in humans—it must have evolved gradually from small beginnings in simpler animals presumably because it had some adaptive advantages. Some years ago a questionnaire was sent to many neuroscientists asking them to rank animals in terms of degree of consciousness. As expected, primates and sea mammals ranked highest, then carnivores, then rodents and so on. Serious doubt was expressed concerning the consciousness of flies and worms (Thompson, 1993).

This of course is only opinion. Remember that consciousness cannot be measured directly.

It may be useful to consider dissociation between consciousness or awareness expressed verbally and performance that is not "conscious" (i.e., not expressed verbally).

Implicit memory is an interesting example of such a dissociation between "consciousness" and measurable performance. In implicit memory tasks the subjects cannot describe these memories explicitly in verbal terms, yet the memories are easily measured in performance (see Schacter & Tulving, 1994). In a typical implicit memory priming task subjects are given words to study and later presented with the first three letters of the words, together with words they have not studied. They are asked to respond with the first word they think of. They respond with the previously studied words at a significantly higher rate than do subjects who had not earlier studied the words. Yet they are "unaware" of this. Some evidence suggests that visual association areas of the cerebral cortex may be critical for visual implicit memory performance. These brain regions are quite different from the medial temporal lobe—hippocampal system necessary for explicit or "conscious" memory performance (Schacter & Tulving, 1994; Squire et al., 1992; Tulving et al., 1994).

Threshold judgments are another kind of example of dissociations between awareness and performance. At absolute auditory threshold subjects state that they are guessing much of the time, even under circumstances where their performance is better than chance. This observation is easily accounted for in signal detection theory (Green & Swets, 1966). Performance depends on criterion level. If subjects are instructed to respond with a high degree of certainty, then their performance is accurate (high hit rate and low false alarm rate) and corresponds more closely with awareness. But if instructed to guess (lower hit rate and higher false alarm rate), they can perform above chance to a degree without awareness. So here awareness is a matter of criterion.

In our studies of brain substrates of behavioral detection of threshold-level auditory stimuli in the rabbit we found that the animals performed in an all-or-none manner. They gave a substantial conditioned response (eye blink) or no response at all at 50% threshold performance. Interestingly, this threshold did not correspond to neural unit activity evoked in primary auditory structures (ventral cochlear nucleus, ventrolateral division of the central nucleus of the inferior colliculus, or the ventral division of the medial geniculate body). Instead, neural activity in these structures was reliably evoked and equal in amplitude by both the behaviorally detected and nondetected threshold stimuli (see figure 3.1). The auditory system reliably detected all the stimuli at behavioral threshold. However, when we recorded neural activity in a cortical structure (hippocampus), unit activity corresponded exactly with behavioral detection, that is, there was a stimulus-evoked unit response in the hippocampus on the behavioral detection trials but not on nondetection trials (see figure 3.1). The auditory system reliably *detected* the stimuli, but the cortical system *decided* to respond or not respond. Perhaps for the rabbit the hippocampal response corresponds to "awareness" of the stimulus.

Actually, the hippocampus and the associated medial temporal lobe system in primates and humans appear critical for one kind of memory, namely declarative or recognition memory, particularly of one's own experience, as in episodic memory, which is generally equated with awareness (Squire, 1992; Tulving, 1983).

Brain injury can yield striking dissociations between awareness (verbal report) and performance. A case in point is "blindsight" (Weiskrantz, 1986). People with destruction of the visual cortex insist they are blind—they cannot see at all. Yet, if such a person is forced to point to a light source in the visual field, he or she will point accurately, all the while insisting there is no light at all. The remaining visual system can subserve visual localization but the awareness of visual experience is lost. These observations do not, of course, demonstrate that visual consciousness is in the visual cortex, only that this region of cortex is necessary for visual awareness. The primary visual cortex might simply serve as a necessary relay to visual and other association areas that play a more direct role in sensory awareness. Note again that sensory awareness is here measured by verbal report. But dissociations such as these that occur with brain damage or callosal section are so striking because they are exceptions to the normal correspondence between verbal reports and other behavioral measures.

In my view Roger Sperry (e.g., 1992, 1993) has written among the most provocative characterizations of the mind and awareness. To quote:

> Mental states as dynamic emergent properties of brain states cause behavior but are not dualistic, because they are inextricably interfused with their generating brain processes. Mental states in this form cannot exist apart from the active brain. At the same time, mental states are not the same as brain states. The two

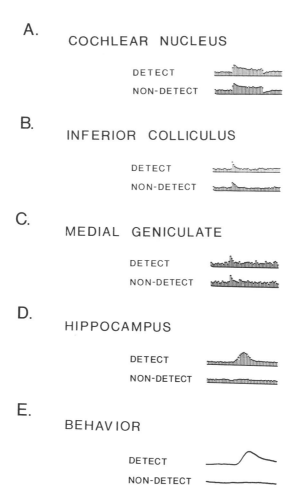

**Figure 3.1   Histograms of neural unit cluster responses recorded from three pri-
mary auditory nuclei and from the hippocampus (CA1) on behavioral (conditioned eye blink) detection and nondetection trials at 50% behavioral response
threshold. Responses were created for a 750-ms period (total trace duration)
beginning 201 ms before the onset of the 350-ms constant intensity threshold
level white noise–conditioned stimulus (−20 dB spectral level) from a total of
more than 200 detection trials and an equal number of nondetection trials. The
histogram bin width is 15 ms. The behavioral response (E) is eye blink closure
(actually extension of the nictitating membrane) indicated by upward movement
of the trace in detect. Note that the behavioral and cortical (hippocampal) unit
responses are all (DETECT)-or-none (NON-DETECT) but the auditory unit
responses are identical on behavioral detect and non-detect trials. The auditory
system "detects" but the cortical system "decide." (From Kettner and Thompson,
1982, 1985.)**

differ in the way a dynamic emergent property differs from its component intrastructure. It is characteristic of emergent properties that they are notably novel and often amazingly and inexplicably different from the components of which they are built. The recognized methodologic difficulties posed by the use of introspection, however, are not remedied. (Sperry, 1993, p. 180)

So for Sperry, mind emerges from the brain and acts back on the brain. The common view in neuroscience today is indeed that the mind, whatever it may be, is an *emergent* property of the activity of the brain. But the meaning of the term "emergent" is not so simple. To quote from an earlier discussion (Thompson, 1994):

The properties of water are emergent from the properties of hydrogen and oxygen atoms, their subatomic wavicles, and the ways they interact to form water, and can be deduced from quantum mechanics (reductionism); however, it is so much simpler to measure the properties of water directly. As Sperry said, "These subatomic features are the same for any macro entity, be it a great cathedral or a sewage outlet" (Sperry, 1993, p. 880).

Churchland and Sejnowski (1992) provided a nice example in neuroscience of emergent properties, using the stomatogastric ganglion of the spiny lobster, studied in detail by Selverston (1988). This ganglion has 28 neurons, all of which have been identified, and acts to drive the muscles controlling the teeth of the gastric mill so food can be ground up for digestion. The output, measured as muscle or motor neuron activity, is rhythmic to produce the regular grinding actions. A great deal has been learned about the biophysical properties of these neurons and about the anatomy of their interconnections. Putting together all this information should make it possible to predict the behavior of the system, rhythmic output, but it does not. No one cell is responsible for the output; it is due to the interactions among the cells as well as their intrinsic properties. Churchland and Sejnowski (1992) concluded, "The lesson is that micro level data are *necessary* to understand the system, but not *sufficient*"

(p. 5). Although I do not agree with this conclusion, it will come as no surprise to psychologists and others who work with neural networks. I would say rather that the interactions among the neurons in the circuit are too complicated for humans to analyze at a verbal-conceptual level but are a simple exercise for a computer, that is to say, a sufficiently detailed computational model of the ganglion. At another extreme are parallel-distributed processing neural-like networks that can model such complex, emergent properties of the human brain as language acquisition (Seidenberg & McClelland, 1989).

It seems to me that there is a very fundamental difference between these examples and the mind. The emergent properties of water, of the ganglion, and of neural networks can be measured physically, whereas the mind cannot be measured directly; we must still depend on verbal and other behavioral measures.

Sperry was very unhappy with this state of affairs but regretfully acknowledged the fact that the only measure of the mind we have available is verbal or other behavior (personal communication). Where does this leave us? As we learn more about the brain and its patterns of activity, we can draw closer parallels between brain activity and "awareness" or verbal report. Mental images provide an example. Although currently a little controversial, some evidence suggests that when one imagines a visual stimulus, the pattern of activation in the visual areas of the cerebral cortex is very similar to the pattern that develops when one actually sees the same stimulus (Kosslyn et al., 1993). The field of human brain imaging that provided these data has really only begun.

My own view is that we will never be able to measure "mind" or "consciousness" more directly than with verbal or other behavioral report. As we learn more about brain processes, the links between patterns of brain activity and behavioral reports will grow ever closer, to the point where there is no longer any need to postulate intervening variables such as "mind" or "awareness."

The acid test of my view will come from the field of computer science. It seems inevitable that true Turing machines will someday be developed, systems like Hal in *2001*. Does such a system have a mind and consciousness? It will say so and describe its sensations, perceptions, feelings, and thoughts in a manner indistinguishable from human reports. So the answer must be yes—such systems do have mind and consciousness, "emergent" properties from their circuitries, just as our minds are emergent properties of our neural circuitries. The hardwares may differ but the principles need not. The difference, of course, is that we have complete understanding only of the silicon circuits.

Perhaps the most important advances regarding the "mind" in the 21st century and beyond will come from (1) the development of "artificial" minds that are equal or superior to the human mind in all its aspects, and (2) the increasing characterization of brain substrates of verbal and other aspects of behavior. As these developments occur, the mysteries of the mind and consciousness will gradually fade from our collective awareness.

References

Boring, E. G. (1929/1950). *A history of experimental psychology*. New York: Appleton-Century-Crofts.

Churchland, P. S., & Sejnowski, T. J. (1992). *The computational brain*. Cambridge, MA: MIT Press.

Green, D. M., & Swets, J. A. (1966). *Signal detection theory and psychophysics*. New York: Wiley.

Jacobson, E. (1931). Electrical measurements of neuromuscular states during mental activities: VII. Imagination, recollection and abstract thinking involving the speech musculature. *American Journal of Physiology, 97,* 200–209.

Kettner, R. E., Shannon, R. V., Nguyen, T. M., & Thompson, R. F. (1980). Simultaneous behavioral and neural (cochlear nucleus) measurement during signal detection in the rabbit. *Perception & Psychophysics, 28,* 504–513.

Kettner, R. E., & Thompson, R. F. (1982). Auditory signal detection and decision processes in the nervous system. *Journal of Comparative and Physiological Psychology, 96,* 328–331.

Kettner, R. E., & Thompson, R. F. (1985). Cochlear nucleus, inferior colliculus, and medial geniculate responses during the behavioral detection of threshold-level auditory stimuli in the rabbit. *Journal of the Acoustical Society of America, 77,* 2111–2127.

Kimble, G. A. (1994). A new formula for behaviorism. *Psychological Review, 101*, 254–258.

Kosslyn, S. M., Alpert, N. M., Thompson, W. L., Maljkovic, V., Weise, S. G., Chabris, C. S., Hamilton, S. E., Rauch, S. L., & Buonanna, S. S. (1993). Visual mental imagery activates topographically organized visual cortex: A PET investigation. *Journal of Cognitive Neuroscience, 5*, 263–297.

Posner, M. I. (1989). *Foundations of cognitive science*. Cambridge, MA: MIT Press.

Posner, M. I., & Shulman, G. L. (1979). Cognitive science. In E. Hearst (Ed.), *The first century of experimental psychology* (pp. 371–405). Hillsdale, NJ: Erlbaum.

Schacter, D. L., & Tulving, E. (1994). What are the memory systems of 1994? In D. L. Schacter and E. Tulving, *Memory systems 1994* (p. 1–38). Cambridge MA.: MIT Press.

Seidenberg, M. S., & McClelland, J. L. (1989). A distributed, developmental model of word recognition and naming. *Psychological Review, 96*, 523–568.

Selverston, A. J. (1988). A consideration of invertebrate central pattern generators as computational data bases. *Neural Networks, 1*, 109–177.

Skinner, B. F. (1990). Can there be a science of mind? *American Psychologist, 45*, 1206–1210.

Sperry, R. W. (1968). Hemisphere deconnection and unity in conscious awareness. *American Psychologist, 23*, 723–733.

Sperry, R. W. (1992). Turnabout on consciousness: A mentalist view. *Journal of Mind and Behavior, 13*, 259–280.

Sperry, R. W. (1993). The impact and promise of the cognitive revolution. *American Psychologist, 48*, 878–885.

Squire, L. R. (1992). Memory and the hippocampus: A synthesis from findings with rats, monkeys, and humans. *Psychological Review, 99*, 195–231.

Squire, L. R., Ojemann, J. G., Miezin, F. M., Petersen, S. E., Videen, T. O., & Raichle, M. E. (1992). Activation of the hippocampus in normal humans: A functional anatomical study of memory. *Proceedings of the National Academy of Sciences, 89,* 1837–1841.

Thompson, R. F. (1993). *The brain: A neuroscience primer* (2nd ed.). New York: Freeman.

Thompson, R. F. (1994). Behaviorism and neuroscience. *Psychological Review, 101,* 259–265.

Tulving, E. (1983). *Elements of episodic memory.* Oxford; Clarenden London Press.

Tulving, E., Kapur, S., Craik, F. I. M., Moscovitch, M., & Houle, S. (1994). Hemispheric encoding/retrieval asymmetry in episodic memory: Positron emission tomography findings. *Proceedures of the National Academy of Science, 91,* 2016–2020.

Watson, J. B. (1913). Psychology as the behaviorist views it. *Psychological Review, 20,* 158–177.

Weiskrantz, L. (1986). *Blindsight.* New York: Oxford University Press.

4   FACT: The First Axiom of Consciousness and Thought

Endel Tulving

Writing about the future is much easier than writing about the past: One need not worry about whether what one writes is true, or even about whether what one says is believable or plausible. But there are several ways of making absolutely sure that one's ruminations about the future will not come back to haunt one, directly or indirectly. A rather effective stratagem is to consider the future whose happenings are too far away for anyone alive today to be able to verify. Another is to refuse at the outset to accept any responsibility for what one says.

Shortly after I accepted my assignment from the editor of this book, I experienced a remarkably fortunate incident: I was visited by a young person of indeterminate gender who said that It was an emissary of a committee that had become aware of my problem of writing something meaningful about the brain/mind sciences of the 21st century and that the committee had decided to send It to help me. What was remarkable was not the offer of help as such but rather the fact that the visitor said that It was visiting me from the future, from the year A.D. 2096 to be exact, and that the purpose of the visit was directly connected with my assignment. The thing explained that despite Its relative youth (It did not mention Its age, but looked forty-something to me) and the fact that It had not yet completed its formal education, It had developed some interest in the history of sciences. Among other things, It had recently completed a 4.4-megabyte Condensed History of C-Sci in the 21st Century that had qualified It for membership in the committee that It now represented. It offered to share the contents of Its CH with me. Being of the mischievous kind. however (as It freely admitted upon questioning), It stipulated that I could only read the compendium, that I could not copy it or take any written notes, and that if I wanted to use the 2096 history of the past as a basis for my 1996 predictions about the future, a thought that indeed had already occurred to me, I was welcome to do so, provided that I relied on my TACIT memory

(Text-Analysis-and-Comprehension-of-Infinite-Transversality in translation into 1996ese, It kindly explained). I cleverly refused to waste time on further discussion of either that term or the issue of the 2096-style classification of memories). Thus, no notes or copies or tangibly accessible records of any kind—I had to rely purely on mind.

Therefore, the wobbliness and incompleteness of what follows are to be attributed to the infelicities of my TACIT memory; the account itself that I read was exceedingly clear and complete. Especially remarkable was my own reaction to what I read: time after time I was struck with the lucidity of the story, with its unmistakable character of "of course—it could not have been otherwise—but naturally—indeed, self-evidently true—how could we have missed it back in 1996?" Just about everything I read in the compendium about the *early* 21st century made perfect sense to me, although I began struggling with the developments after about 2020 and essentially had to give up trying to understand the details after 2040. This is also why, despite my essay being all about C-Sci in 2096, it deals mostly with the early 21st century.

What follows, then, is what my TACIT memory informs me of what I read. I cannot be sure of course how veridical everything is. Fortunately, however, because there is no such thing as a "true history" anyway, some additional noise introduced into the fallible account of history by the fallibility of human memory is not going to change anything very much: we still end up with a fallible account. It is like adding infinity to infinity and still getting only infinity. The only thing that I am reasonably sure about is that the various footnotes (*identified as such in the general text by italics*) were in the original, apparently placed into the account by various committees or their members at different times, with a few contributed by myself by way of explicating what I had read, or communicating what It had said.

Prehistory of C: The Late 20th Century

In the early days of C-Sci there was science but no C. As late as the 1990s; what we today know as C was referred to in English by the cumbersome term "consciousness." The topic was immensely popular, probably because of its earlier suppression: consciousness had been a taboo word in science for the most part of the 20th century. Of all the terms designating something that no one could define, or observe, or point at, or describe, or measure— "consciousness" was by far the most fashionable thing to talk about. A truly rich literature was created on the topic, contributed to by scientists representing all existing disciplines, as well as many others without any discipline.

A curious custom at the time was to designate many things other than consciousness with the same term. Apparently most of the early thinkers thought these other things were somehow meaningfully related to consciousness, and because of a scarcity of words in any language, especially English, they had decided to let the same term stand for everything. For instance, while they referred to what we think of as C as "consciousness" they, or at least some of them, also believed that lifeless machines were "conscious," that is, that machines could "have" consciousness. Also, most of the time they did not make any distinctions between concepts that today are distinguished, such as "consciousness" and "awareness," or "consciousness" and "attention." Even more mysteriously, they identified "consciousness" with grespy ("*general responsivity" in the early 21st century, "arousal" and "alertness" during the heyday of folk psychology*). Historians are a bit clearer on the reasons for this last-named feat of duplicity—but that is another story.

The terminological confusion contributed greatly to the state of affairs that some contemporaries thought was sorry and sad while others labeled it exciting and promising. There were, of course, attempts made by rare individuals to try to straighten out the terminology, but these efforts came to nought, for two reasons: (1) Few people were interested in what others were saying, and (2) it is well known fact that the terms of a scientific discipline can be no better than its concepts. Because concepts can only emerge from an interplay between observing nature and thinking hard about the observations, and because there was little in the early (late 20th century) study of consciousness that could be regarded as empirical observations of consciousness, the concepts of consciousness had not changed over many hundreds of years.

Indeed, the lack of "hard" facts about consciousness was probably the major determinant of the state of affairs. There were essentially two kinds of thinkers interested in and committed to a scientific study of consciousness, and the efforts of neither kind helped much with the dearth of facts and verifiable phenomena about consciousness. The first kind did not particularly care about anything other than the "facts about consciousness" that were obvious to them through the exercise of their own intelligence. These people could be readily identified by examining their papers and books on consciousness: There were no data in them, no tables, no graphs, no measurements, indeed usually no illustration—just words. (*This essay here is a perfect example of the genre.*) The second kind, who frequently complained about the first kind, did care about and did include various kinds of data in their published works. Their efforts, however, usually foundered on the general inability of researchers to extricate C from other aspects of mental activity. Even when, toward the end of the 20th century, memory researchers began to distinguish between what they called "conscious" and "nonconscious" memory, it was never quite clear exactly in what sense the distinction was made: everyone agreed that test persons exhibiting conscious memory were as conscious as those engaged in nonconscious memory. Some timid attempts were made to attribute the different states of C to the *contents* of memory, but that did not work, because it was not known how to measure the consciousness of a remembered bit of information without the mediation of the (always conscious) test person. (*As we will see later, the problem was solved by making it disappear by the magic of what came to be known as The First Axiom.*)

Thus it was that a great deal was written about "consciousness," but little was achieved. Endless energy was wasted talking about consciousness, especially toward the end of the 20th century, when the term became a true buzzword and exquisitely fashionable. Conferences were organized, books were written, journals were established, prizes were given about, on, and around consciousness, and thinkers interested in and committed to a scientific study of consciousness competed with one another in making claims about designated regions in the brain where their theories said consciousness resided. It was all preparadigmatic, however, to use the terms of Thomas Kuhn, a perceptive 20th-century thinker.

A major symptom of the preparadigmatic nature of the enterprise was the near-total lack of agreement on anything pertaining to consciousness. At the time when scientific conferences still adhered to the primitive form in which individuals lectured to large audiences, it was nearly impossible to go to a conference on consciousness, with scores of speakers, and find anyone who had anything agreeable to say about anyone else. The topics were always the same, having to do with issues such as what consciousness is and what it is not, whether it exists or does not, whether it is real or epiphenomenal, whether it can be studied or not, whether respectable scientists (like, for example, molecular biologists) should be studying it, or if they were, whether they should admit it publicly, and in general what it means to study consciousness "scientifically," given all the doubts about its existence to begin with. Large numbers of papers (*"paper" was the 20th-century term for scifiles, because they were actually typed on paper* [sic!]), and many sections of papers, were entitled "The Problem of Consciousness." (*This was another quaint custom of unknown origin that keeps baffling our historians, because there were few scientific papers written, in any century, under the comparable titles such as "The Problem of Universe," or "The Problem of Life," or "The Problem of Behavior," and it was not at all clear why these other huge categories invented by the human mind had escaped being problematic.*)

The Beginning of the End?

As the reader can surmise, the "Problem of Consciousness" was in deep trouble near the end of the 20th century, and it seemed to be slipping deeper into it year by year. Its future was decidedly bleak. Some made heroic efforts to resuscitate the ghost of consciousness by using positron emission tomography (PET) to identify brain activity of test persons who did nothing other than think conscious thoughts. Yet these efforts ran aground when the technical experts pointed out that the findings were meaningless, because the correlational nature of the data was ambiguous and essentially uninterpretable. One could surmise that the data showed the effect of the brain on the PET images, but one could equally readily argue that the data in fact reflected the effect of the PET scan on the test person's brain. This why the PET studies of consciousness just fizzled out. (*By way of a sad footnote it should be mentioned that one old professor, who had dabbled in PETting of the mind, had to be sheltered, because through all his waking hours he kept shouting, over and over again, in a loud voice, "I knew that correlation was an invention of the Devil, I knew it, I knew."*)

Just when the fortunes of the study of consciousness were at their lowest, and the stories of the "Problem of Consciousness" read at their bleakest, things started to change again, and in fact to turn around, and eventually blossom into C Science, or C-Sci as we say. The turning point was initially imperceptible, and many historians at first thought that it was so for a good reason: there was in fact no single cause of the turnaround, no single event, or even series of events, that could have been pointed at and declared to be the markers of the "birth" of C-Sci. It was only the remarkable and indefatigable ingenuity of our historical committees that led to the revision of the history. Many happenings have now been identified that could be mentioned as playing a pivotal role in the inevitability of the unfolding of the C universe according to what now seem to have always been its natural laws. Our committees have in fact been able to pinpoint a number of Significant Historical Happenings (SHHs). They have further distinguished between minor SHHs and major SHHs.

An example of a minor SHH is the dazzling insight of a first-year graduate student at the University of NIET (Northern Independent Eastern Townships, once a part of a country called Canada), at the turn of the millennium, that the cumbersome and nonfunctionally long but exceedingly popular and frequently used word "consciousness" could be replaced with the word C, which would serve the purpose as aptly and distinctively as "consciousness." (*From early on she was fond of telling the story how she had recognized the blinding nature of her insight immediately, because the thought had been instantly followed by a flash of light brighter than a thousand suns. Later in life, as she became old and famous as a sciam— "science administrator," one of the most popular and revered careers in the second half of the 21st century, a subcategory of "government bureaucrat"—she came to believe that the light had in fact accompanied the thought, and still later that it had most certainly preceded and thereby inspired the brilliant insight.*) Her proposal to replace "consciousness" with C, surprisingly, was almost immediately accepted, thereby greatly shortening speeches and scifiles about C. It was more convenient, indeed less painful, to refer to C-scientists, or C-ers, as we say today, rather than to use the tiresome phrase "thinkers interested in and committed to a scientific study of consciousness" or any of its tedious equivalents.

Another minor significant historical happening that has been identified as relatively noncontroversial was the gradual switch (*remember the initial imperceptibility?*) from "What is the problem of consciousness?," which had been the central issue at the end of the 20th century, to "What is the matter with the people that are interested in and committed to a scientific study of consciousness?" The redirection of the focus of concern had no single identifiable origin, and seemed to have simply risen, as mist rises from a marsh, from the enormous frustration felt by many. At one point it must have become increasingly difficult to further ignore something that is exceedingly clear to us, with our wisdom of hindsight: Given the enormous effort made by large masses of thinkers interested in and committed to a scientific study of consciousness, it was most incongruous that nobody really knew much more about consciousness at the end of the 20th century than William James and other enlightened minds had known at the end of the 19th. (*Some observers even liked to liken the story of C to the story of parpsy— "parapsychology" of the old. In parpsy, too, masses of highly intelligent practitioners had their minds wonderfully concentrated on obviously interesting problems, they had at their disposal all the tools of modern science, they observed and measured and described and used t-tests and drew conclusions, they used intuition, logic, and the Bayesian theorem, yet all to no avail: a hundred years later they were where they had been a hundred years earlier.*) At any rate, these and similar kinds of thoughts, totally unacceptable for almost a hundred years after William James, were at the root of the shift of emphasis from C to C-ers. The assumption was that if one could fix the C-ers the problem of C would also be fixed.

The 2018 TeleCongress

It is the firm belief of most history committees, although there is little direct evidence to support it, that the role of the gradual shift of the focus of concern from C to C-ers was much more profound than people realized at the time, because the shift prepared the ground for one of the most profoundly important major SHHs in the history of our subject. This event, which transpired in 2018, was a virtually assembled international telecongress sponsored by NATO, the reborn SEATO, and HFSP to solve what by then had become generally acknowledged as the "Problem of C-ers." The problem was, specifically, What are we to do with them? The world governments had already made their decision, which most decisively did answer the question, but they needed the international congress to prove the wisdom of the decision.

The congress participants (*they will be referred to as "delegates" in this essay, although in 2096 they were known as "telparts"*) were typical for the age—a mixture of government bureaucrats representing all six levels of government, their advisors, lawyers, accountants, and a sprinkling of representatives of the public, together with some scientists, including some bona fide C-ers. The idea that science was far too important to be left to scientists had been gaining ground extrascientifically in the 20th century. Its growth culminated in the establishment of comsci (*"Committee science" in the 1996 parlance*) with its own unique but now widely known procedures, practices, and traditions, including the one of not contaminating scientific conferences with large proportions of scientists. The idea, ironically, mirrored a similar idea that had been brewing intrascientifically, within scientific circles, namely, that publication of research findings is far too important to be left to those who had done the research. (*There were many reasons for it, but the most telling argument was that researchers are too close to their projects and experiments to be able to render an unbiased assessment as*

to what it was that they had done, why they had done it, and what the findings meant.)
The remedy to the problem, as already mentioned, paralleled the extrascientific
developments: scientific publications came to be written by committees, consisting of editors, consulting editors, editorial consultants, referees, reviewers,
and other experts. It was the committees that wrote the reports, on the basis of
the data provided by researchers. The researchers were initially included as
coauthors, but eventually a more satisfying solution was adopted: the committee would thank the researchers in a footnote for their contribution to the
joint research. This was the origin of what by the beginning of the 21st century had been known as "compub" (*committee publishing*). But this, too, is another story, and we should not be distracted from the main line. (*Narrator's
note: I cannot resist the temptation, however, of just mentioning, very briefly, what It,
the emissary of the 2096 history committee, told me in private discussions when It visited
to let me read the compendium. In the early days of comsci, scientists offered a great deal
of resistance to the plans made for them by the government bureaucrats, like the peasants
did in the Soviet Union when Stalin forced collectivization on them. They referred to
the governments' efforts as "alien obstruction" before the phrase was decreed politically
incorrect and its use punished by having the offenders wear baseball caps, the visor
pointing right, to committee meetings. But only when the governments resolutely put an
end to the counterinsurgency through the venerable stratagem of stopping paying any and
all research expenses of scientists did most scientists get the message and abandon the
fight as futile. Some took early retirement, others retrained as government bureaucrats,
took jobs as their advisors, or became lawyers, accountants, and mental healthcare
workers looking after the remaining scientists.*)

The agenda of the 2018 congress was long, detailed, and thorough. The
problem was that many of the delegates, all brilliant minds, had been C-ers in
their previous careers, or had C-ers in the family tree, or had read and heard
enough about C to feel fully qualified to talk about C. Thus it came about that
instead of immediately coming to grips with their mission, to seal the fate of
C-ers, the delegates decided to spend some time initially on what the participants later described as the "last-gasp effort to solve the problem of C." At
that point, not surprisingly, it took only two short days of debate for the tele-
discussion to veer around to the seductively alluring and beguiling problem of
machine consciousness. The delegates then spent the next 16 days in furious,
frequently acrimonious, and always emotionally charged discussion of the
topic.

Aristotle to the Rescue

In the late evening of the 18th day of the telecongress, with no end of the debate in sight, a young scholar of Sanskrit, appointed to the congress as a delegate by the Committee for the Protection of Incomprehensible Minor Scholars, made a proposal that changed the history. Her name, Geanne Ovida Darche, was unusual, but since names had been getting more and more unusual over many preceding decades, delegates paid more attention to, and thereby became more aware of, what she had to say than her name. (*For brevity's sake, in what follows, only her initials are used.*)

G.O.D. was not only at home in Sanskrit, but in 46 other dead languages. She also knew everything about what in the 19th century had been called "classics." Her suggestion to the delegates was stunningly original: she proposed to solve the problem of machine consciousness by using Aristotelian reasoning. She explained to the delegates who Aristotle had been, how reasoning had been used in the past to solve problems, how Aristotle even had thought it could be used to arrive at the truth, and how Aristotle's system had worked. (*Aristotle's name and his method of arriving at the truth were unknown to most delegates for two reasons. First, general knowledge of dead philosophers had been declining precipitously ever since the governments had decided, around the turn of the millennium, that "There are no votes in the humanities," and told the universities to stop teaching humanities. Second, the "modern" values had been eroding for a while even in the 20th century and they were eventually replaced by "postmodern" values: facts were replaced by faith, logic by beliefs, and truth by feelings.*)

G.O.D. then presented her case forcefully and articulately. (*Historians' opinions are divided as to whether she had carefully planned the operation for over some time, or whether it had come to her naturally on the spur of the moment. In either case, all agreed that it was startlingly brilliant.*)

In the beginning, G.O.D. presented her first syllogism, as follows:

PREMISE 1: Matter can exist without life.

PREMISE 2: Living matter can exist without consciousness.

CONCLUSION: Consciousness can exist regardless of whether the conscious system is alive or not.

There was little discussion of the conclusion, either because of the late hour or because there was nothing to discuss. (*A very old man tried to question*

G.O.D. on the legitimacy of her syllogism, muttering something like "it does not look like a syllogism to me," but G.O.D. just looked him deeply in the virtual eye, and he fell silent.) After the delegates had voted both premises true, and G.O.D. had explained that therefore the proposed conclusion was syllogistically valid, everybody cheered. At that point G.O.D. pulled out her first trump card. She pointed out that although the conclusion was a valid conclusion, that is, logically conclusive, it was empirically inconclusive. She explained that it was this theoretical problem—logically conclusive but empirically inconclusive conclusion—that had been responsible, throughout the 20th century, for (1) the interminable discussions about machine consciousness that had wasted thousand of C-er years, and (2) the fact that the discussions were interminable. (*Although many delegates could not quite follow G.O.D.'s reasoning, it felt good, and no one demurred.*)

Then G.O.D. proposed her second syllogism:

PREMISE 1:   Life cannot exist independently of matter.

PREMISE 2:   Consciousness cannot exist independently of living matter.

CONCLUSION: Consciousness cannot exist unless the conscious system is alive.

She also offered a corollary to the conclusion.

COROLLARY: Artifacts that are not alive, even if produced by living systems, cannot be conscious.

(*According to the personal testimony of the 2096 emissary, and not part of the official record, it had been verified that at this point some delegates became alarmed, because they thought she had said "coronary." They calmed down, however, when G.O.D. explained the difference. According to the same personal testimony, again not found in the records, the same very old man again tried to question G.O.D. on her syllogism, but when G.O.D. asked other delegates how they felt about the syllogism, and they said they believed the syllogism was a syllogism, the old man was ignored for the rest of the proceedings.*)

Delegates unanimously voted premise 1 to be true. There was some discussion about premise 2. Some delegates questioned it, because, they said, there was no experimental evidence for it, or even any other kind of empirical evidence. But by this time general ennui really had set in, and the debate became pretty one-sided. G.O.D. claimed that one cannot question premise

2 on the grounds of empirical evidence any more than one could question premise 1 on the same grounds, and pointedly asked whether any delegate had contrary opinions. None did. Not wishing to leave anything to chance, however, G.O.D. decided to drive her point home by asking whether any delegate had any empirical proof of the existence of a real world outside their own phenomenal experience, and when none did, she asked how many of them nevertheless thought that the world really existed. All did. With the audience thus softly prepared, G.O.D. invited another young scholar of Sanskrit, whose name was Jeanne Charisma, and whose qualifications were very similar to those of G.O.D., and whom G.O.D. apparently knew quite well, to explain the doctrine of solipsism to the delegates. (*Knowledge of philosophical ideas had gone the way of philosophers.*) As J.C. delivered her monologue, most delegates kept solemnly nodding their heads, as was clearly seen on the transvideo. J.C. then took the opportunity of occupying the center and reminded the delegates that if there were any secret doubters left they should realize that accepting premise 1 but rejecting premise 2 would imply that there may be more things in the universe that are conscious than there are things that are alive, and that that surely could not be true, because it would violate the Third Law of Evolution. (*Again, some historians have speculated that the powerful argument delivered by J.C. was not totally unrehearsed, but evidence on the point has remained fuzzy.*) By this time all the delegates had pushed the "Call Vote" button, and when the vote was taken, the conclusion of G.O.D.'s second syllogism and its corollary were overwhelmingly accepted as valid.

FACT: The First Axiom of C and T

In the dying minutes of the telecongress, with the weary delegates heady with a warm glow of feelings of accomplishment—after all, they had managed to put their collective finger on at least one of the C-er problems—the second young Sanskrit scholar, J.C., proposed that for the conclusion just accepted to be really effective in guiding future thinking about C, it would be desirable to elevate the conclusion and its corollary to the status of an axiom. The proposal was overwhelmingly accepted. There were no contrary votes, although 14 delegates, representing computer, chip, and cable manufacturers, abstained. Quickly capitalizing on the now irrepressibly jubilant mood of the delegates (some spontaneous singing of Beethoven's "Ode to Joy" was heard in the cosmic background of the universal transmission of the proceedings) G.O.D., seconded by J.C., made what she promised was her final proposal: To extend the First Axiom from C to T. (*T by the year 2096 had been derived from the word "thought" by the sociolinguistic mechanism subserving Zipf's law; thought and thinking preoccupied the society almost as much as C, E, and X, where E stands for what was generically known as "entertainment" back in the 20th century, and X stands for what in the dying days of that century had been called "gender."*) She explained that even without the cumbersome reasoning required by Aristotelian syllogisms, or even without reasoning by analogy, it was exceedingly clear that thought was always accompanied by awareness, and because awareness was nothing but expression of consciousness, talking about nonconscious thought and related ideas ("thinking machines") made sense and was excusable only in situations where it was necessary to come up with the most powerful example of the concept of "oxymoron."

Thus came about what later in C-Sci became known as the First Axiom of C and T, or the FACT—*If a thing is not alive, it cannot be conscious, nor can it think.* After the fateful congress of 2018, it has never been seriously questioned. Indeed, in our own time, near the end of the 21st century, it would be difficult to find an educated person over 8 years of age who does not think of the FACT as something whose verity is utterly beyond any doubt.

The acceptance of the First Axiom turned out to be a truly pivotal event in the history of C. Not only did it save the C-ers and their activities from experimental extinction envisaged by the governments (after the 2018 congress C-ers seemed to be coming out of the woodwork in hordes), it also provided a surprisingly clean new beginning to the study of C. (*It was surprising, because no one would have predicted that as slight a realignment of thought as that involved in decisively rejecting the possibility of machine consciousness would make much of a difference in the study of those aspects of C that were, or could be seen as being, free from any dependence on the issue. Nevertheless it did. It was as if the C-ers' creative powers were set free from the ominous influence of a dark cloud that had been hanging over them, not physically preventing them from thinking productive thoughts about C, but somehow paralyzing them by its mere presence.*)

The brilliance of the solution crafted by G.O.D. and J.C., although doubted by some traditionalists at the outset, became more generally clear over some 20 years of thought following the 2018 congress. By 2040 everybody agreed that it had saved C as an object of scientific interest. (*This indeed is why some referred to the First Axiom as "salvation," rather than merely as a "solution."*) However, different people liked different things about it.

Some thought the solution was brilliant because it freed thinkers from being frustrated by the historical Turing problem, doing so the same way that Alexander the Great had dealt with the Gordian knot. It was now realized that the Turing problem was not just trivial, but also boring: Surely you can build clever machines, or even intelligent ones, whose actions can fool all the people some of the time and some people all the time. So what? The important issue is not machine intelligence, but machine C. And C is what the machines do not have, by definition, like an ordinary human does not have wings, or silicon chips in its frontal lobes, by definition. (*This was yet another breakthrough discovery: There may be people who will always want to argue about machine consciousness—after all there are people who believe that the earth is flat—and we can let them do that. No problem, as they used to say. But machine C is ruled out the same way as studies of sexual reproduction of machines is ruled out.*)

Other commentators were full of admiration for the First Axiom, because it most ingeniously shifted the whole burden of decision from the difficult How do we know that X is not conscious? to the much easier How do we know that X is alive? Most people were ready to believe that the criterion of life was DNA, and thus they agreed on how to distinguish living things from nonliving ones: Does it or does it not have DNA that looks like DNA and acts like DNA and comes about the same way as does DNA? So they were happy that they did not need the Turing test, or any exotic room test, or any kind of a symbol-crunching test. All they needed, they said, was a test for DNA. Once they had established that the object under scrutiny had DNA they could proceed, and frequently did, to ask and find out what kind of C it did have. If it had no DNA, it had no C of any kind. It was as simple as that.

Still others thought that the main virtue of the First Axiom lay in the clear establishment of C as a biological phenomenon, freeing it from the strictures of quantum mechanics as much as from the dogmas of metaphysics. (*Although some argued that quantum mechanics was quite relevant to the understanding of C, the consensus was that although true in principle, the claim was in the same logical category as the claim that principles of internal combustion are relevant to the understanding of the dynamics of traffic jams.*)

Finally, a small minority liked the thought of all the trees (in the earlier years of the debate) and all the electricity (later on) that had been saved (*salvation again?*) by eliminating the endless, futile, and totally unneeded arguments over the possibility of consciousness of rocks, marble statues, waterfalls, windmills, cuckoo clocks, household robots, desktop computers, and Barbie dolls who speak accent-free Estonian.

The important point is that there was universal agreement that the First Axiom had in fact totally changed the history of C. The FACT was taught in all schools and thus it became not just generally known but greatly admired. Many mortals came to think of it as the most lucid human thought ever expressed. Many theologians were surprised when told the story of its birth, because on the pure face of it, it was difficult to reject the impression that it must have been of divine origin.

Author's Note

The ideas expressed in the essay, like all other ideas that scientists have, owe their existence to an unknown mix of what has already been stated by others and what has not yet been expressed, or not yet been expressed in quite the same form. It would be impossible to do perfect justice to all the previous thinkers who have wrestled with the many problems that the term "consciousness" can conjure up in the active minds of conscious people. I know explicitly that my own thoughts on the matter have been stimulated by at least the papers and books that are listed in the bibliography, and probably many more. It is safe to assume, therefore, that any similarity between my thoughts and those expressed before by many others is highly unlikely to be purely accidental. The same is probably true of the similarity between thoughts in this essay and the similar ones that can be found in papers and books I have not listed. As of 1 January, 1996, there were over 10,000 entries that responded to the *keyword* search for "conscious" or "consciousness" (restricted to human studies in the MEDLINE (1975–1995), and over 18,000 entries that responded to the same search in the PsycLIT (1970–1995). The richness of the literature is largely attributable to the fact that just about anything that has something to do with the behavior of organisms and cognitive phenomena of human beings has been seen to be related to consciousness. Thus there are endless papers (mostly book chapters, because these do not go through a very strict refereeing process) written on consciousness and X, where X might be any one of hundreds of items such as action, activity, amnesia, anesthesia, aphasia, artificial intelligence, attention, biology, brain, classical conditioning, cognition, cognitive science, computational models, connectionist models, cortical activity, dreaming, emergence of language, evolution, experience, frontal lobes, hemispheric laterality, hippocampus, intelligence, intentionality, language, lateral asymmetry, learning, memory, mental imagery, mind, neglect, neurotransmitters, ontogenesis, parallel distributed processing, perception, phenomenology, phylogenesis, prosopagnosia, qualia, quantum physics, reductionism, scientific method, sensation, skill learning, sleep-waking cycle, spatial organization, teleology, temporal organization, theory of relativity, thought, time, and universe.

Acknowledgment

E. T.'s research is financed by an endowment by Anne and Max Tanenbaum in support of research in cognitive neuroscience, and by a grant from the Natural Sciences and Engineering Research Council of Canada.

Bibliography

Baars, B. J. (1988). *A cognitive theory of consciousness*. Cambridge, England: Cambridge University Press.

Bunge, M., & Ardila, R. (1987). *Philosophy of psychology*. New York: Springer-Verlag.

Cabanac, M. (1996). On the origin of consciousness, a postulate and its corollary. *Neuroscience and Biobehavioral Reviews, 20*, 33–40.

Crick, F., & Koch, C. (1992). The problem of consciousness. *Scientific American, 267*, 152–159.

Delacour, J. (1995). An introduction to the biology of consciousness. *Neuropsychologia, 33*, 1061–1074.

Dennett, D., & Kinsbourne, M. (1992). Time and the observer: The where and when of the consciousness and the brain. *Behavioral and Brain Sciences, 15*, 183–206.

Donald, M. (1995). The neurobiology of human consciousness: An evolutionary approach. *Neuropsychologia, 33*, 1087–1102.

Farthing, G. W. (1992). *The psychology of consciousness*. Englewood Cliffs, NJ: Prentice Hall.

Gardiner, J. M. (1995). On consciousness in relation to memory and learning. In M. Velmans (Ed.), *The science of consciousness: Psychological neuropsychological, and clinical reviews*. London: Routledge.

Gazzaniga, M. S. (1985). *The social brain: Discovering the networks of the brain*. New York: Basic Books.

Hirst, W. (1995). Cognitive aspects of consciousness. In M. S. Gazzaniga (Ed.), *The cognitive neurosciences* (pp. 1307–1319). Cambridge, MA: MIT Press.

Ingvar, D. H. (1985). "Memory of the future": An essay on the temporal organization of conscious awareness. *Human Neurobiology, 4,* 127–136.

James. W. (1890). *Principles of psychology*. New York: Holt.

Kinsbourne, M. (1995). Models of consciousness: Serial or parallel in the brain? In M. S. Gazzaniga (Ed.), *The cognitive neurosciences* (pp. 1321–1329) Cambridge, MA: MIT Press.

Mandler, G. (1975). *Mind and emotion*. New York: Wiley.

Markowitsch, H. J. (1995). Cerebral bases of consciousness: A historical review. *Neuropsychologia, 33,* 1181–1192.

Moscovitch, M. (1995). Models of consciousness and memory. In M. S. Gazzaniga (Ed.), *The cognitive neurosciences* (pp. 1341–1356). Cambridge, MA: MIT Press.

Perner, J., & Ruffman, T. (1995). Episodic memory and autonoetic consciousness: Developmental evidence and a theory of childhood amnesia. *Journal of Experimental Child Psychology, 59,* 516–548.

Revonsuo, A., Kamppinen, M., & Sajama, S. (1994). General introduction: The riddle of consciousness. In A. Revonsuo & M. Kamppinen (Eds.), *Consciousness in philosophy and cognitive neuroscience* (pp. 1–23). Hillsdale, NJ: Erlbaum.

Rugg, M. D. (1995). Memory and consciousness: A selective review of issues and data. *Neuropsychologia, 33,* 1131–1141.

Schacter, D. L. (1989). On the relation between memory and consciousness: Dissociable interactions and conscious experience. In L. Roediger III & F. I. M. Craik

(Eds.), *Varieties of memory and consciousness: Essays in honour of Endel Tulving* (pp. 355–389). Hillsdale, NJ: Erlbaum.

Searle, J. R. (1992). *The rediscovery of the mind.* Cambridge, MA: MIT Press.

Shallice, T. (1988). *From neuropsychology to mental structure.* Cambridge, England: Cambridge University Press.

Stuss, D. T., & Benson, D. F. (1986). *The frontal lobes.* New York: Raven Press.

Velmans, M. (1991). Is human information processing conscious? *Behavioral and Brain Sciences, 14,* 651–726.

Weiskrantz, L. (1994). Neuropsychology and the nature of consciousness. In H. Gutfreund & C. Toulouse (Eds.), *Biology and computation: A physicist's choice* (pp. 323–336). Singapore: World Scientific Publishing.

II   Brain and Mind in the 21st Century

5 Infusing Cognitive Neuroscience into Cognitive Psychology

EDWARD E. SMITH

Like others in this book, I am going to predict (i.e., guess) that in the next few decades cognitive psychology will increasingly move in the direction of neuroscience. Moreover, I suspect that the nature of this movement will not be restricted to the growth of cognitive neuroscience as a separate area, but will also include the infusion of findings and ideas of cognitive neuroscience into cognitive psychology. Twenty or 30 years from now, cognitive psychology students will routinely learn something about brain-cognition relations, just the way they now learn something about mathematical models and statistics.

The reason that I am making this prediction is that it has already started to happen. Even in the domains of memory and higher-cognitive processes—which are the foci of this chapter—there are now research programs that apply biological methods and measures to bread-and-butter issues in cognition.

This infusion of neuroscience into cognition is very different from prior work in cognitive psychology. The seminal work that brought about the "cognitive revolution" (e.g., Bruner et al., 1956; Miller et al., 1960) was as much concerned with fighting the then dominant paradigm of behaviorism as it was with promoting cognitive psychology; consequently, that work focused on tasks which involved high-level processing and which were removed from anything going on in the neurobiology of that time. The next generation of cognitive psychologists maintained this emphasis on the purely cognitive level. The gap between cognition and neuroscience, if anything, broadened in the late 1970s and early 1980s when a chunk of cognitive psychology became part of the cognitive science movement. The guiding wisdom then was that one could understand cognition without worrying about its neural underpinnings, just as one could understand the workings of computer software without knowing anything about the underlying hardware.

Why, then, are many cognitive psychologists now turning to cognitive neuroscience for new insights about cognition, and why should this trend grow in the future? In the main body of this chapter, I will try to spell out three reasons for this change in view. To preview, I want to argue the following:

1. Contrary to the software/hardware viewpoint of the 1970s and 1980s, cognitive science, biologically oriented work, can substantially alter our *cognitive* theories of memory and the higher mental processes. I am not alone in believing this, and the main reasons for the change in view are that (a) neuroscientists have found out a great deal about the neural bases of memory and related processes in the last 15 years, and this work places constraints on our cognitive theories, and (b) in the last decade, physicists and neuroscientists have developed neuroimaging techniques like positron emission tomography (PET) and functional magnetic resonance imaging (fMRI) that for the first time allow us to get a "picture" of changes in brain function while the organism is actively engaged in various tasks.

2. It is not just a matter of cognitive neuroscience providing constraints, or more data, about cognition. Neuroimaging techniques may eventually provide more informative and more directly interpretable information than that obtained in strictly cognitive experiments. (Since "strictly cognitive experiments" use only behavioral measures, I will also refer to them as "strictly behavioral experiments.") Furthermore, as we learn more about the functions of different anatomical regions, the power of neuroimaging data will increase greatly.

3. Cognitive neuroscience can also contribute by suggesting new ways of dividing cognition into meaningful areas of study. Every science has to determine how to carve nature at its joints, and cognitive neuroscience has some new ideas about how to do this.

The rest of my chapter will develop these three points in more detail. As will be evident, as I move from topics 1 to 3, my comments will become increasingly speculative. Also, throughout this chapter I will be emphasizing the results of neuroimaging experiments, especially studies using PET. I do not mean to minimize the contributions of other methodologies in cognitive neuroscience—particularly studies of the selective deficits shown by brain-damaged patients, and experiments that measure electrical activity in the brain—but in this brief chapter I will be selective.

Constraints from Cognitive Neuroscience: A Case Study

It is hard to have a discussion about how cognitive neuroscience will do this or that without a concrete example in hand. The example I will use is taken from work that John Jonides and I have done on the nature of what used to be called "short-term memory" and is increasingly referred to as "working memory."

First some comments about the concepts of working memory. By working memory, I mean a system that can keep active only a limited amount of information (say, 7 ± 2 items), for a brief time period (a matter of seconds), where that information is rapidly accessible (on the order of milliseconds). Something like this concept was explicit in the writings of William James (1890) but it became far more influential in the modern cognitive era. In particular, Waugh and Norman (1965) and Atkinson and Shiffrin (1968) proposed "dual-memory" models, which contained separate stores for short-term memory and long-term memory plus a rehearsal process that transfers information between them. The next major conceptual step was taken by Baddeley and Hitch (1974). They argued that short-term memory does more than store information briefly until it can be coded into long-term memory. Short-term memory is also the structure in which mental calculations take place, operations of the sort needed in reasoning, problem solving, and language understanding. Hence short-term memory is a "working memory," a mental blackboard that is used in the service of higher cognitive processes.

During the period from the late 1950s through 1980, hundreds of experiments on short-term or working memory were published. What is striking about this literature is that the vast majority of it deals with only verbal materials. There is relatively little consideration of the possibility of a separate working memory for nonverbal materials. In the last decade, however, Baddeley and his coworkers (e.g., Baddeley, 1986) have proposed separate stores for verbal (phonological) information and visuospatial information. There are now a number of strictly behavioral experiments that try to dissociate the verbal store from the visuospatial one (reviewed in Jonides et al., in press). Although these studies provide some evidence for the visual-verbal distinction, they are weakened by the fact that each of the tasks used seems to include both verbal and visuospatial components, when ideally purer tasks are needed (see Jonides et al., in press).

This is where cognitive neuroscience and neuroimaging come in. The basic idea is to have subjects perform either a purely verbal task or a purely spatial task while their brain activity is measured. The neuroimaging technique that we have used to measure brain activity is PET. The logic behind it is this:

• Ideally, we would like to know what regions of the brain increase in neural activity when a particular task is performed (for the regions that show the increase presumably are the ones that mediate performance). Alas, we cannot measure localized neural activity directly in humans.

• However, we can measure what regions of the brain show an increase in blood flow when a particular task is performed, and it is known that increases in regional blood flow are linearly related to increases in neural activity.

• To measure regional blood flow, one inserts a radioactive tracer into the subject's bloodstream; then counts of the radioactive tracer in various regions (which is what PET measures) tell us about regional increases in blood flow, which in turn inform us about regional increases in neural activity.

With this as background, now I need to get specific for a while so that I can get my concrete example across. In our research (see, e.g., Smith et al., 1996), we had subjects lie in a PET scanner while they performed either a spatial or a verbal working memory task. On each trial of the spatial task, three dots were presented briefly; subjects had to store the positions of these dots during a 3-second retention interval, and at the end of the interval had to decide whether a probe circle matched one of the stored positions. This task clearly recruits spatial working memory. In contrast, on each trial of the verbal task, four letters were presented briefly; subjects had to store the names of these letters during a 3-second retention interval, and at the end of the interval had to decide whether a probe letter matched one of the stored letters in name. This task clearly involves verbal working memory.

The top of figure 5.1 contains a simple, two-dimensional schematic of a brain that shows areas with significant increases in activation (blood flow) during the spatial task. There are a number of things you need to know to interpret this schematic. First, the areas listed reflect mainly memory processes because the activations due to perceptual and response processes have been subtracted out of them. (This was accomplished by having the subjects perform a control task that required the same perceptual and response processes as

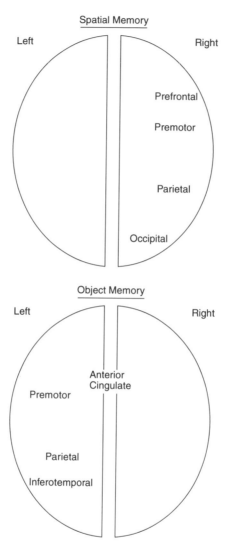

Figure 5.1 Two-dimensional schematic diagrams of the brain that show the statistically significant areas of activation in two working memory tasks. The top of the figure contains the schematic for the spatial task; the bottom contains the schematic for the verbal task. The locations of the areas in the schematic correspond roughly to their locations in the brain, with respect to the left-right and anterior-posterior dimensions. Note that in the spatial task, all four significant foci of activation are in the right hemisphere, whereas in the verbal task most of the significant activations are in the left hemisphere.

the spatial memory task but no memory, and then subtracting the PET results in the control task from that of the spatial memory task.) Second, the locations of the areas in the schematic correspond roughly to their locations in the brain with respect to the left-right and anterior-posterior (front-back) dimensions; there is no indication, however, of the height of the activated area in the brain. Third, the left (right) side of the schematic corresponds to the left (right) side of the brain, whereas the top of the schematic corresponds to the front of the brain and the bottom of the schematic to the back of the brain. Thus all four significant areas of activation in the spatial task are in the right hemisphere, with some of them in the back of the brain and some in the front. By way of contrast, the schematic for the verbal task is in the bottom of figure 5.1 (again, activations due to perceptual and response processes have been subtracted out, so the areas shown reflect only memory processes). Strikingly, most of the significant areas of activation are now in the left hemisphere. At this *global level* of analysis, then, there is a *dissociation* between spatial and verbal working memory, with the mechanisms underlying spatial working memory housed in the right hemisphere and the mechanisms mediating verbal working memory located in the left hemisphere. We consider this strong evidence for the claim that there are qualitatively different working memories for different kinds of information.[1]

One can learn far more about the processes of interest by going beyond this global level of analysis to a *regional level* of analysis, that is, an analysis that looks at the specific neuroanatomical area involved and focuses on its known functions. For the spatial task, two of the right-hemisphere regions activated are in the back of the brain, one in the posterior parietal cortex and the other in the anterior occipital cortex. Studies of brain-damaged patients indicate that the parietal region is involved in spatial processing and spatial memory (e.g., McCarthy & Warrington, 1990), whereas other neuroimaging experiments suggest that the occipital region of interest is involved in the maintenance of visual images (e.g. Kosslyn et al., 1993). It is plausible, then, that in our spatial task, subjects computed the spatial positions of the target locations and maintained an image of them. The two regions activated in the front of the brain in the spatial task can also be given a functional interpretation, albeit a speculative one. These regions are sufficiently close to motor areas to suggest that they may play a role in some kind of implicit eye movements, which may be used to rehearse the visuospatial material (analogous to how implicit speech is used to rehearse verbal material; see below). Thus our regional analysis suggests a two-component theory of spatial working memory: a storage component mediated by structures in the back of the brain, and a rehearsal component mediated by regions in the front of the brain.

A regional analysis of the results in the verbal task argues for the same kind of two-component architecture. Specifically, in the verbal task, the most activated area was in the left-hemisphere posterior parietal cortex, which is the region most likely to be damaged in patients who show a deficit in verbal short-term memory tasks (see Shallice, 1988). This strongly suggests that this region has a role in the storage of verbal information. Furthermore, all of the frontal regions activated—including Broca's area, the premotor area, and the supplementary motor area—are known to be involved in mediating higher-level aspects of speech (see Fuster, 1995), and therefore it is likely that they mediated an implicit speech or verbal rehearsal process in the verbal task.

The above results provide strong converging evidence for there being distinct verbal and spatial working memories. Indeed, this conclusion seems unavoidable if one assumes that the cortical regions activated implement the cognitive mechanisms involved. So our findings seem as relevant to the cognitive study of working memory as they do to the analysis of brain-cognition relations. These findings are just a piece of a rapidly accumulating set of neuroimaging results that provide converging evidence for distinctions that have been drawn at the cognitive level. Thus, cognitive researchers (e.g., Schachter, 1989) routinely distinguish between *explicit memory* (memory as revealed by conscious recollection of a past event) and *implicit memory* (memory as revealed by improvements in performance), and recent PET studies show that performing an explicit memory task leads to *increased* activation in several regions, including the hippocampal system, whereas performing an implicit memory task leads to *deceased* activation in numerous sites (Squire et al., 1992). There seems little doubt, then, that cognitive neuroscience can supply converging evidence—about cognitive processes—to that obtained in strictly behavioral studies of cognition. Given our specific example of cognitive neuroscience in action, we can now proceed to more general considerations.

What's Special About Cognitive Neuroscience Data?

There is a possibility that data from cognitive neuroscience can contribute something special to an analysis of cognition, something that one cannot get from strictly behavioral studies. I do not mean the obvious—that only cognitive neuroscience can tell us about the neural bases of cognition. Rather I am going to suggest that compared with strictly behavioral data, findings from cognitive neuroscience may be (a) more informative and (b) more directly interpretable in terms of underlying cognitive functions. I will consider a couple of reasons for why this may be so, touching on the first one briefly, and treating the second reason in some detail.

DIRECTNESS OF DISSOCIATIONS

Consider again our PET case study. At our global level of analysis, we showed two things: (a) There are brain regions that are active when storing spatial information, but inactive when storing verbal information (this is a dissociation between memory for spatial and memory for verbal information). (b) There are other brain regions that are active when storing verbal information, but not when storing spatial information (another dissociation). Such *double dissociations* are generally accepted as strong evidence for two mechanisms being in play (see, e.g., Shallice, 1988).

One can also find such dissociations with strictly behavioral data, but their implications are less direct.[2] To see this, consider an idealized behavioral double dissociation between spatial and verbal working memory. Subjects are required to store items in working memory while concurrently performing a secondary task. If the material being stored in working memory is spatial, then the secondary task will interfere with memory performance only if it involves spatial processing; in contrast, if the material being stored in working memory is verbal, then the secondary task will interfere with memory performance only if it involves verbal processing. This behavioral double dissociation is as extreme as the PET one we obtained, but the implications are less direct. The implications of the PET dissociation are that mechanisms that underlie spatial processing were active in the spatial memory task but not in the verbal memory task, and vice versa for mechanisms that underlie verbal processing. But one cannot go directly from the strictly behavioral pattern of dual-task interference to underlying mechanisms. For example, knowing that a verbal secondary task, but not a spatial one, interferes with verbal-memory performance does not directly imply that the mechanisms underlying spatial processing were inactive. In this sense, neuroimaging data may provide a more direct connection to underlying mechanisms.

MULTIPLE DEPENDENT MEASURES AND THEIR DIRECT FUNCTIONAL
INTERPRETATION

The preceding point focused on a global level of analysis. When we turn to
a regional level of analysis, I can make an even stronger case for the special
quality of neuroimaging data.

The critical point is to think of each brain region that has a *known functionality* as a dependent variable, with the activation level of this region being
the value of the dependent variable. Consequently, any neuroimaging experiment, in principle, has numerous dependent variables or measures, whereas
most strictly behavioral studies of cognition have only one or two dependent
variables. In this respect, neuroimaging studies are more informative than
strictly behavioral ones. Furthermore, as we learn more about the function
of more regions, the informativeness of neuroimaging studies will increase.
Indeed, if someday we know the function of 50 distinct regions of the human
brain, then every neuroimaging study will have 50 dependent variables or
measures, which far exceeds what any strictly behavioral study could supply.
Call this the "multiple-measures" argument.

In addition to neuroimaging providing a multitude of measures, note
that each of these measures permits a direct functional interpretation. That is,
to the extent that an area of known function is active, one can infer that that
function was involved in the task of interest. Call this the "direct interpretation" argument.

Let me illustrate the multiple-measures and direct-interpretation arguments by again referring to our PET case study. Suppose we knew in advance
of the experiment the complete functionality of eight of the regions that
proved significant: (1, 2) two right-hemisphere regions in the back of the brain
that maintain visual images of spatial positions; (3, 4) two right frontal regions
that mediate implicit eye movements; (5) a left-hemisphere parietal region that
is involved in the storage of phonological material; and (6–8) three left frontal
regions that are involved in the planning and preparation of speech. (All we
are supposing here is that the functions we suggested earlier for these areas are
indeed the true functions of these areas.) Then we could describe our results
by saying that the spatial memory task produced positive readings on measures
1 to 4 but null readings on measures 5 to 8, whereas the verbal memory task
produced positive values on measures 5 to 8 but null readings on measures 1

to 4. The interpretation of these findings could not be more straightforward: The spatial memory task involved maintaining visual images and rehearsing them via implicit eye movements, whereas the verbal memory task involved storing phonological representations and rehearsing them via implicit speech. In essence, the areas activated give us a functional decomposition of the task.

In contrast, suppose that we focus on just the behavioral data in this experiment, which consist of the usual response accuracies and latencies. We have far fewer results, values on just two measures rather than eight, and there is no straightforward way of interpreting these values in functional terms. Knowing that the average reaction time for the verbal task was 800 ms, for example, one cannot infer anything about the functions of the underlying mechanisms. (In contrast, knowing that Broca's area showed a 10% increase in blood flow, one can infer that implicit speech was involved.)

Alas, there are problems with the above arguments. For one thing, it is not clear that a single neuroanatomical region should be the unit of analysis. Different regions tend to be correlated in their activation patterns, perhaps because all of the correlated regions are needed to implement a single psychological function. If the resulting configuration of regions is taken as the unit of analysis, then there is no longer such a multiplicity of dependent measures.[3] This problem is not that severe, though. Just because units are correlated does not mean that we cannot learn something by looking at the individual units. And even if we do take as our unit of analysis a configuration of neuroanatomical areas (or even an entire circuit), there are still going to be more of these than there are useful behavioral measures; hence the more-measures argument stands even if it is now on the order of $20:2$ rather than $50:2$. Also, even if we take a configuration or regions as our unit of analysis, direct interpretation of that configuration is still possible (e.g., the function or the speech-planning neural circuit is implicit speech) unlike the case with behavioral measures. Thus the direct-interpretation argument is unaffected by the size of the unit.

A second problem with our multiple-measures and direct-interpretation arguments is more severe. It says that, when it comes to memory and higher cognitive processes, we are still so ignorant about the function of any brain region that the immediately preceding example about spatial and verbal working memory is too fanciful to take seriously. More generally, any argument for using neuroimaging to study memory and higher mental processes that rests on the known function of brain regions is suspect, given how little is actually known about the functions of brain regions.

My first reaction to this "ignorance" criticism is to note the obvious. There is substantial variation in how much we know about the function of different regions, ranging from enough to use it in confidently interpreting new results to essentially nothing. As examples, consider some of the regions that figured in our case study. There is a good deal of evidence that the left-hemisphere premotor and supplementary motor areas are involved in higher-level aspects of motor behavior, including speech (see Fuster, 1995, for a recent review). There is some evidence that Broca's area or part of it is involved in articulation (see Dronkers, et al. 1992). Alas, there is virtually no evidence linking right-hemisphere premotor cortex to the function of implicit eye movements. Hence the amount known regarding the function of various areas is a continuous variable.

In principle we *can learn* about the function of neuroanatomical areas. Therefore, the proper rebuttal to the ignorance criticism is simply this: re-searchers will use neuroimaging experiments—along with studies of selective impairments in brain-damaged patients, and other kinds of experiments—to learn more and more about the function of more and more brain regions, and each new piece of knowledge will make the next neuroimaging study more interpretable. Indeed, this bootstrapping operation is what I see as the main agenda item for cognitive neuroscience in the coming years. What is needed is increasingly more precise specification of the psychological functions of vari-ous neuroanatomical areas, that is, "brain mapping" (Worden & Schneider, 1996, make the same point). The cumulative character of brain mapping might give cognitive psychology a cumulative nature, something which seems to be currently lacking in the field.

There is another fundamental problem with the multiple-measures and direct-interpretation arguments that plagues the brain-mapping proposal as well. We keep talking about "brain areas," but what exactly is such an area? An answer to this question must take into consideration cytoarchitectural pat-terns—for example, what kinds of neurons are found in the various layers of cortex—as is done in the standard division of the brain into Brodmann's areas. But we already know that some Brodmann's areas are associated with multiple functions, so a brain region of interest may be smaller than a Brodmann's area (or a configuration of interest would include regions smaller than Brodmann's areas). Indeed, while there are only about 50 Brodmann's areas, Worden and

Schneider (1996) have estimated that there may be as many as 1000 human brain areas with distinct psychological functions (their estimate hinges on scaling up from the known number of functional areas in the macaque monkey). Perhaps the most obvious way to determine these areas is via neuroimaging studies that try to isolate a specific psychological function. For example, it may turn out that a task requiring the production of speech activates one part of Broca's area, whereas a task requiring judgments of the grammaticality of word strings recruits another part of Broca's area (Worden and Schneider, 1996); in this way, we will have divided Broca's area into two areas of interest. Again, then, the answer to the problem at hand potentially lies in future research of just the sort that is now being carried out.

In sum, the game plan is this. The next wave of cognitive neuroscience studies (including studies of brain-damaged patients as well as neuroimaging experiments) will increase our knowledge about the specific psychological functions of specific brain areas, which will allow us to interpret the subsequent wave of neuroimaging studies more directly and with more dependent measures, which in turn will lead to the next wave of cognitive neuroscience studies, and so on. It requires a lot of bootstrapping, but there seems to be no principled reason why it will not work.[4]

Does Cognitive Neuroscience Offer a New Way to Look at Cognition?

Now I am going to get even more speculative, and suggest that cognitive neuroscience can do more than provide more informative and interpretable data—perhaps it can provide a new way of dividing cognition into topics of study. That is, I am suggesting that cognitive neuroscience may parse cognition differently than does strictly behavioral work or computational analyses. There are some indications that this may be the case, and in what follows I consider a few of them.

CONTENT DIFFERENCES IN PERCEPTION AND MEMORY

The nature of the material that gets processed—the qualitative nature of the contents in a task—looms far larger in cognitive neuroscience than in cognitive psychology. In fact, in cognitive neuroscience the nature of the to-be-processed material becomes a primary means for dividing up cognition. This point was the major take-home message from our PET case study of working memory, which showed that different neural circuits underlie working memory for spatial and verbal materials. And this finding is only the tip of an iceberg. Here are some other dramatic content effects that have emerged from cognitive neuroscience and related biological work.

• About 15 years ago, ablation studies with nonhuman animals showed that the visual system has two distinct tracts, one that involves occipitoparietal circuits and that mediates spatial localization (*where* an object is), and one that involves occipitotemporal circuits and that mediates object perception (*what* an object is) (Ungerleider & Mishkin, 1982). More recently, PET studies have demonstrated the operation of these same two systems in humans (Haxby et al. 1992). Hence the study of perception needs to be parsed into two areas: spatial localization and object recognition.

• The spatial vs. object distinction applies to memory as well. This has been demonstrated in studies with nonhuman primates, which measure activity in single cells while the animal is doing various tasks. When the animal is performing a task that requires it to briefly store spatial information, cells in a particular region of its frontal cortex are active, but when the animal is performing a task that requires it to briefly store object information, cells in a different region of its frontal cortex are active (Wilson et al., 1993). Recently, we have used PET studies to demonstrate the same kind of spatial- vs. object-working memory dissociation in humans (Smith et al., 1995). Furthermore, there is evidence from brain-damaged patients of comparable spatial-object dissociations in long-term memory and visual imagery (e.g., Levine et al., 1985).

• Studies of memory in brain-damaged patients indicate that lesions in left-hemisphere parietal cortex are routinely associated with impairments in short-term memory for verbal materials but not with impairments for visual materials. Other studies show that lesions in right-hemisphere regions are associated with deficits in processing visual materials but not verbal ones (McCarthy & Warrington, 1990; Shallice, 1988).

And so on. In general, the cortex is organized around distinctions based on spatial vs. object information, and, in the case of humans, around a visual vs. verbal distinction as well. This provides a way of parsing cognition that has not always been widely used in cognitive psychology (with the exception of imagery research, e.g., Kosslyn, 1980; Shepard & Cooper, 1982).

CONTENT EFFECTS IN CATEGORIZATION

There are more subtle content effects as well. To illustrate, let us move from the topic of memory to that of concepts and categorization, and consider the study of categorization in brain-damaged patients. The general finding of interest is that there are patients who are impaired in their ability to categorize certain classes of objects but not others. These phenomena are referred to as *category-specific deficits*, and they again indicate the importance of what particular contents are to be processed. The best-known category-specific deficit is probably *prosopagnosia*—a selective inability to categorize familiar faces. Another such deficit is the inability to categorize living things, particularly animals, while the ability to recognize nonliving things or artifacts remains relatively intact (e.g., Warrington & Shallice, 1984). A patient with this deficit, for example, can name pictured artifacts (tools, clothing, etc.) about as well as normals, but scores far below normals when asked to name familiar animals.

Taken at face value, these findings suggest that there may be different cortical regions responsible for concepts of animate and inanimate objects. Numerous researchers, however, have suggested instead subtle content differences between animals and artifacts. As one example, Farah and McClelland (1991) suggest that animals tend to be mentally represented mainly in terms of their perceptual features, whereas artifacts may be mentally represented as much by their functional as by their perceptual features. To the extent that functional features are tied to the motor system, this perceptual/functional proposal fits with the basic split between perception and action systems in the brain. In a related argument, Damasio (1990) notes that our experiences with most artifacts involves manipulating them, whereas, typically, manipulation is not part of our interaction with animals. Consequently, our representations of artifacts may be more motor-based than our representations of animals, and again the animal/artifact distinction reduces, in part, to a perception/action distinction. Neuroimaging experiments will likely prove useful in evaluating these proposals in the future. Regardless of how the details play out, again we have evidence for the importance of a content difference—perceptual vs. motoric information—that has not played much of a role in cognitive psychology.

PLANNING

Some topics are given more emphasis in cognitive neuroscience than in strictly behavioral studies. Consider the topic of planning. While it is a central topic in artificial intelligence, in cognitive psychology planning is generally treated as a component of problem solving and given relatively short shrift (as evidenced by the reduced treatment it gets in most cognitive psychology textbooks). But in cognitive neuroscience, particularly in the study of brain-damaged patients, the analysis of planning is of considerable importance. This is because deficits in planning are among the most striking symptoms of those patients who have suffered damage to the frontal lobes, and these deficits can drastically reduce the quality of the patients' lives. A frontal patient with planning deficits, for example, may be completely unable to carry out routine actions like making a cup of coffee or balancing a checkbook, even though they can carry out the individual components that constitute these activities. Because of considerations like this, planning is a bigger part of the "cognition pie" in cognitive neuroscience than in cognitive psychology.

This difference in the emphasis on planning in cognitive psychology vs. cognitive neuroscience reflects a general difference between the two fields that has broad implications. In cognitive psychology, all questions, of course, are about psychological functions, for example, Is selective attention a component of planning? In cognitive neuroscience, some questions are strictly functional, but others concern the relations between psychological functions and brain regions, for example, What is the function of this particular cortical area? Such brain-cognition questions are a natural consequence of working with brain-damaged patients and observing that lesions in particular areas are correlated with particular functional deficits. The fact that the two fields are asking somewhat different questions is worth emphasizing, for it alone could lead the two fields to parse the domain of cognition differently.

In sum, I have mentioned two general differences between cognitive neuroscience and cognitive psychology that lead the two approaches to divide cognition differently: (1) The major functional distinctions known about the cortex—verbal vs. visual information; spatial vs. object information, perceptual vs. motoric information—do not seem to have a comparable status in cognitive psychology, and (2) brain-cognition questions play a major role in cognitive neuroscience, but by definition they are not part of purely cognitive approaches. Likely, there are other general differences between cognitive psychology and cognitive neuroscience that lead to different views of cognition—for example, inhibitory processes may be emphasized more in cognitive neuroscience because of the importance of inhibition at the neuronal level—but hopefully the preceding discussion is sufficient to convince the reader that cognitive neuroscience offers something of a new "world view."[5]

Concluding Comments

I have argued that cognitive neuroscience can add to cognitive psychology in three distinct ways by providing (1) converging evidence, or additional constraints, on cognitive theories; (2) more informative and more directly interpretable data about cognitive processes; and (3) new ways of parsing the domain of cognition into researchable topics. Although my examples have emphasized the domain of memory, I believe the same three points apply to other broad cognitive domains as well. Assuming there is merit to these three points, the future might expect to see cognitive psychologists building on cognitive neuroscience results, and, for example, focusing strictly behavioral studies on issues like differences in processing verbal vs. visual materials. More radically, the future might see a blurring of the distinction between cognitive neuroscience and cognitive psychology, as every student of cognition would know and appreciate the relation between the brain and cognitive processes.

Acknowledgments

Preparation of this report was supported by a grant from the Office of Naval Research. I thank John Jonides, Patti Reuter-Lorenz, and Robert Solso for comments on the manuscript.

Notes

1. The results in figure 5.1 are based on 27 subjects (18 in the spatial task, 9 in the verbal task). PET is not particularly useful for determining how one individual differs from another (fMRI is better for these purposes). However, there is one source of variation among our subjects that does shine through. Women tended to be less lateralized than men, that is, in the spatial task, women showed some activation in left-hemisphere areas as well as right-hemisphere ones.

2. This difference was pointed out to me by John Jonides.

3. I thank John Jonides and Patti Reuter-Lorenz for these points.

4. In trying to make the case for the added methodological power of neuroimaging, I have underplayed the analytic power of strictly behavioral measures, particularly reaction time. Thus, Sternberg (1969) developed a method of analyzing reaction times that permits strong inferences about underlying processes, and Meyer et al. (1988) have shown how this method can be fruitfully applied to biologically based studies of cognition. Still, the point remains that knowing the value of a single reaction time provides less information about function than does knowing the level of activation of a single brain region.

5. The claim that cognitive neuroscience has a distinct way of parsing cognition has been argued in the literature on selective brain damage (e.g., Shallice, 1988). Here the critical point seems to be that the set of specific functions lost with brain damage provides a better estimate of the basic set of normal psychological functions than that derived from mainstream cognitive psychology. This position is compatible with the arguments I presented in the text, as long as the finding from brain-damaged patients converge with those from neuroimaging studies.

References

Atkinson, R. C., & Shiffrin, R. M. (1968). Human memory: A proposed system and its control processes. In K. W. Spence (Ed.), *The psychology of learning and motivation: Advances in research and theory* (vol. 2, pp. 89–195). New York: Academic Press.

Baddeley, A. D. (1986). *Working memory*. Oxford: Oxford University Press.

Baddeley, A. D., & Hitch, G. J. (1974). Working memory. In G. H. Bower (Ed.), *The psychology of learning and motivation* (vol. 8). New York: Academic Press.

Bruner, J. S., Goodenow, J. J., & Austin, G. A. (1956). *A study of thinking*. New York: Wiley.

Damasio, A. R. (1990). Category-related knowledge defects as a clue to the neural substrates of knowledge. *Trends in Neurosciences, 13,* 95.

Dronkers, N., Shapiro, J., Redfern, B., & Knight, R. (1992). The role of Broca's area in Broca's aphasia. *Journal of Clinical and Experimental Neuropsychology, 14,* 52–53.

Farah, M., & McClelland, J. (1991). A computational model of semantic memory impairment: Modality specificity and emergent category specificity. *Journal of Experimental Psychology: General, 120,* 339–357.

Fuster, J. M. (1995). *Memory in the cerebral cortex.* Cambridge, MA: MIT Press.

Haxby, J. V., Grady, C. L., Horwitz, B., Ungerleider, L. G., Mishkin, M., Carson, R. E., Herscovitch, P., Schapiro, M. B., & Rapoport, S. I. (1992). Dissociation of object-spatial visual processing pathways in human extrastriate cortex. *Proceedings of the National Academy of Sciences of the United States of America, 88,* 1621–1625.

James, W. (1890). *Principles of behavior.* New York: Holt.

Jonides, J., Reuter-Lorenz, P., Smith, E. E., Awh, E., Barnes, L., Drain, Glass, J., Lauber, E., Patalano, A., & Schumacher, E. (in press). Verbal and spatial working memory. In D. L. Medin (Ed.), *The Psychology of Learning and Motivation.*

Kosslyn, S. M. (1980). *Image and mind.* Cambridge, MA: Harvard University Press.

Kosslyn, S. M., Alpert, N. M., Thompson, W. L., Maljkovic, V., Weise, S. B., Chabris, C. F., Rauch, S. L., & Buonanno, F. S. (1993). Visual mental imagery activates topographically organized visual cortex. *Journal of Cognitive Neuroscience, 5,* 263–287.

Levine, D. N., Warach, J., & Farah, M. J. (1985). Two visual systems in mental imagery: Dissociation of "what" and "where" in imagery disorders due to bilateral posterior cerebral lesions. *Neurology, 35,* 1010–1018.

McCarthy, R. A., & Warrington, E. K. (1990). *Cognitive neuropsychology: A clinical introduction.* New York: Academic Press.

Meyer, D. E., Osman, A. M., Irwin, D. E., & Yantis, S. (1988). Modern mental chronometry. *Biological Psychology, 26,* 3–67.

Miller, G. A., Galanter, E., & Pribram, K. (1960). *Plans and the structure of behavior.* New York: Holt, Rinehart, & Winston.

Schacter, D. L. (1989). Memory. In M. I. Posner (Ed.), *Foundations of cognitive science.* Cambridge, MA: MIT Press.

Shallice, T. (1988). *From neuropsychology to mental structure*. Cambridge, England: Cambridge University Press.

Shepard, R. N., & Cooper, L. A. (1982). *Mental images and their transformations*. Cambridge, MA: MIT Press.

Smith, E. E., Jonides, J., Koeppe, R. A., Awh, E., Schumacher, E., & Minoshima, S. (1995). Spatial vs. object working memory: PET investigations. *Journal of Cognitive Neuroscience, 7*, 337–358.

Smith, E. E., Jonides, J., & Koeppe, R. A. (1996). Dissociating spatial and verbal working memory using PET. *Cerebral Cortex, 6*, 11–20.

Squire, L R., Ojemann, J. G., Miezin, F. M., Petersen, S. E., Videen, T. O., & Raichle, M. E. (1992). Activation of the hippocampus in normal humans: A functional anatomical study of memory. *Proceedings of the National Academy of Sciences of the United States of America, 89*, 1837–1841.

Sternberg, S. (1969). The discovery of processing stages: Extensions of Donders' method. In W. G. Koester (Ed.), Attention and performance 11 (special issue). *Acta Psychological, 30*, 276–315.

Ungerleider, L. G., & Mishkin, M. (1982). Two cortical visual systems. In D. J. Ingle, M. A. Goodale, and R. J. W. Mansfield (Eds.), *Analysis of visual behavior*. Cambridge, MA: MIT Press.

Warrington, E. K., & Shallice, T. (1984). Category-specific semantic impairments. *Brain, 107*, 829–853.

Waugh, N. C., & Norman, D. A. (1965). Primary memory. *Psychological Review, 72*, 89–104.

Wilson, F. A. W., O Scalaidhe, S. P., & Goldman-Rakic, P. S. (1993). Dissociation of object and spatial processing domains in primate prefrontal cortex. *Science, 260*, 1955–1958.

Worden, M., & Schneider, W. (1996). Cognitive task design in *f*MRI. *International Journal of Imaging Science and Technology, 6*, 253–270.

6   Imaging the Future

MICHAEL I. POSNER AND DANIEL J. LEVITIN

One thousand years ago it was not universally held that the mind was located within the brain. One hundred years ago, the firm conviction that brain and mind were related led phrenologists to map the topography of the scalp and face (figure 6.1). In the last 10 years, cognitive psychologists studying mental operations have embraced neuroimaging techniques to localize mental operations in the brain, and to study their orchestration as humans perform a variety of tasks (figure 6.2). What will we find as scientists explore and chart the brain in the next 10 years, 100 years, or 1000 years?

Extrapolating the Current Scene

Before speculating about the future, it seems appropriate to begin with a brief account of what we already know (or at least the two of us think we know) of the brain through current methods (Posner & Raichle, 1994). As we reach the last half decade of the 20th century it still amazes us that we can see pictures of our own minds at work. If a thought process can be sustained for only a few seconds, the snapshot revealed positron emission tomography (PET) or functional magnetic resonance imaging (fMRI) can show us which parts of our brain anatomy are active and to what degree. We know already that there are specific brain anatomies for reading (Posner & Raichle, 1994), listening to music (Marin, 1982; Sergent, 1993), mentally practicing your tennis serve (Roland, 1994), calculating numbers (Dehaene, 1995), and imagining a friend's face (Kosslyn, 1994). The methods for revealing the macroanatomy (in the range of millimeters to centimeters) of any mental process are clearly available.

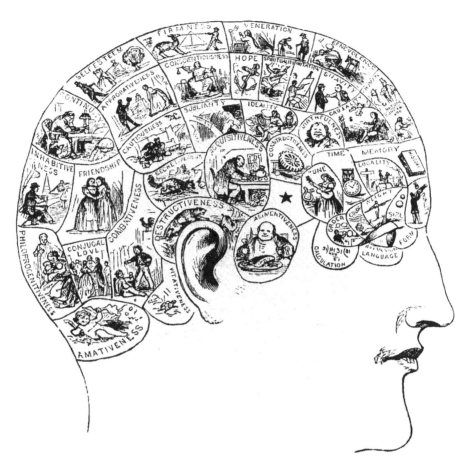

Figure 6.1 A picture of classic phrenology. The areas of the brain come from studies of bumps on the head and the cognition represents the faculty psychology common at the turn of the century. (From Krech, D., and Crutchfield, R., *Elements of Psychology*. © 1958 by David Krech and Richard S. Crutchfield. © 1969, 1974 by Alfred A. Knopf, Inc.)

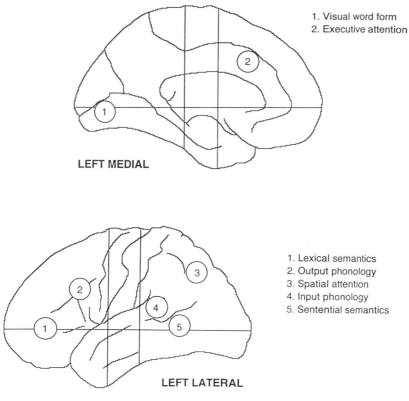

1. Visual word form
2. Executive attention

LEFT MEDIAL

1. Lexical semantics
2. Output phonology
3. Spatial attention
4. Input phonology
5. Sentential semantics

LEFT LATERAL

Figure 6.2   Modern phrenology. The areas of the brain summarize studies using PET and fMRI to observe changes in blood flow under experimental and control conditions. The cognition represents ideas of the types of computation involved in many cognitive tasks.

Anatomy

One clear finding that emerges from these methods is that every cognitive task entails a particular network of brain areas; often we can link these brain areas to a specific computation required by the task. Some brain areas are very specific to a given cognitive domain so that they are only active if the task involves language or recognizing a face. Other brain areas appear to carry out very general computations that may be important in any task domain. For example, the lateral cerebellum appears active in both sensory and motor timing, as if it represented a central clock (Ivry & Keele, 1989).

In the coming decades, we can expect our maps of brain anatomy to yield greater detail and spatial resolution, even if no new methods are invented. However, the attraction of young physicists formerly working on military problems to the study of the brain is such that we can be fairly certain that new and unanticipated ways of imaging brain activity will arrive. How should we use this increased resolution? Not just to make finer and finer maps! Rather, we need to seek principles of how important cognitive activity becomes distributed in brain regions.

In neuroscience, the cortical column is seen as the basic unit of organization of the human brain. Imaging methods have already shown that adjacent brain areas seem to become active as tasks change slightly. This forms the starting point for a principled approach to cortical organization at a macro level. The parietal lobe is involved in shifts of covert attention, but high up in its most superior regions it is active when the shift is to a purely visual event for which little response is required. When the shift of attention involves more detailed analysis of the nature of the visual event, or when overt orienting is allowed, the areas of activation appear to involve more inferior areas of the parietal lobe. When the task is purely one of recognition and no shift of attention is needed, the mid- to inferior temporal lobe is active.

Similarly, when a task is mostly passive (listening to a voice or music) different areas of the frontal midline show activity than those active when one begins to respond rapidly to a task (such as shadowing a word). Moreover, practicing a task can alter the brain areas involved. In one type of experiment, subjects are shown a noun and asked to respond with a word describing how it is used (e.g., "pound" to the word "hammer"). During this task, there are strong activations in the anterior cingulate, and in the left lateral posterior and anterior cortex. These activations disappear with practice but this is accompanied by an increase in activation in other brain areas that appear to be involved in automated (or "overlearned") tasks such as reading a word (Posner & Raichle, 1994). Perhaps our colleagues in the 21st century will be able to integrate these findings into a set of principles that will describe the organization of the brain for cognition.

COMPARATIVE ANATOMY

As principles emerge in the study of the human brain these areas of activation can be viewed in relation to the known areas of primate brains to advance evolutionary analysis of cortical development. Some advances in this area have already taken place. For example, the visual word form area appears to involve portions of the brain that are also important for processing color. This relatively recent evolution suggests that the processing of visual words takes advantage of the high spatial frequency analysis available with the parvocellular areas of the visual system. Similarly, there is reason to think that the grammar of human language may take advantage of brain areas originally developed for hierarchical mechanisms of motor programming (Greenfield, 1991).

There are other advantages of exploring relationships between neuroimaging in human and animal models. The neuroimaging methods have been confined to an anatomy in the millimeter range, while cortical columns are in the micron range. The *micro*anatomy is important for understanding how *computations* are made by neurons. We already have some idea of the power of this method from studies of how mental rotations are computed in the monkey motor system (Georgopolis et al., 1989) and how perceptual motions are computed within area MT of the monkey (Newsome, et al., 1994). The coming period should confirm and expand our knowledge of these mechanisms. We can then build on what we know about the details of neuronal computation in animals as additional constraints in the development of models of complex human tasks. As such models emerge it will be important to be able to examine the circuitry involved in human cognition to confirm predictions from models and to shape the agenda for the kinds of animal studies that will be needed.

CIRCUITRY

Today it is also possible to observe the orchestration of many brain areas in real time. So far this has been accomplished mainly by relating the distribution of activity visible in event-related electrical and magnetic fields to generators found active in anatomical studies (Snyder et al., 1995).

Circuitry and Reading   One of the areas for which the most knowledge is already available is in reading of words. During the reading of a foveal word (Posner et al., in press), computations occur in the right posterior occipital lobe at about 80 ms that relate to *features* of the word. By 130 to 180 ms the "visual word form" of the left posterior cortex is activated. For simple, clearly visible words, this is followed by activity in a frontal midline attention system by 170 ms and in a left lateralized frontal semantic system by 220 ms.

These activations contribute to organizing the saccade for the next fixation which typically begins by about 270 ms (Posner et al., in press). It is known from cognitive studies that the saccade is influenced by knowledge of the meaning of the current word. Therefore, it is necessary that information about the meaning of the word be available before the eyes are moved. Before the saccade begins there is more activation in anterior semantic areas related to word meaning, as well as higher-level frontal attentional areas. We should not think that these activations are purely in the direction of posterior to frontal. Rather there is feedback of information from frontal systems into posterior areas. Thus, in imagining a scene, frontally based attention and semantic systems can be used to activated posterior areas related to the visual form of the scene (Kosslyn, 1994).

While we can expect some of the details of these findings will likely be modified by future work, the way is clearly open for a detailed description of the time courses of mental operations in high-level human tasks.

There is also much scope for improvement in our ability to image noninvasively the circuitry involved in brain activity. While at present, electro- and magnetic activity recorded from outside the head are all that are available, the development of new statistical tools, including Bayesian analyses to constrain the solution space, will allow us to project the probable three-dimensional source of activation deep into the brain (Tucker et al., 1994). Future advances in dense sensory array measurement (e.g., 128 or 256 channels) of the brain's electrical and magnetic fields at the head surface promise new insights into the sources of these fields.

By combining the surface measurement with accurate information on the tissues of the head and brain from magnetic resonance imaging (MRI), the electrical (electroencephalogram or EEG) and magnetic (magnetoencephalogram or MEG) studies may be guided by additional constraints for localizing the neural sources. Unlike metabolic or blood flow (PET or fMRI) methods that have a poor temporal resolution, the EEG and MEG techniques provide a millisecond temporal resolution that is better suited to the time course of cognitive operations performed by neural circuits.

PLASTICITY

In cognitive science there has been a long-standing interest in the nature of expert performance (Chi et al., 1988). These studies show that there are major differences in representation of the same information by novices and by experts, and changes in representation that accompany the development of expertise within an individual. Very familiar to most cognitive psychologists is the impressive achievements of chess masters. Simon has estimated that this skill is based on many thousands of hours of practice and produces an elaborated semantic memory that allows reproduction of the chessboard in lawful master-level games (Chase & Simon, 1973). Chase and Ericsson (1982) have observed these changes in memory with practice in students trained to have numerical digit spans of up to 100 items. In these cases we do not yet know how the brain is altered by the experience involved.

While it has not yet been possible to understand the achievements of chess masters in *neural* terms, some studies of the neural basis of expert performance have already taken place. Familiar to most cognitive psychologists is the phenomenological change that accompanies learning to read. The ability of a skilled reader to recognize each letter of a lawful word at a lower threshold than the letter in isolation shows that learning the skill provides a visual chunk that eliminates the need to scan and integrate the letters. For this effect we already have a candidate neural system in the left medial occipital lobe (Posner & Raichle, 1994) that appears to be involved in performing this recognition function. It appears that this skill requires years of practice and produces signs of an adult "word form system" only at about age 10 (Posner et al., in press).

The studies outlined above suggest the continued plasticity of some aspects of brain circuitry with new learning. However, there is already evidence of critical periods in the learning of skills. Weber-Fox and Neville (1996) studied the learning of English by immigrants from China who came to the United States at ages ranging from 2 years to adulthood. They found that the brain circuitry involved in understanding the meaning of lexical items was similar regardless of age of immigration. However, the circuitry underlying grammatical judgments resembled American natives for those who immigrated as young children, but was very different in those whose immigration was late. A similar critical period has now been reported in learning the violin. Children who begin lessons prior to age 12 show changes in somatosensory cortical representation between the left and right hands that are not present even in expert violinists who began their lessons late (Elbert et al., 1995).

At present we have only a rudimentary understanding of how the anatomy, circuitry, and plasticity of the brain are involved in the performance of high-level human skills. It is clear that the accuracy and replicability of these findings is likely to improve steadily as new methods and more laboratories examine the results. However, it appears unlikely that we will ever be able to describe playing chess, for example, in terms of every brain area of computation that is invoked during a masters game. What will our goals be then and what progress toward their attainment can we expect?

Dynamic Brains

The study of psychology during the period from World War II to the mid-1980s was a study of how information was transferred between people and within a person. Psychology then was the study of the logic of how information was perceived, transformed, stored, and communicated. The brain was a black box, opaque to the physical substrate required to perform the functions specified by psychological models of mental events. A dominant metaphor was that psychologists studied software and for the logic of the programs it really didn't matter what hardware was required to run them. The current scene that we have described above—in which the hardware is also of interest—was ushered in by two related events. First, methods of neuroimaging opened up the human brain to investigation. It was now possible to image parts of the brain and see how they cooperated during performance. Second, a new class of models were developed, based on the idea of complex computations resulting from simple neuronlike units. These two events have allowed psychologists to describe the anatomy, circuitry, and plasticity of higher forms of human performance. In this section we try to speculate on what the consequences of this new opportunity will be.

A series of very important studies by Merzenich and colleagues (Merzenich & Sameshima, 1993) has found that the brain of the sensory systems of higher primates can change with experience. What is new as the century draws to a close is our capacity to also observe these changes in humans as they acquire skills.

We have barely begun to understand the capacity for change in the human brain. In a recent functional magnetic resonance study (Spitzer, Kwong, Kennedy, Rosen & Belliveau, 1995) showed evidence that brain areas that coded the concept "animal" were separate from the brain areas that were responsive to pictures of furniture. Whereas the areas active for these concepts were generally located within brain areas related to semantic processing, the number, the exact location, and the extent of the activation appeared to differ among people. Putting these observations together with the learning-dependent changes in brain maps shown in Merzenich's work, we may expect that spending a month furnishing your apartment would lead to an expansion of "furniture" representational areas in your brain, while working in a zoo might change the extent and depth to which animals are represented in the brain. These findings might well explain the common observation that our thoughts and even our dreams tend to be dominated by events related to current experiences—observations that on a more micro scale are seen in laboratory studies of priming.

LEARNING

Cognitive science, which views humans as intelligent, learning, and thinking creatures, is beginning to have an influence in the field of education. To bridge the gap between theory and practice in this important arena, a number of cognitive psychologists have moved into the classroom. A recent book (Bruer, 1993) describing the significance of cognitive work for classrooms has received an award from the American Federation of Teachers.

    We believe that in the future the field of cognitive neuroscience will be likely to also have a large impact on education. This may seem at first a somewhat unrealistic idea. There have been so many false starts, so many pop theories of brain functions, that many people (perhaps even the two of us) are wondering if we can learn things about the brain of sufficient importance to describe to those entrusted with the education of children. Nonetheless, we think that the new methods available to us both in terms of cognitive theory and brain imaging are stronger then ever before and we really must attempt to relate our findings to educational issues.

RECOVERY OF FUNCTION

Possibly the first area to benefit from the study of brain imaging will be the field of cognitive retraining following strokes or other closed head injuries. There has been evidence of some success in attempting to improve outcome from new forms of learning. However, since the mechanisms of recovery are not known, it has proved difficult to know whether these improvements in behavior are related to the training or due to spontaneous recovery that may also occur with delay after the injury. The ability to image the brain should allow much more detailed evidence of what the learning might do to change the anatomy or circuitry involved in cognitive tasks. In time we should know whether—and under what conditions—the relearning influences recovery within the damaged tissue, allows new areas to take over, or produces wholly new strategies that involve very different brain areas than those involved in the original task.

School Subjects

Already some tasks involving reading, music, and arithmetic have been studied in terms of anatomy and circuitry. Is there anything likely to emerge in cognitive neuroscience that will influence how these subjects are taught? One recent report illustrates what might be possible. Dehaene (1996) has argued that areas of the posterior parietal cortex are important for understanding the *quantity* of a number. He argues that this area of the brain is active when subjects are required to compare quantity, and moreover, lesions of this area produce a deficit in comparing and otherwise understanding quantity. Dehaene argues that this area may be common to both humans and animals and underlies our ability to know about quantity.

Griffin and colleagues (1994) has argued that children who are at risk of failing arithmetic in elementary school have a deficit in understanding the quantity of numbers so that they are unable to compare numbers. When this deficit is corrected by intensive education, they show marked improvement in their ability in arithmetic courses. These findings raise the possibility that we may be able to detect difficulties in comprehension related to specific brain areas and perhaps observe changes in activation of these areas that occur following the training. If so, our ability to diagnose a wide variety of learning disabilities in children may improve and benefit from neuroimaging in much the same way as described above for recovery of function following brain damage.

Individuality

The science of human differences has been heavily influenced by psychometric methods on the one hand, and on the other by the promise of twin studies that have suggested the genetic basis of personality. Work at three different levels of understanding in particular hold great promise: (1) genetic approaches, including the human genome project, (2) neuroimaging, and (3) phenotypic approaches to defining personality. As these methods are refined and the different levels related to one another, there is the promise of new excitement in the study of individual differences in cognition, emotion, and personality.

GENETIC LEVEL

According to recent estimates, the full sequence of the human genome will be completed ahead of schedule, by 2005. We now know that the brain has 3195 distinctive genes, and that roughly 17% of these are involved with cell signaling. It is conceivable that in the near future we will have found connections between particular genes in the brain and individual differences in personality traits. Whether particular genes will indicate a propensity for certain behaviors or determine those behaviors will undoubtedly be the subject of much popular debate. However, the currently available evidence—based on studies of identical twins separated at birth—is quite convincing that genetics is not deterministic of behavior; it merely provides a statistical model that accounts for only a portion of behavior variability (Lykken et al., 1992, 1993), and then only for the behavior of groups, not individuals. Thus, although certain gene markers might become associated with the potential for particular behaviors, the existence of a particular gene will not likely determine one's behavior.

What we still do not know much about is the way in which genes are translated first into biological substrates in the brain, and then into psychological mechanisms, such as a trait, nature, attitude, or preference. Moreover, we still know very little about the relation between traits and behavior, as the power of situational forces can often confound our predictions based on traits (Malle, 1995; Ross & Nisbett, 1991). The findings of behavior geneticists and personality and social psychologists will need to be integrated in the coming years to advance our understanding of these issues.

NEUROIMAGING

The genome findings, taken in concert with imaging studies, promise to illuminate the anatomical basis for many types of individual differences. The development of fMRI allows ready superposition of changes in blood flow and brain structure. Thus we can see how activation of brain areas relates to the structure of individual brains. We have already reviewed evidence that the structure and function of the brains of violinists differ if practice is started early enough (Elbert et al., 1995). We should be able to determine which differences depend upon practice and which may involve genetic differences that perhaps lead to the acquisition of high-level skill. In current cognitive psychology both genetic and learning views of individual differences have advocates; it seems likely that the use of imaging methods will provide a basis for separating and relating these approaches.

Phenotypic Structure

Although we use thousands of words to describe how people differ from one another, mathematical analyses show that our perception of human traits clusters in an orderly fashion, such that most of the traits on which people differ can be described by a location in a five-dimensional coordinate system, the "Big Five" personality model (Goldberg, 1993). This finding seems to hold up across a variety of cultures and languages, adding to the growing body of evidence that the strong version of the Whorf–Sapir hypothesis in untenable.

A subset of work on personality differences concerns one particular constellation of traits, those associated with what we loosely call "intellect." The recent, more inclusionary definitions of "intelligence" that allow for athletic, spatial, artistic, and other "nonacademic" intelligences (Gardner, 1983) broaden our notions of what it means to be intelligent. These new definitions also provide an expanded framework for the study of expertise. The near future may see changes in how we teach our children, as a result of the formal acknowledgment by academia that disparate forms of accomplishment exist.

Sociopathy

An example of how these three levels of research are merging comes from recent studies on criminal and aggressive behaviors. Geneticists have speculated that an "aggression" or "criminality" gene may soon be found. fMRI studies of the brains of murderers have shown clear differences in blood flow between them and normals: murderers tend to show far less frontal lobe activity, a possible indicator that they are less able to regulate feelings of aggression in a normal way. Obviously this evidence is merely correlational, and it does not demonstrate a causal link. Yet, some researchers believe that violent behavior will turn out to be physiologically determined. Raine (1993) predicts that the next generation of clinicians and the public will "reconceptualize non-trivial recidivistic crime as a psychological disorder."

At the phenotypic level, the constellation of traits that seem correlated with criminality appear clustered along the negative axis of one of the Big Five dimensions conscientiousness/undependability. The degree to which criminal behavior is a matter of genetics, anatomy, environment, or personality is a problem that may become subject to scientific resolution. A recent, forward-looking integration of many of these ideas in sociopathy may be found in Lykken (1995).

Some have predicted that within 10 years we will be able to actually diagnose those people with a propensity for committing violent acts before they have committed them, possibly during childhood or preadolescence (Gibbs, 1995). How this information is to be used will undoubtedly become a source of considerable public debate in the coming decades, and psychologists will likely be called upon to participate in this debate. But any "individual differences screening" based on anatomical or genetic markers can yield only statistical probabilities for a group. That is, we might be able to say that $X\%$ of a group that shows the propensity for violence will go on to commit violent acts, but we cannot predict with any certainty *how a given individual will behave.* Consequently, the most responsible use of such information might be never to gather it in the first place. It is our worst fear that screening information might be used to force medical interventions or incarceration on individuals who have demonstrated only that they are part of a group with a statistical chance of violent behavior, a course that would parallel the ugly history of the eugenics movement in the United States in the early 1930s. A concomitant fear is that future public policy might ignore the findings of science: even seemingly benign interventions that result from the best intuition and intentions can backfire (McCord, 1978).

The one thread common to these three approaches to the study of individuality seems to be an emerging consensus that the brain contains a great deal of "hard-wiring" of systems that are specialized for particular functions, or the expression of particular behaviors. But this hard-wiring is only a framework, one that holds tremendous plasticity, and is malleable as a result of experience and environmental input. Although the range of human differences appears infinite, these differences are contained within a system that is finite in its genetic, anatomical, and phenotypic description.

Theory of Consciousness

The coming decades should hold more interaction among researchers in the various fields that study human behavior. The neuroimaging methods have already brought together many fields in an effort to map the human brain. One theoretical topic that has united philosophy with the sciences is the effort to understand the physical basis of our conscious experience.

The question of what it is to be conscious has recently again become a central one in many serious scientific circles. Proposals range from the anatomical—for example, locating consciousness in the thalamus or in thalamic-cortical interactions—to the physical—for example, the proposal that consciousness must rest on quantum principles. Will all of these speculations provide a basis for understanding the centuries-old philosophical problems of how our mental experiences arise and how they relate to the brain?

One aspect of experience that has traditionally been related to or equated with consciousness is attention (James, 1890/1950). The images of human brains at work have revealed brain areas that seem closely related to programming the order of our mental computations. The areas responsible for programming amplify particular computations or suppress others, and they comprise various networks supporting selective attention. So far, these studies have supported three fundamental working hypotheses that together constitute current efforts to produce a combined cognitive neuroscience of attention. First, the brain possesses an attentional system that is anatomically separate from the various data-processing systems that can also be activated passively by visual, auditory, and other input. Second, attention is accomplished through a network of anatomical areas; it is neither the property of a single brain area nor is it a collective function of the brain working as a whole. Third, the brain areas involved in attention do not carry out the same function, but specific computations are assigned to specific areas (Posner & Raichle, 1994).

One major source of our feelings of conscious control involves the act (or illusion!) of voluntary control over behavior and thought. Volitional control is by no means total as the (presumably unwanted) tendency of depressed people to dwell on negative life events clearly shows. Yet all normal people have a strong subjective feeling of intentional or voluntary control of their behavior. Asking people about goals or intention is probably the single most predictive indicator of their behavior during problem solving. The importance of intention and goals is illustrated by observations of patients with frontal lesions (Duncan, 1994) or mental disorders (Frith, 1992) that cause disruption in either their central control over behavior or the subjective feelings of such control. Despite these indices of central control, it has not been easy to specify exactly the functions or mechanisms of central control.

Nonetheless there are some cognitive models of executive control that outline subsystems serving to control cognitive processing (Norman & Shallice, 1986). According to this model, attentional systems involve two qualitatively different mechanisms. The first level of control corresponds to routine selection (contention scheduling) in which the temporarily strong activity wins out. However, when a situation is novel or highly competitive (i.e., requires executive control), another supervisory system would intervene and provide additional inhibition or activation to the appropriate schema for the situation. Norman and Shallice (1980, 1986) have argued that the supervisory system would be necessary for five types of behaviors or situations in which the routine or automatic processes of the contention scheduling mechanisms would be inadequate and executive control would be required. These are (1) situations involving planning or decision making; (2) situations involving error correction; (3) situations where the response is novel and not well-learned; (4) situations judged to be difficult or dangerous; and (5) situations that require overcoming habitual responses.

One of the most interesting findings from the era of neuroimaging is that tasks involving these properties have all activated areas on the midline of the frontal lobe (Posner & DiGirolamo, in press). Moreover, lesions in this general area produce a remarkable loss of spontaneous thought and action. Damasio (1994) has recently described the effects of lesions of this area as follows: "Their condition is described best as suspended animation, mental and external—the extreme variety of an impairment of reasoning and emotional expression. Key regions affected by the damage include the anterior cingulate cortex, the supplementary motor area, and the third motor area." While more recent studies of surgical lesions of this area have not produced the devastating loss of mental function, so we do not know the extent or the neural system involved.

A new debate has emerged over whether consciousness is a function or a process, and thus over whether consciousness will be found to exist in a particular place in the brain. Elsewhere, one of us has argued that the anterior cingulate is likely to be a necessary and important component of tasks that are associated with consciousness (Posner, 1994), but that consciousness is a distributed, multifaceted function. The other of us has argued the not inconsistent idea that consciousness is an emergent property of the brain-as-a-whole, and that it is a *process*, not a *thing* (Luu et al., 1996). Thus, just as we don't expect to find "gravity" at a particular location in the middle of the earth, we shouldn't expect to find consciousness at a particular place in the head.

We can only speculate about the consequences of these new developments in the theory of attention for philosophical views about the relationship of brain to mental experience. Although we feel some confidence about the scientific predictions made in this chapter, we have relatively little idea what effect they might have upon the philosophical disputes that have attended the issue of consciousness. However, we can express our hope that the new developments in neuroimaging that will take place over the coming decades might help psychologists and philosophers to overcome the inhibitions of the hundreds of years of separation between mental and physical events. With an understanding that knowledge of the brain's anatomy provides constraints for more conceptual—or traditional cognitive—models, the psychologist and the philosopher will thus be able to reason, each from his or her understanding of neuroscience and of cognition. This joint approach will provide the basis for understanding the mechanisms of awareness and cognitive control as elements of consciousness.

References

Bruer, J. T. (1993). *Schools for thought: A science of learning in the classroom.* Cambridge, MA: MIT Press.

Chase, W. G., & Ericsson, K. A. (1982). Skill and working memory. In G. H. Bower (Ed.), *The psychology of learning and motivation* (Vol. 16). New York: Academic Press.

Chase, W. G., & Simon, H. A. (1973). The mind's eye in chess. In W. G. Chase (Ed.), *Visual Information processing.* New York: Academic Press.

Chi, M. T. H., Glaser, R., & Farr, M. J. (1988). *The nature of expertise.* Hillsdale, NJ: Erlbaum.

Damasio, A. R. (1994). *Descartes' error: Emotion, reason, and the human brain.* New York: G. P. Putnam.

Dehaene, S. (1996). The organization of brain activations in number comparisons: Event related potentials and the additive-factors method. *Journal of Cognitive Neuroscience, 8*, 47–68.

Duncan, J. (1994). Attention, intelligence and the frontal lobes. In M. S. Gazzaniga (Ed.), *The cognitive neurosciences* (pp. 721–734). Cambridge, MA: MIT Press.

Elbert, T., Pantex, C., Wienbruch, C., Rockstroh, B., & Taub, E. (1995). Increased cortical representation of the fingers of the left hand in string players. *Science, 270,* 305–306.

Frith, C. D. (1992). *The cognitive neuropsychology of schizophrenia.* Hillsdale NJ: Erlbaum.

Gardner, H. (1983). *Frames of mind: The theory of multiple intelligences.* New York: Basic Books.

Georgopoulos, A. P., Lurito, J. T., Petrides, M., & Schwartz, A. B. (1989). Mental rotation of the neuronal population vector. *Science, 243*(4888), 234–236.

Gibbs, W. W. (1995). Seeking the criminal element. *Scientific American, 272*(3), 76–83.

Goldberg, L. R. (1993). The structure of phenotypic personality traits. Presented at Sixth European Conference on Personality. *American Psychologist, 48*(1), 26–34.

Greenfield, P. M. (1991). Language, tools and brain: The ontogeny and phylogeny of hierarchically organized sequential behavior. *Behavioral and Brain Sciences, 14*(4), 531–595.

Griffin, S., Case, R., & Siegler, R. S. (1994). Rightstart: Providing the central conceptual prerequisites for first formal learning of arithmetic to students at risk for school failure. In K. McGilly (Ed.), *Classroom Lessons: Integrating Cognitive Theory and Classroom Practice.* Cambridge, MA: MIT Press/Bradford Books.

Ivry, R. B., & Keele, S. W. (1989). Timing functions of the cerebellum. *Journal of Cognitive Neuroscience, 1*(2), 136–152.

James, W. (1890/1950). *The principles of psychology.* New York: Dover.

Kosslyn, S. (1994). *Image and brain.* Cambridge, MA: MIT Press.

Luu, P., Levitin, D. J., & Kelley, J. M. (in press). Brain evolution and the process of consciousness. In P. G. Grossenbacher [Ed.], *Consciousness and brain circuitry: Neurocognitive systems which mediate subjective experience*. Philadelphia: John Benjamins.

Lykken, D. T. (1995). *The antisocial personalities*. Hillsdale, NJ: Erlbaum.

Lykken, D. T., Bouchard, T. J., McGue, M., & Tellegen, A. (1993). Heritability of interests: A twin study. *Journal of Applied Psychology, 78*(4), 649–661.

Lykken, D. T., McGue, M., Tellegen, A., & Bouchard, T. J. (1992). Emergenesis: Genetic traits that may not run in families. *American Psychologist, 47*(12), 1565–1577.

Malle, B. F. (1995). The person and the situation: Conceptual issues in theories of social behavior. Unpublished manuscript.

Marin, O. S. M. (1982). Neurological aspects of music perception and performance. In D. Deutsch (Ed.), *The psychology of music*. San Diego: Academic Press.

McCord, J. (1978) A thirty-year follow up of treatment effects. *American Psychologist, 33*(3), 284–289.

Merzenich, M. M., & Sameshima, K. (1993). Cortical plasticity and memory *Current Opinion in Neurobiology, 3*(2), 187–196.

Newell, A., & Simon, H. (1972). *Human problem solving*. Englewood Cliffs, NJ: Prentice Hall.

Newsome, W. T., Shadlen, M. N., Zohary, E., Britten, K. H., & Movshon, J. A. (1994). Visual motion: Linking neuronal activity to psychophysics performance. In M. S. Gazzaniga (Ed.), *The cognitive neurosciences* (pp. 401–413). Cambridge, MA: MIT Press.

Norman, D. A., & Shallice, T. (1980). *Attention to action: Willed and automatic control of behavior* (Technical Report No. 99). Center for Human Information Processing.

Norman, D. A., & Shallice, T. (1986). Attention to action: Willed and automatic control of behavior. In R. J. Davidson, G. E. Schwartz, & D. Shapiro (Eds.), *Consciousness and self-regulation* (pp. 1–18). New York: Plenum Press.

Posner, M. I. (1994). Attention: The mechanism of consciousness *Proceedings of the National Academy of Sciences of the United States of America, 91*(16), 7398–7402.

Posner, M. I., Abdullaev, Y. G., McCandliss, B. D., & Sereno, S. E. (in press). Anatomy, circuitry, and plasticity of reading. In J. Everatt (Ed.), *Visual and attentional processes in reading and dyslexia.*

Posner, M. I., & Raichle, M. E. (1994). *Images of mind.* New York: Scientific American Library.

Posner, M. I. & DiGirolamo, G. J. (in press). Conflict, target detection and cognitive control. In R. Parasuraman (Ed.), *The attentive brain.* Cambridge: MIT Press.

Raine, A. (1993). *The psychopathology of crime.* New York: Academic Press.

Roland, P. (1994). *Brain activation.* New York: Wiley-Liss.

Ross, L., & Nisbett, R. E. (1991). The person and the situation: Perspectives of social psychology. New York: McGraw-Hill.

Sergent, J. (1993). Mapping the musician brain. *Human Brain Mapping, 1,* 20–38.

Shallice, T. (1988). *From neuropsychology to mental structure.* New York: Cambridge University Press.

Snyder, A. Z., Abdullaev, Y., Posner, M. I., & Raichle, M. E. (1995). Scalp electrical potentials reflect regional cerebral blood flow responses during processing of written words. *Proceedings of the National Academy of Sciences of the United States of America, 92,* 1689–1693.

Spitzer, M., Kwong, K. K., Kennedy, W., Rosen, B. R. & Belliveau, J. W. (1995). Category-specific brain activation in fMRI during picture naming. *NeuroReport, 6,* 2109–2112.

Tucker, D. M., Liotti, M., Potts, G. F., Russell, G. S., & Posner, M. I. (1994). Spatio-temporal analysis of brain electrical fields. *Human Brain Mapping, 1,* 134–152.

Weber-Fox, C. M., & Neville, H. J. (1996). Maturational constraints on functional specializations for language processing: ERP and behavioral evidence in bilingual speakers. *Journal of Cognitive Neuroscience, 8,* 231–256.

7 What to Do with Your Own Personal Brain Scanner

ALAN GEVINS

The Man Who Wanted to Speak with the Dead

Before I talk about what I think will happen in T★H★E★ N★E★X★T M★I★L★L★E★N★N★I★U★M, I should mention something about our Lab. (What's the big deal about the year 2000? There will be some great parties and the date function on a lot of software is going to break.) I guess you could say that our Lab is not a typical lab, but really it is, especially if you compare it to something other than a lab, for instance, an insurance office.

I'm not sure where to start the story of the Lab, maybe in 1935 when Charles Levant Yeager, M.D., Ph.D., started the first EEG (brain wave) lab at the Mayo Clinic in Rochester, Minnesota. He and Emily drove there in a Model T Ford (figure 7.1). He had to build his own EEG recorder because you couldn't buy them back then. Or maybe, I should start after World War II when Dr. Yeager came to the Langley Porter Neuropsychiatric Institute at the University of California School of Medicine in San Francisco in 1947 to start a clinical EEG lab there. Being a ham radio enthusiast, he built a radio transmitter for brain waves so that a patient's brain could be monitored while he or she was walking around on the ward. It was a good idea, but at the time most of the psychiatric patients were in straitjackets and couldn't walk around.

I think I'll start the story in 1974 when Dr. Yeager retired (figure 7.2) and I, an uppity computer programmer and would-be Zen philosopher with a beard and ponytail, a Brooks Brothers suit, and a four-cylinder Honda 750 motorcycle with twice the horsepower of a VW microbus, became the Lab director. I first came to the Lab 2 years before to use the excellent but idle PDP-15 computer for my research on the effects of alternating magnetic fields on the brain. The computer, which was appropriately called JOHN, was donated to the Lab by Dr. Yeager's brother-in-law, Mr. John E. Fetzer. Mr.

Figure 7.1 In 1935, Charles and Emily Yeager drove their Model T Ford to Rochester, Minnesota, where Dr. Yeager established the first EEG lab at the Mayo Clinic. After World War II, Dr. Yeager started an EEG lab at the Langley Porter Neuropsychiatric Institute at the University of California School of Medicine in San Francisco. Programmers working late at night at our Lab still take naps in the green leather chair Dr. Yeager bought in 1947 for patients to sit in while their EEGs were recorded.

Fetzer owned the Detroit Tigers, as well as a number of radio and TV stations in the Midwest. He was very interested in extrasensory perception and, being in the broadcasting business, thought brain waves had something to do with it. JOHN was the hottest lab computer there was in those days. It was about 12 ft long, 3 ft deep, and 7 ft tall, and about as powerful as one of today's electronic appointment schedulers that fits in your pocket. It kept the Lab warm in the winter though, which is something that no pocket scheduler can to.

Mr. Fetzer once tried to repair JOHN by laying his hands on the central processing unit and concentrating on some kind of healing mantra. It's amazing what you can do if you're rich. For some reason, I didn't make any snide remarks when the computer remained broken. One time Brian Cutillo, who

Figure 7.2   Even after he retired in 1974, Dr. Yeager liked to come in and work on JOHN, our PDP-15 computer.

was the Lab's resident expert on cognition and was also a highly respected translator of obscure but actually quite relevant Tibetan Buddhist psychological texts, and I went to visit Mr. Fetzer at his winter home in Arizona to ask for some money to buy the Lab a new computer. Mr. Fetzer asked me if with our research we could learn how to communicate with the dead. I diplomatically (I thought) said that there were some more basic issues we needed to understand about consciousness and the brain first and that maybe communicating with the dead wasn't as important in the big scheme of things as learning how people could use their brains better, or even understanding how we move a finger. Apparently that wasn't the right answer because we didn't get a new computer, just some macadamia nuts and martinis before dinner and a few thousand dollars for the Lab as a consolation prize. Shortly after that Mr. Fetzer endowed the John E. Fetzer Foundation for Energy Medicine with about $150 million and built a large pyramid in the woods near Kalamazoo for its headquarters. I think energy medicine has to do with vibes and auras, but I'm not sure if it includes healing computers. Thinking back on it, maybe it wouldn't have been so bad to have a small, necessarily secret, part of the Lab doing research on communicating with the dead. Since dead people don't have brain waves, there probably would have been plenty of time left over to look into those more basic issues. I'd like to tell you the story of the Lab during the last 20 years and how it all leads up to the subject of this chapter, the Personal Brain Scanner (will you mind if I call it PBS?). In fact, I wrote quite a bit about the Lab, which is kind of a mix between a football team, a rock band, and a library, but I had to cut it out because this chapter is supposed to be very short. Sorry. Perhaps another time?

Bevis, Butthead, Bakunin, and CBS, PBS, and DSP

As predicted by the visionaries in think tanks worldwide, the 21st century is almost here. It's a sure bet that computers will continue to get smaller-faster-cheaper, that traffic and parking in the city will get worse, that the stock market will go up and down and then up again, and that the length of skirts will increase and decrease.

As go computers, so go brain wave machines, since an EEG device is just a computer with some wires touching the head and a little amplifier. It's only a matter of a few years before you won't even notice that there's an EEG machine there at all since the electrodes and amps may be built into a baseball cap. No wires will connect the EEG machine to a computer. You and your brain will be like a wireless modem, beaming data about your state of alertness and level of attention and mental effort directly into the computer. (I hope that if this sort of thing catches on, there won't be any unexpected problems, like, for instance, your computer picks up your neighbor's brain waves and thinks they're yours.) Actually, your brain will not be like a wireless modem. Modems are two-way devices which both transmit and receive data. The technology I'm describing is one-way, from your brain to the computer, and not the other way around. There's been lots of science fiction about computers transmitting all kinds of stuff into your brain, but I'll leave discussion about that sort of thing to the likes of Issac Asimov, William Gibson, and their esteemed science fiction writing colleagues since there isn't much I could say at this time about your brain directly receiving messages from a computer.

Just like with word processors, spreadsheets, and e-mail, what makes a computer into an EEG machine is software. Many kinds of software are needed to turn a computer into an EEG analyzer, but the most important kind is digital signal processing (DSP) software. DSP software is used to clean the EEG data to remove contaminants generated by eye movements, scalp muscle activity, and the like. DSP software also can remove the blurring of EEG signals as they are conducted from the brain through the highly resistive skull. Most important of all, DSP software extracts the brain signals related to alertness, level of attention, and degree of mental effort from the background electrical chatter of the brain. In a way, this is like trying to determine from outer space about how many fans are cheering at football games in each major city of the United States on a Sunday afternoon.

The PBS will also be able to determine the degree to which you're using each of your major cortical brain systems (hereinafter, CBS; the cortex, which is the outermost part of the brain, is critically involved in all sensory, motor, and higher cognitive functioning). This needs some explanation. Let's say you are working at a computer, writing a term paper analyzing Bevis and Butthead from the point of view of Bakunin's theory of anarchy. Visual input and motor output areas of your brain are of course engaged in the task of looking at the screen and pounding the keyboard, but many other areas are active as well. You might be thinking how to express the next few words as you type. If so, language output areas in the left front and rear part of your cortex (if you are right-handed and for some lefties) are active, as are other areas in the front and back of your cortex needed for maintaining representations and thoughts in the forefront of your mind. The pattern of which major cortical areas are active in performing a particular task or producing a particular brain state is the degree to which you're using each of your CBSs.

There has been a tremendous amount of progress in the past few decades in extracting specific information about thinking from EEG signals (figure 7.3), and progress is certain to continue. But please don't take this to mean that it will be possible to read the specific contents of someone's mind with EEGs. Engineering considerations aside, this may not be possible in principle because the brain's code for a specific word may not be the same from one instant to the next.

Eight Things That You Can Do with Your PBS

Let's imagine ahead a few years, not so many, to a time when EEG machines are simply an inexpensive peripheral that can conveniently communicate with your computer at home, your computer at work, the main computer in your car, and even your wearable sports training computer. When you buy your PBS, the first thing you will have to do is to calibrate it to your unique brain signal patterns. After that, without having to make any special effort, if you wish to, you will be able to communicate to all the computers in your life how alert you are, how hard you're concentrating, and which of your CBS's are busy and working together. That's nice, but what good does it do you if your computer knows you're falling asleep or not paying attention? Here are some ideas that I've thought about. I'm sure you can think of others.

I can think of four main areas where your PBS would be useful to you, namely to perform mental checkups on yourself, to help you improve basic mental functions like concentration and learning faster, to enhance performance, and just for fun.

Mental Checkups: Very Short, Short, Medium, and Long-Term Scales

VERY SHORT: AM I FALLING ASLEEP AT THE WHEEL?

I've stayed up almost all night packing and have been finishing up a zillion details, first at the office and then at home, so I can start out on that long-awaited backpacking trip. It took a lot longer than I expected to finish up. It's almost 9 P.M., and I'm looking at driving all night to get to Joshua Tree National Monument down near the Mexican border around dawn. I've been down Interstate 5 many times before and it's on my top 10 list of the most boring roads in the world. It's all farmland, no lights, no towns, hardly any other cars at night. There's not even a turn in the road until after Bakersfield. Naturally, I'm worried about falling asleep at the wheel. No problem. I put on my PBS headset and set the system to Alertness Monitoring mode, confident that it will warn me even before I close my eyes and start to nod off. To be on the extra-safe side, I set the PBS to command the car to reduce its speed, put on the blinkers, sound the horn, and pull off to the side of the road if it detects incipient drowsiness. Long-haul truck drivers might also like this feature of a PBS.

SHORT: IS THIS A BAD HAIR DAY?

I've got a very important and delicate negotiating meeting today at which I'll have to help achieve a consensus between two parties whose interests are not squarely aligned and who don't get along with each other to boot. The problem is that I just don't feel as sharp as I normally do. My mind feels like it's in a thick fog. The stakes are high and it would be better to postpone the meeting than come to it with less than a full deck of cards upstairs. I put on my PBS, sit down at my computer, and do a few simple standard mental tasks that test some key mental functions. After a few minutes, the PBS tells me that I'm not focusing my attention as well as I normally do despite the fact that I'm exerting a greater-than-normal degree of mental effort. Yes, this is a bad hair day. It would be better to postpone that meeting.

MEDIUM: I'M RECOVERING FROM A HEAD INJURY. AM I READY TO GO BACK TO WORK?

I was trying out the highly touted off-road capabilities of my new Jeep Grand Cherokee a couple of weeks ago. I guess I should have taken some lessons first. I was trying to go up a very steep embankment a little too fast and definitely at the wrong angle. It flipped and I got a pretty nasty bang on the head. I've had some headaches and couldn't focus my attention the way I normally do. My doc says to take Tylenol for the headaches, not to worry, I should recover completely in a few more weeks or so, and please feel free to call him if I have

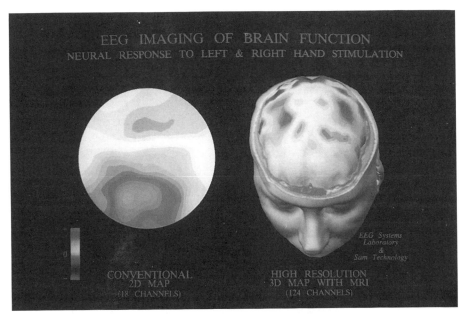

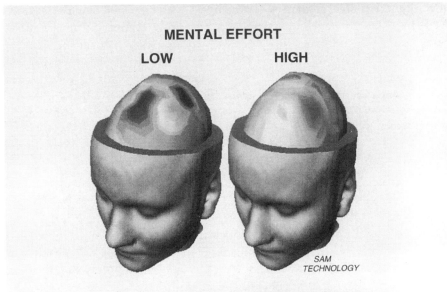

Figure 7.3   (*Top*) There hasn't been that much interest in improving EEGs. By contrast, vast sums of money have been spent developing other technologies for measuring brain function such as positron emission tomography (PET) and magnetic resonance imaging (MRI). I was once told by an executive at the division of General Electric that makes MRI scanners that the reason they weren't interested in EEGs was that EEGs were too cheap and they couldn't make enough money from them. That may be so, but EEGs are sensitive measures of mental activity in the brain and are worth further developing. There is a lot of untapped spatial detail that could be obtained from EEGs. The first step is increasing the number of recording electrodes on the scalp, and the second step is removing the blurring of EEGs as they pass through the highly resistive skull. The left head outline shows a conventional EEG topographic map made from 18 electrodes. There is nothing about the appearance of the map that would indicate that fingers on the left and right hands are being stimulated. There's just a big blob at the left front of the head (the nose is at the bottom). The right head shows the same stimulation conditions, but recorded with 124 electrodes and with the blurring removed using a deblurring method we developed which combines information about brain function from EEGs with information about brain structure from MRIs. It is immediately apparent from the islands of high activity on the left and right side of the brain that fingers on left and right hands have been stimulated. The improvement in spatial detail is quite dramatic, but it still must be remembered that even the best EEG cannot provide a true three-dimensional image of function throughout the entire brain. EEGs are particularly useful for measuring activity on the outer surface of the brain, the cerebral cortex. This isn't so bad if one is interested in thinking because a lot of the action in thinking takes place in the cerebral cortex. Besides costing perhaps 50 to 100 times less, EEGs have some advantages as compared with other methods, though. They can capture events in the brain that are 1000 times briefer than other methods, and they can measure brain function while a person is engaged in ordinary everyday life situations, which isn't possible if you are immobilized inside the cannon-barrel-like magnet of an MRI. (*Bottom*) This is a high-resolution EEG image we made during a recent study of working memory. It shows a particular instant in time when a subject was doing either an easy or a difficult task. Such studies are providing the scientific basis for your Personal Brain Scanner.

any more questions. I'm tired of hanging out watching the soaps and puttering around the garden. I think I can go back to work, but I'm an air traffic controller, and if I lose my concentration people could die. I select the PBS's Personalized Mental Stress Test. About a half hour later, after doing a whole battery of difficult tasks, my brain feels like it's been in a microwave oven. The report appears on the screen. It confirms what I feel. Better to spend a few more days at home.

LONG-TERM: AM I GETTING SENILE?

Sometimes I just can't remember the name of a restaurant I've been to, or the name of someone I've met several times. Is this a sign of incipient Alzheimer's, that I'm already starting to lose my marbles? I select my PBS's Long-Term Checkup option and choose several of the memory tests. After a few minutes, the PBS tells me that the brain electrical patterns of my memory functions are no different from what they were last year, the year before, and the year before that. Nothing to worry about, yet.

Improving Basic Mental Functions and Learning

HOW DO I CONCENTRATE BETTER?

There's nothing wrong with my concentration. It's just that it could be a lot better than it is. For example, I might be trying to picture where each guest will sit at a large dinner party I'm having next week and I keep getting distracted by one train of thought or another, like the last time I saw one of the guests named Susanna. Or I might be trying to debug a computer program and just can't quite keep all the conditional interrelations between the different functions of the program in my mind's eye. I know that if I could, I would find the bug. There are lots of other examples from everyday life in which I don't have enough control over my own attentional processes to be able to efficiently carry out one task or another. My PBS has a Personal Brain Trainer function which will take me through a series of exercises to help me improve my ability to deploy my attention. Its good for this purpose because, unlike exercises that rely only on my behavioral responses to indirectly infer whether my attention was focused or diffuse, my PBS can actually measure the neural signals of my attention in real time. But I know that if I'm serious about improving my mental abilities, I will have to work hard at it every day for quite a while. The PBS will not instantly and effortlessly improve me. I have to do it myself. No pain, no gain.

Can I Learn Faster?

I'd like to learn Japanese, and bought a nifty new computer-based language teaching program that interfaces with my PBS. Whenever I make a mistake the language program asks the PBS whether I was alert and paying attention, or whether I was drifting off. If the PBS says r was concentrating, the language program knows that I didn't understand the concept it was trying to teach me and will try a different explanation. By contrast, if the PBS says I wasn't paying attention, the language program might ask me if I'd like to stop now and try again later after I've had some coffee.

Here's another example. I'm a jet mechanic and I'm trying to learn how to assemble a new type of engine. The computer-aided instruction system I'm using notices that I'm having a hard time putting together the pieces for a particular subassembly. Areas on the left side of my brain responsible for language comprehension and generation are quite active, while the right parietal area of my cortex, crucial in visualizing spatial relations, is relatively silent. The training program encourages me to try to visualize the spatial relations between the parts more and rely less on naming them and making up a story about how they fit together. I try this out and am able to do the problem. By having information about the degree to which I'm using each of my CBSs, the teaching program can adapt what its doing to optimize the learning process for me.

Enhancing Performance

How Do I Make That Perfect Golf Stroke?

I know there are times when I'm right in the groove and the shot is perfect. I think it has something to do with getting my mind centered, whatever that is, at the instant before I start the swing. Maybe if I run my PBS in Pattern Recognition Training mode while I do a bunch of strokes, I'll get enough samples of ordinary and exceptionally good strokes for the PBS to tell them apart. Once it has an image of my "right stuff" brain state, it can tell me when

I'm in it, and maybe I'll learn to produce the right stuff state more frequently. It might even be able to compare my right stuff profile with that of some great pros and give me some hints.

Entertainment

CAN I PLAY A VIDEO GAME WITH THIS THING?

Don't hold your breath if your waiting to be able to control a rapidly moving space ship through an asteroid belt just by thinking about it, but there might be some fun things you could do with a PBS and a video game. For instance, the PBS could provide the game with the information it needs to create a nasty opponent that shoots at you when you're not paying attention.

Is All This California Dreaming?

Do these applications exist today? Of course not. Are they far-off science fiction? Not really. They are somewhere in-between. For all of these applications, the basic science knowledge about appropriate signals of higher brain function is, in principle, known or knowable. Nor are there insurmountable engineering obstacles to producing practical, inexpensive technologies. Rather, it is mostly a matter of designing and running many experiments to settle hundreds of little details. These details make the difference between what is just another interesting basic science result and a practical, useful technology. Unfortunately, there are no shortcuts. Even under the best of circumstances it will take a number of years to carry out several rounds of experiments and technology development. The data from many hundreds of subjects will have to be recorded, analyzed, and reanalyzed to make a viable, practical system in each of the application areas. I would be remiss if I didn't warn you to watch out for the inevitable Killer Clowns from Inner Space who will claim to have made a PBS without successfully completing all the difficult, tedious, and expensive prerequisite research. Not only will their pseudo-PBSs not really work (figure 7.4), they will make it harder to develop the real thing by prematurely raising hopes and expectations and then causing disappointment and resentment (that's why they're called Killer Clowns). But not to worry, there are many crusty scientists like me, and we will all do our best to neutralize the Clowns if they start to cause trouble.

Figure 7.4   When the first supposed brain treatment devices came out around a hundred years ago, they bore a family resemblance to cerebral blood flow scanners of the 1970s, but lacked any of the essential components of a real device, for instance, electronic circuits or detectors of radioactivity. Although I'm sure that extravagant claims were made about the wondrous capabilities of these devices, their acceptance was very limited because they didn't really do anything. When real EEG machines, real regional cerebral blood flow measurement devices, and real PET and functional MRI scanners were invented, their acceptance was virtually instantaneous because they actually worked. Watch out for Clowns with unproved devices they claim can help you develop your brain's full potential.

I hope that when you have your own PBS someday soon, it will help you on your voyage of self-discovery and self-development, and also help you in many other ways to have a better life. So, goodbye for now. I think the best is yet to come.

Acknowledgments

Our Lab's research is supported by competitive grants from several U.S. federal agencies and departments, including the National Institutes of Health and Mental Health, the Air Force, NASA, and the National Science Foundation.

Bibliography

Gevins, A., Leong, H., Smith, M. E., Le, J., & Du, R. (1995). Mapping cognitive brain function with modern high resolution electroencephalography. *Trends in Neurosciences*, *18*, 429–436.

Gevins, A. S., Bressler, S. L., Cutillo, B. A., Illes, J. Fowler-White, R. M., Miller, J., Stern, J., & Jex, H. (1990). Effects of prolonged mental work on functional brain topography. *Electroencephalography and Clinical Neurophysiology*, *76*, 339–350.

Gevins, A. S., & Cutillo, B. A. (1993). Spatiotemporal dynamics of component processes in human working memory. *Electroencephalography and Clinical Neurophysiology*, *87*, 128–143.

Gevins, A. S., Doyle, J. C., Cutillo, B. A., Schaffer, R. E., Tannehill, R. S., Ghannam, J. H., Gilcrease, V. A., & Yeager, C. L. (1981). Electrical potentials in human brain during cognition: New method reveals dynamic patterns of correlation. *Science*, *213*, 918–922.

Gevins, A. S., Doyle, J. C., Schaffer, R. E., Callaway, E., & Yeager, C. (1980). Lateralized cognitive processes and the electroencephalogram. *Science*, *207*, 1005–1008.

Gevins, A. S., Morgan, N. H., Bressler, S. L., Cutillo, B. A., White, R. M., Illes, J., Greer, D. S., Doyle, J. C., & Zeitlin, G. M. (1987). Human neuroelectric patterns predict performance accuracy. *Science*, *235*, 580–585.

Gevins, A. S., & Remond, A. (1987). Methods of analysis of brain electrical and magnetic signals. In A. S. Gevins & A. Remond (Eds.), *Handbook of electroencephalography and clinical neurophysiology* (vol. 1). Amsterdam: Elsevier.

Gevins, A. S., Schaffer, R. E., Doyle, J. C., Cutillo, B. A., Tannehill, R. S., & Bressler, S. L. (1983). Shadows of thought: Shifting lateralization of human brain electrical patterns during a brief visuomotor task. *Science, 220,* 97–99.

Gevins, A. S., Smith, M. E., Le, J., Leong, H., Bennett, J., Martin, N., McEvoy, L., Du., R., & Whitfield, S. (1996). High resolution evoked potential imaging of the cortical dynamics of human working memory. *Electroencephalography and Clinical Neurophysiology, 98*(4), 327–348.

Gevins, A. S., Zeitlin, G. M., Doyle, J. C. Yingling, C. D., Schaffer, R. E., Callaway, E., & Yeager, C. L. (1979). EEG correlates of higher cortical functions. *Science, 203,* 665–668.

8

The Deep and Surface Structure of Memory and Conscious Learning: Toward a 21st-Century Model

Karl H. Pribram

Sir Arthur Eddington, the British astronomer, once remarked that "You cannot believe in astronomical observations before they are confirmed by theory." Much the same applies to the experiments we do in biology: we can begin to believe in results only if we have an adequate grasp of the theories that seek to explain the nature of the systems we study.

—Gordon M. Shepherd (1988, p. 91)

What might theories within the brain-behavioral sciences be like a decade or two hence? Despite some considerable trepidation, I shall ruminate on two topics because of their abiding interest to me: (1) the deep and surface structure of memory and (2) conscious learning as self-organization. I will do this in terms of outlines of models based on my own experience, with the hope that these outlines provide the skeleton for current and future work that will flesh them out.

The Deep and Surface Structure of Memory

Memory loss due to brain injury ordinarily encompasses a category of processing: prosopagnosia (inability to recognize faces); tactile agnosia; aphasia (inability to speak), and so forth. But the category can be narrowly restricted—for instance, to living vs. nonliving items or unfamiliar perspectives on familiar objects. Furthermore, whenever we wish to recall something or other, we find it useful to employ a very specific trigger that provides entry into the retrieval structure. Still, specific memories (engrams) are rarely "lost" due to brain injury. This has given rise to the view that, ultimately, storage of experience in the brain is distributed. What kind of brain process can account for both the specificity of memory and distribution?

From a 21st-century vantage, I will conceive of the organization of memory storage to resemble somewhat the organization proposed by Chomsky (1965) for language: memory has a deep and a surface structure. The deep structure of memory is distributed in the connection web of brain tissue; its surface structure is encompassed in specific circuits which are dispositions toward patterned propagation of signals preformed genetically or on the basis of experience, or both. Retrieval entails a process whereby brain circuitry addresses the distributed store. Smolensky (1986) has captured the formal essence of the process that characterizes the retrieval process, the surface structure of memory: "The concept of memory retrieval is reformalized in terms of the continuous evolution of a dynamical system [embodied in the function of a circuit] towards a point attractor [a trigger] whose position in the state space [the distributed store] is the memory. You naturally get dynamics of the system so that its attractors are located where the memories are supposed to be. . . ." (pp. 194–281). In short, the process of remembering operates on a dismembered store by initiating a temporary dominant focus of excitation in the dendritic net. Smolensky's suggestion is made more plausible if the "location" of attractors is content determined, that is, if the process is essentially content addressable—by a similarity matching procedure—rather than location addressable.

In everyday life, we experience the type of process described above if we have mastered two languages. When speaking either language, we readily address the contents of our stored experience, our memories (deep structure), but we do so in a totally different manner in each language. The difference is so great that unless one is an experienced translator, one has great difficulty in shifting from one language structure to the other. But the "items" of stored experience, such as the clothes we wear, the places we work and live in, the relationships we practice, are accessible to both languages. More on this presently.

DEEP STRUCTURE

Neurons are nerve cells that are made up of a cell body, small-diameter branching extensions from the cell body (dendrites), and often another single extension (an axon), usually larger and possessing properties different from the dendrites. As axons approach the dendrites of another neuron, the axons branch and thus resemble dendrites in that their diameters are also very small.

This is an important consideration because the amplitude and speed of propagation of an electrical signal in an axon are proportional to the diameter (actually the membrane circumference) of the nerve fiber—thus, in the terminal axon branches signals become of such low amplitude that for the most part, a chemical booster has to be released to influence the postsynaptic site. Furthermore, because of the marked slowing of signals, they interact by passive spread rather than by an active propagation, as in large axonic or nerve trunks.

With guarded hope, I foresee that during the 21st century, it will become evident to everyone that the deep distributed structure of memory storage is taking place within the brain's connective web, that is, at the synaptodendritic level of processing. One of the most intractable problems facing brain neurophysiologists has been to trace the passage of signals through the dendritic trees of neurons. The received opinion is that such signals accumulate from their origins at synapses, by simple summation of excitatory and inhibitory postsynaptic potentials, to influence the cell body and its axon and thus the cell's output. This is not the case. Each synaptic site "is functionally bipolar ...; it both projects synapses onto and receives synapses from many other processes.... Hence input and output are each distributed over the entire dendritic arborization ... where[ever] dendrodendritic interactions are important" (Selverston et al., 1976, quoted by Shepherd, 1988, p. 82). The anatomical complexity of the brain's connective web has led to the opinion summarized by Szentagothai: "The simple laws of histodynamically polarized neurons indicating the direction of flow of excitation ... came to an end when unfamiliar types of synapses between dendrites, cell bodies and dendrites, serial synapses etc. were found in infinite variety" (Szentagothai, 1985, p. 40).

The received opinion also focuses on the transmissive nature of synapses: Thus the term "neurotransmitters" is, more often than not, ubiquitously applied to the variety of chemical molecules secreted at axon terminals when these are stimulated by the arrival of depolarizations of axon branches at the presynaptic site. This focus on transmission appears to me to be misplaced. In any signal processing device, the last thing one wants to do if unimpeded transmission is required is to physically interrupt the carrier medium. Interruption is necessary, however, if the signal is to be processed in any fashion. Interruption allows switching, amplification, and storage to name a few purposes which physical interruptions such as synapses could make possible.

At the behavioral and experiential level, these processes make possible the distinction between memory storage processes that depend on attention—

that is, on conscious experience on the one hand and automatic processing on the other (Pribram 1971). Early on it became evident that automatic behavior and awareness are often opposed—the more efficient a performance, the less aware we become. Sherrington (1911/1947) noted this antagonism in a succinct statement: "Between reflex (automatic) action and mind there seems to be actual opposition. Reflex action and mind seem almost mutually exclusive—the more reflex, the less does mind accompany it." Additionally, however, over the past decades it has been shown that automaticity holds not only for behavior but also for processes such as attention and memory. Thus, we now distinguish between automatic and controlled processing (Bolster & Pribram, 1993) in attention and between implicit and explicit memory (Schacter & Tulving, 1994).

Evidence (Pribram, 1971) indicates that automatic processing is programmed by neural circuitry mediated by nerve impulses, whereas awareness, which provides an opportunity for conscious learning, is due to delay in processing occurring in the brain's connective web. The longer the delay between the initiation in the dendritic network of postsynaptic arrival patterns and the ultimate production of axonic departure patterns, the longer the duration of awareness and the opportunity for distributed storage. This opportunity becomes constrained as skills develop.

Daniel Alkon and his colleagues showed that as the result of Pavlovian conditioning there is an unequivocal reduction in the boundary volume of the dendritic arborizations of neurons (Alkon and Rasmussen, 1988). These neurons had previously been shown to increase their synthesis of messenger ribonucleic acid (mRNA) and specific proteins under the same Pavlovian conditions. Although these experiments were carried out in molluscs, such conditioning-induced structural changes may be akin to the synapse elimination that accompanies development as the organism gains in experience.

Before such constraints become operative, signal transmission in the dendritic network is far from straightforward. As Alkon points out in a 1989 *Scientific American* article: "Many of the molecular [and structural] transformations take place in ... dendritic trees, which receive incoming signals. The trees are amazing for their complexity as well as for their enormous surface area. A single neuron can receive from 100,000 to 200,000 signals from separate input fibers ending on its dendritic tree. Any given sensory pattern probably stimulates a relatively small percentage of sites on a tree, and so an almost endless number of patterns can be stored without saturating the system's capacity" (pp. 42–50).

The picture becomes even more complicated when we consider the spines that extend perpendicularly from the dendritic fiber—hairlike structures (cilia) onto which axon branches terminate. Each spine consists of a bulbous synaptic head and a narrow stalk which connects the head to the dendritic fiber. Thus, synaptic depolarizations and hyperpolarizations become relatively isolated from the dendritic fiber because of the high resistance to the spread of polarization posed by the narrowness of the spine stalk. It appears, therefore, "that there is an isolation of the activity at a given site from the ongoing activity in the rest of the cell. . . . Part of the strategy of the functional organization of a neuron is to restrict synaptic sites and action potential sites to different parts of the neuron and link them together with passive electronic spread" (Shepherd 1988, p. 137). Furthermore, "it has been shown that synaptic polarization in a spine head can spread passively with only modest decrement into a neighboring spine head" (Shepherd et al., 1985, p. 2192). The interactions among spine-originated dendritic potentials (that need to become effective at the cell's axon) thus depend on a process which is "discontinuous and resembles in this respect the saltatory conduction that takes place from node to node in myelinated nerve" (Shepherd et al. 1985, p. 2193). For details as to how this occurs, see the Appendix.

THE SURFACE STRUCTURE

With regard to the systems that encompass the brain circuitry, there is considerable agreement to the effect that at least three broad classes of memory processes can be discerned: one class encodes and decodes experiences that refer to our environment; a second class codes experienced episodes of events that relate to our interests; and a third class organizes the practice of skills. The three processes can be crudely encapsulated as encoding the what; the when and whence; and the how of experience. Within the primate forebrain, the what systems involve the distance receptor processing performed by the posterior cerebral convexity; the when and whence systems involve the fronto-limbic formations; and the how systems entail the centrally located somatic motor and sensory mechanisms. It is within these systems, with their cortical and subcortical components, that the memory *circuits* necessary to retrieval become established. But the circuits composing each of the posterior, central, or frontal cortical systems can be divided into extrinsically connected (to receptors and effectors) projection systems and so-called association systems intrinsically connected in large measure to other brain and brain stem structures.

J. Z. Young (1962), over 30 years ago, developed the theme that the primary sensory projection systems of the brain have evolved to map the sensory environment, whereas the more intrinsically connected "association" cortex performs abstract computations on the mapping functions. In discussing his paper, I (Pribram, 1963) presented evidence that the abstract computations were composed by sampling the maps in a top-down fashion. More recently, a great deal of interest has been generated by Shiffrin and Schneider's (1984) observations of the conditions that predispose humans toward automatic processing as opposed to those which predispose them toward consciously controlled processing of sensory input. Automatic processing was considered to operate in parallel on maps of the input; controlled processing was considered to entail scans (searches) of the input.

Experiments by Efron have called attention to the fact that a variety of hitherto conflicting or unexplained observations—especially with regard to differences in hemispheric function—can be understood in terms of the order in which sensory input is sampled, or scanned (for a review, see Efron, 1989). Scanning was shown to occur during a postexposure period and thus to be independent of eye movement. Some central brain process—the same as that which provides the surface structure of memory?—shown to be influenced by prior experience was inferred to be responsible.

Studies were undertaken to investigate under what conditions sampling entailed scan and what extent of intrinsic cortex might be involved in sampling procedures. Tasks were modified from Treisman's (1969) "disjunctive" vs. "conjunctive" displays in keeping with Shiffrin and Schneider's (1984) procedures: the display *set*—the nature and number of distractors in an array—was manipulated. Such procedures had, in other studies (Douglas et al., 1969; Douglas & Pribram, 1969; Pribram, 1960), been shown to be sensitive to the effects of brain damage.

The results showed that when reaction times are prolonged, differences in stimulus-evoked brain electrical responses are recorded from intrinsically connected association cortex and not from projection cortex. Furthermore, such differences were obtained from *all* three locations within the intrinsic cortex from which recordings were made. This suggests that more than one single process is responsible for the increase in reaction times, and thus, for the scanning procedure necessary to the organization of the surface structure of memory: (1) location search (parietal), (2) generating a scanplan to deal with the covarying contingencies that characterize a shared feature distractor set (frontal), and (3) bias leading to attentional fluidity (not to be confused with automaticity; temporal lobe). The most enigmatic of these factors is bias: fluidity in sampling apparently depends on comprehending not only the featural factors that directly determine the outcome of a search but ancillary task parameters and prior experience, as well.

But a great deal of the memory store is apt to be located in the basal ganglia (caudate, putamen, globus pallidus, nucleus accumbens), a repository that has been neglected in memory research. The surface structure of memory, most likely, will therefore be found to involve thalamocortical-basal ganglia-thalamcortical circuitry. Shunts will occur within the basal ganglia-thalamic portions of the circuits that allow the how, when and whence, and what processes to distribute and retrieve their respective stores within one another's confines.

Thus, during retrieval, the systems continually and rapidly interact so that we know *how* to find *what* we are looking for and monitor and store *when and whence* we find it, so that the process is facilitated the next time around.

As is well known, my bias is that this process entails a stage which is produced by transforming the ordinary space-time configurations of processing into a spectral order much as processing is done in computed tomography (CT) and magnetic resonance imaging (MRI). Only by engaging in such a harmonic transformation can the rapidity of retrieval (as in playing a piano concerto; the processing necessary to making massive correlations; and the magnitude of the memory store) be accounted for (Van Heerden, 1968).

To provide a specific model as to how such a memory storage, coding, and retrieval process might work, let me paraphrase a recent letter addressed to J. McClelland and Bruce McNaughton (6 November 1995)—filled in with appropriate material referred to in the letter:

> Ever since I saw your beautiful data in Tucson, Bruce, I have been stewing on the relationship of your findings to others. As I mentioned to J., when we strychninized the hippocampus proper, we found no exit to neocortical regions, even though *they* all "fire" the hippocampus. There are, however, massive outputs to the amygdala, perirhinal cortex and the region of the

nucleus accumbens septi from the subiculum. Thus, the problem with the model that you propose, at least as it stands, is that we would need some kind of a matching process between hippocampal space-time patterns and cortical space-time patterns. There seems to be no appropriate connectivity to accomplish this. On the other hand, if the matching (convolution/correlation) takes place in the spectral (holographic) domain via the nucleus accumbens, it could be accomplished readily.

Such a model was developed by Landfield (1976) and O'Keefe, (1986). In contrast to your own, their evidence precludes a map or representation of the environment that is in any way geometrically isomorphic with the environment represented. They suggest that the representation is of a holographic nature. O'Keefe describes their model as follows:

Attempts to gain an idea of the way in which an environment is represented in the hippocampus strongly suggest the absence of any topographic isomorphism between the map and the environment. Furthermore, it appears that a small cluster of neighboring pyramidal cells would map, albeit crudely, the entire environment. This observation, taken together with the ease that many experimenters have had in finding place cells with arbitrarily located electrodes in the hippocampus, suggests that each environment is represented many times over in the hippocampus, in a manner similar to a holographic plate. In both representation systems the effect of increasing the area of the storage which is activated is to increase the definition of the representation.

A second major similarity between the way in which information can be stored on a holographic plate and the way environments can be represented in the hippocampus is that the same hippocampal cells can participate in the representation of several environments (O'Keefe & Conway, 1978; Kubie & Ranck, 1983). In the Kubie and Ranck study the same place cell was recorded from the hippocampus of female rats in three different environments: All of the 28 non-theta cells had a place field in at least one of the environments, and 12 had a field in all three environments. There was no systematic relationship amongst the fields of the same neurone in the different environments. One can conclude that each hippocampal place cell can enter into the representation of a large number of environments, and conversely, that the representation of any given environment is dependent on the activity of a reasonably large group of place neurones.

The third major similarity between the holographic recording technique and the construction of environmental maps in the hippocampus is the use of interference patterns between sinusoidal waves to determine the pattern of activity in the recording substrate (see Landfield, 1976). In optical holography this is done by splitting a beam of monochromatic light into two, reflecting one beam off the scene to be encoded and then interacting the two beams at the plane of the substrate. In the hippocampus something similar might be happening.... The beams are formed by the activity in the fibers projecting to the hippocampus from the medial septal nucleus (MS) and the nucleus of the diagonal band of Broca (DBB).

Pioneering work by Petsche, Stumpf and their colleagues (Stumpf, 1965) showed that the function of the MS and DBB nuclei was to translate the amount of activity ascending from various brainstem nuclei into a frequency moduled code. Neurons in the MS/DBB complex fire in bursts, with a burst frequency which varies from 4–12 Hz. Increases in the strength of brainstem stimulation produce increases in the frequency of the bursts but not necessarily in the number of spikes within each burst (Petsche, Gogolak and van Zweiten, 1965). It is now widely accepted that this bursting activity in the MS/DBB is responsible for the synchronization of the hippocampal theta rhythm (O'Keefe, 1986, pp. 82–84).

Let me quote from the November 1995 issue of *Scientific American* as to how such a holographic matching process could work. Of course, in this quotation, the matching process works by way of illuminating crystals, and one would have to develop neural substitutes for this (which our laboratory is currently engaged in with respect to somatosensory cortex):

Given a hologram, either one of the two beams that interfered to create it can be used to reconstruct the other. What this means, in a holographic memory, is that it is possible not only to orient a reference beam into the crystal at a certain angle to select an individual holographic page but also to accomplish the reverse, *illuminating a crystal with one of the stored images gives rise to an approximation of the associated reference beam, reproduced as a plane wave emanating from the crystal at the appropriate angle.*

A lens can focus this wave to a small spot whose lateral position is determined by the angle and therefore reveals the identity of the input image. If the crystal is illuminated with a hologram that is not among the stored patterns, *multiple reference beams—and therefore multiple focused spots, are the result. The brightness of each spot is proportional to the degree of similarity between the input image and each of the stored patterns.* In other words, *the array of spots [weights in a layer of a PDP network] is an encoding of the input image, in terms of its similarity with the stored database of images.* (Psaltis & Mok, 1995, p. 76.)

Putting this together with the McClelland-McNaughton model, which is based on data which do show a representation of the *path* taken by an animal down an alley maze, it occurred to me that encoding in the hippocampus may be both holographic-like *and* patterned in space and time. The hypothesis would be that the transformation from the spectral domain into space-time coordinates is due to a selected movement, to taking a particular path at a particular time. Thus when records are computed according to a chosen arm of the maze, a space-time representation was obtained. When records are computed as to what any cell might do over an extent of trials, a distributed holographic-like representation is found.

As noted, the shift of coordinates is suggested to take place by way of choosing a particular path. Computational models such as those proposed by Harth, Unnikrishnan and Pandya (1987) and by Yasue, Jibu and Pribram (1991) have been developed for vision to account for the shift in coordinates as a result of such a choice. In the Yasue et al. proposal, Euler-Lagrange equations correspond to *paths* taken in configuration space (spacetime coordinates). The shift from the spectral to the configuration domain has been demonstrated in the visual system both at the thalamic and cortical level. Electrical stimulation of temporal or frontal lobe cortex enhances or diminishes the extent of the inhibitory surrounds and flanks of dendritic receptive fields in thalamus and cortex so that the sensory channels can either become multiplexed or fused. As the receptive fields can be described in terms of a spacetime (configuration) constraint on a sinusoid such as the Gabor elementary function, the constraint is embodied in the inhibitory surround of the field. Enhancing the surround enhances the configuration space; diminishing the surround enhances the sinusoidal (spectral domain) aspects of processing. Movement enhances contrast which in turn depends on inhibitory surrounds.

Sincerely, Karl H. Pribram

Conscious Learning as Recoding Through Self Organization

ELEMENTS OF ACQUISITION

As noted, the deep structure of memory storage that takes place in the synaptodendritic process becomes organized into a distributed memory store. This constitutes the first step in the learning process. For these changes to become effective, they must occur both presynaptically and postsynaptically if the results of learning are to become directive to further behavior (Freud, 1895; Hebb, 1949/1961). As detailed above, the processes involving synapses have been found to be much more complicated than conceived by these early theorists. Compartmentalization of activity takes place within a dendritic arborization, even within the dendrites of a single neuron. Recall that the interaction among signals that characterizes classical conditioning turns out to involve the activity in one synaptodendritic compartment where the conditional and unconditional signals come together. Iterations of the temporal association of the signal leads to local changes in enzymes and proteins that alter the amount of potassium ion flow, which in turn alters the electrical excitability of the dendritic membrane.

However, conditioning is a fairly simple form of associative learning and may provide only the very basic element of a model for the learning process we want to occur in the classroom. The surface structure becomes involved when a student comprehends what is being presented. When a student reorganizes that presentation to fit his or her needs, the iteration of processing through the cortical-basal ganglia-thalamocortical circuits must, in some fashion, establish triggers, temporary dominant foci, as aids to retrieval. In accomplishing this, what might be the role of processes intrinsic to the learned material, as compared to those controlled by extrinsic rewards? The answers to these questions are not obvious.

In monkeys who have cheek pouches to temporarily store food, I often observed that peanuts were stored in the pouch whenever a correct response was made; however, when an error occurred, a peanut was popped out of the pouch and gleefully chewed and swallowed. We often advise our friends that when things look bleak, they should go shopping to reward themselves. How does the brain operate to associate chewing a peanut with the longer-range problem-solving process and not with the immediate error just committed? A clue may come from the observation that a challenging problem that is being mastered leads to general excitement: young male monkeys often display erections in such challenging situations. And recall Kissinger's statement that a position of power leading to political success is the best-known aphrodisiac. Some sort of internal state seems to be involved which is modulated by the organizing properties of the material to be learned.

The story of just how these two factors interact can fruitfully begin with an assessment of the effects of bilateral hippocampal gyrus resections on the performance of monkeys in a discrimination reversal procedure. In this task, the hippocampectomized monkeys show normal extinction, and the slope of acquisition of the currently appropriate response does not differ from that of the control monkeys. What does occur is a long series of trials, which intervene between extinction and acquisition, during which the monkeys select cues at random. They receive a reward approximately 50% of the time, which is sufficient to keep them working (Pribram et al., 1969). There is no obvious event that pulls them out of this "period of stationarity"; quite suddenly the hippocampectomized monkeys resume the acquisition of more rewarding behavior. What goes on during the period of stationarity, and what prolongs this period for monkeys who have had their hippocampal gyrus resected?

There are currently no techniques for directly assessing what goes on during the period of stationarity. It is clear, however, that rearrangement of the association between cue and reward has occurred when reversal is finally effected and that this rearrangement must be perceived before it can be acted on. Rearranging must be processed efficiently and appears to take effort (Pribram & McGuinness 1975, 1992; Pribram 1986, 1991).

Reinforcement—A Redefinition

On the basis of this and other neurobehavioral investigations, some neglected aspects of the response-reinforcement relationship can be evaluated. During the heyday of stimulus-response psychology, reinforcing events were considered to be either drive inducing or drive reducing. This view foundered on neuro-behavioral demonstrations that after lesions of the ventromedial hypothalamus, a rat would become obese if given food ad libitum but would starve if it had to overcome an obstacle or press a panel in order to obtain a reward (for review, see Pribram, 1970). How could a rat have both increased and decreased drive depending on the situation? How could reward be both drive inducing and drive reducing depending on the situation? The cognitive construct *effort* came closer to describing the results of the experiment than did the stimulus-response construct *drive*.

What then might effort be? Under what circumstances would effort be expended? What is the relationship between effort and reinforcement? In a seminal study, David Premack (1965) provided the first steps toward an answer to this question. Premack showed that reinforcement occurs whenever a response with a lower independent rate coincides, coheres, with stimuli that govern the occurrence of a response with a higher independent rate. Thus, the organism tends to increase the response of the lower rate to approach the rate of the response of the higher independent rate. The organism expends effort. Premack used running in an activity wheel and licking a drinking tube to measure behavioral rates of response, and showed that the reinforcing relationship was reversible depending on deprivation circumstances.

This conclusion was confirmed and enhanced by the results of an experiment performed by Herrnstein and Loveland (1975), who found that the crucial variable in reward sequences is not the probability that a response will be rewarded but rather the amount of food that appears at a given location in the environment per unit time (see Gallistel, 1990, for a thorough review).

The point of these observations is that it is the consequences of behavior that stand in relation to one another, not the behaviors per se. Premack's manipulations dealt with consequential behaviors, not just any behaviors. To be consequential, the behavior must be relevant to the organism.

To be relevant (from the Latin *relevare*, to lift up), a consequence must stand out in a situation to which the organism has become habituated, a familiar situation. Relevance depends on one or more of several factors:

1. Uncompleted behavioral sequences initiated by physiological drive stimuli, such as those that produce hunger and thirst

2. Uncompleted behavioral sequences initiated by the behavioral acts themselves, such as writing a letter and finding a box to mail it (Zeigarnick, 1972)

3. Uncompleted behavioral sequences initiated by environmental contingencies, such as earthquakes or final exams

In all cases, it is the uncompleted behavioral sequences that result in relevance. And we have already noted that the behavioral response rates in Premack's experiments refer to behavioral consequences. Thus, uncompleted sequences of consequences, or more briefly the consequences per se, generate effort on the part of the organism to lift up contingencies in a situation, that is, to make them relevant.

Consequences are sequences of situations that are in some sense consonant. An organism will sense a situation to be consequential when the contingencies describing that situation covary, that is, they are consonant, coherent, with those describing prior situations. Note that it is also coherence in the conditioning situations used by Alkon, that compartmentalized changes in the synaptodendritic network occur. The experienced prior situations provide the context within which the current contingencies become relevant—that is, consequential.

In such a sequence, it is necessary to parse situations into episodes—some of which are prior to the current situation. The episode thus becomes a unit of action that is initiated and terminated by an orienting reaction. The episode provides the context within which events, defined as eventualities, consequences, occur. Events (the Latin equivalent of outcome, *ex + venire*) thus are the consequences of actions, for example, the consequence "8" on the throw of dice. Each throw rearranges the event structure, "relevating" a new count on the dice. The terms *outcome*, *event*, and *consequence* are therefore synonymous as they refer to the reinforcing process in behavioral psychology.

In short, during learning the organism tends to expend effort to reduce dissonance and enhance consonance—that is, stability—by its behavior. This is accomplished by producing environmental contingencies that covary—that is, are consonant with those that have, on prior occasions, provided temporary stabilities. In the terminology of nonlinear dynamics (chaos theory), such contingencies serve as attractors for subsequent behavior. Appropriate here is Smolensky's description (1986) of memory retrieval, which is also relevant to the storage of the surface structure of memory: "The concept of memory retrieval is reformalized in terms of the continuous evolution of a dynamical system [embodied in the function of a circuit] towards a point attractor [a trigger] whose position in the state space [the distributed store] is the memory. You naturally get dynamics of the system so that its attractors are located where the memories are supposed to be...." (pp. 194–281). But the relationship between the reinforcing process, event structures, and deterministic chaos is a story of which the details need still to be worked out and thus are left for another day.

Meanwhile, the enigma of reinforcement is gradually yielding its secrets. The question is: What is the nature of the stored representation of prior reinforcing environmental contingencies that makes it possible for an organism to select current environmental contingencies consonant with such a representation?

The direction that can be taken by research into the process by which the environmental contingencies can be represented has been explored in detail for timing behavior. Killeen and Fetterman (1988) and Killeen (1994) presented a comprehensive review of the literature and a computational model of timing (as well as generalization and discrimination) based on their own research with rats and pigeons. The model consists of an internal, biological clock and an environmentally driven counter or accumulator. The pacemaker is based on a neural oscillator, probably of the relaxation type, which generates pulses. The process is described by a quantal model akin to that which produces Gabor functions for the visual system (Pribram & Carlton, 1986). The counter accumulates these pulses and creates a signal when the accumulation equals or exceeds some present value. The signal defines the animal's transit from one behavioral state to the next: that is, in the terminology used in the current chapter, the transit from one episode to the next.

The pacemaker is affected by a variety of biological variables such as drugs (Pöppel, 1972), temperature (Hoagland, 1935), and time of day. In addition, timing behavior is influenced by arousal (Treisman, 1969). Killeen et al., (1978) then showed that arousal is directly proportional to the rate of reinforcement and thus a function of the accumulator in the model. We are, therefore, returned to the argument, based on Premack's data, that the density of environmental outcomes of behavior is the critical variable in determining future behavior. In the model presented by Killeen and Fetterman (1988) the rate of reinforcement is reflected in the interresponse interval plotted as the mean density of a Poisson process. According to the data presented here, the pacemaker would most likely be diencephalic (hypothalamic), the amygdala system would signal change of state (episode), and the striatum (basal ganglia) would act as accumulator (see Pribram & McGuinness, 1975, 1992, for this aspect of the brain-behavior relationship). An event (computed by the hippocampal system) would perhaps correspond to the reciprocal of the mean density of the Poisson distribution of interresponse intervals. Then the process described in the letter to McClelland and McNaughton takes over.

The Big Picture: What The Relation Between the Organization of Learning and Memory and That of the Brain Can Tell Us About the Mind-Brain Connection

Often the future is a return to views expressed in the past but with new insights based on technical innovation and experimental results. With regard to science in the 21st century, we may well see a turn of the wheel toward a world view which has been submerged during the past three centuries during which attention has been focused on the composition and workings of material things. For the cognitive and neurosciences, this submergence has resulted in the received opinion that psychological processes such as learning and memory are essentially the emergent properties of brain function. The alternative view holds that, though brain is critical, brain processes reflect, in a nontrivial form, more universal orderings.

At least since the time of Newton and Leibnitz, these two rather different conceptual schemes have dominated scientific thinking: one emphasizes the lawful relation between observed events (Newton); the other emphasizes the observational medium within which observations occur. This difference in emphasis leads Newtonians to stress forces relating particles (entities) while Leibnitzians stress fluctuations (changes) composing fields. In the Leibnitzian view, entities, such as human organisms, partake of these changing fields.

The following statements place the Leibnitzian view into succinct apposition with the currently received view held by most neuroscientists:

1. The received view: Brain, by organizing the input from the physical and social environment as obtained through the senses, constructs mental phenomena.

2. The Leibnitzian view: Mental phenomena are Platonic ideals, pervasive organizing principles of the universe, which includes the brain.

Paradoxically, while almost all behavioral, cognitive, and neuroscientists would today subscribe to some form of statement 1, statement 2 reflects the belief of many influential theoretical physicists such as Dirac (1930, 1951), Einstein (1961), Heisenberg (1969), Schrödinger (1944), and Wigner (1939). Mathematicians and mathematical physicists have faced the dilemma more directly: How is it that the inventions of their brains so often describe faithfully basic orders in the universe which it then takes physicists many decades to discover?

To anticipate my own resolution to the dilemma: Dirac (1930) pointed out that a basic complementarity in physics is given by the Fourier transform. On one side of the equation are the space-time coordinates within which mass and entropy are described. On the other side of the equation are energy and momentum (measured in terms of frequency and Plank's constant). Feynman et al. (1963) note that this equation is perhaps the most fundamental in physics, and Gabor (1946, 1948) takes off from it to construct both holography and "quanta" of information. I believe that those whose conceptualizations operate primarily in space-time find the emergentist view of mind most compatible, while those who are sensitive to the energy-momentum domain are comfortable with the Leibnitzian view.

Mathematical Holography in Brain Function and Cosmology

The story from my perspective begins with my interactions with Dennis Gabor. In the late 1940s Gabor suggested that the resolution of electron microscopy could be enhanced if, instead of storing images directly, the photographic film would be exposed to the wave patterns of light diffracted (filtered through or reflected from) by the tissue to be examined. Gabor's suggestion was formulated mathematically. Only many years later in the early 1960s was his suggestion realized in hardware. These hardware realizations made it obvious that images of the objects that had initially diffracted the light could readily be reconstructed. Furthermore, Gabor's equations showed that the identical mathematical transfer function (the Fourier transform) transformed image into wave storage and wave storage into image! The storage of interference patterns is thus reciprocally related to the imaging of objects!!

Gabor named the stored interference pattern a hologram, because one of its most interesting characteristics is that information from the object becomes distributed over the whole photographic film. Each point of light diffracted from the object becomes blurred and is spread over the entire surface of the film (the equations that describe this are called spread functions). The spread is not haphazard, however, as the resultant blur would lead one to believe. Rather, ripples become distributed from the point of light somewhat as ripples of waves are formed when a pebble strikes the smooth surface of a pond of water. Throw a handful of pebbles into the pond, and the ripples produced by each pebble will crisscross with those produced by the other pebbles. setting up patterns of interfering wave fronts. The smooth mirror-like surface has become blurred, but the blur has hidden within it an unsuspected orderly pattern. A photograph of the pond at this moment would be a hologram. The photographic hologram is such a frozen record of the nodes of interference among wave fronts.

It seemed immediately plausible that the distributed memory store, the deep structure of memory, of the brain might resemble this holographic record. I formulated a theory based on known neuroanatomy and known neurophysiology that could account for the brain's distributed memory store in holographic terms. In the decades since, many laboratories—including my own—have provided evidence that has sharpened the theory and given it a more precise fit to the known facts.

Essentially, the theory states that at one stage of processing, the sensory systems perform a series of Fourier-like transforms. Not only auditory processing but visual and somatic sensations are initially processed as interference patterns. As noted earlier, processing is accomplished within the connection web of the brain at the junctions of the fine branches of nerve cells.

Holography implies lack of boundaries—but boundaries abound in the brain. When such boundaries are imposed on the Fourier transformations, "quanta of information" are formed. Gabor (1946) described such an information process just prior to his invention of holography in an attempt to determine the maximum efficiency with which a communication could be sent across the Atlantic cable. His mathematics wee formulated in a matrix algebra identical to that used by Heisenberg to describe the microstructure of the atom. Thus he coined the term "quantum of information." As noted earlier, more recent speculations regarding processing in the connection web have suggested that something akin to quantum mechanical processing might, in fact, be operating. (See, e.g., Hameroff, 1987; Epilogue in Pribram, 1991; Penrose 1989, 1994; Hameroff & Penrose, 1995; Jibu et al., 1994, 1996.)

During the 1970s these Gabor functions, or wavelets, as they are now commonly called, were shown to precisely describe visual processing in the brain cortex. I therefore called this process "holonomic" to distinguish it from the unconstrained "holographic" process described earlier. However, the constraints, the boundaries which are due to neural inhibition, are relaxed by electrical excitation of the frontal and related limbic formations of the brain (Spinelli & Pribram, 1967; Lassonde, Ptito, & Pribram 1981). Processing under such circumstances becomes more truly holographic. (For the details of the experiments and their results see Lecture 10, Pribram, 1991.)

THE BRAIN-MIND RELATION

The import of these theoretical and laboratory results to understanding the brain-mind relation can be encapsulated as follows: Take computer programming as a metaphor. At some point in programming, there is a direct correspondence between the programming language and the operations of the hardware being addressed. In ordinary sequential processing configurations, machine language embodies this correspondence. Higher-order languages encode the information necessary to make the hardware run. When the word-processing program allows this essay to be written in English, there is no longer any similarity between the user's language and the binary (on/off) procedures of the computer hardware. This, therefore, expresses a dualism between mental language and material hardware operations.

Transposed from metaphor to the actual mind-brain connection, the language describing the operations of the neural wetware, the connection web, made up of dendrites and synapses and the electrochemical operations occurring therein seem far removed from the language used by behavioral scientists to describe psychological processes. But the distance which separates these languages is no greater than that which distinguishes word processing from machine language.

However, the mind-brain connection is different from that which characterizes the program-computer relationship. The mind-brain connection is composed of intimate reciprocal self-organizing procedures at every level of neural organization. High-level psychological processes such as those involved in cognition are therefore the result of cascades of biopsychological bootstrapping operations.

If we take seriously the possibility that at the level of the connection web something is occurring that is akin to a computer being programmed in machine language, the Gabor or some similar function fulfills the requirements. This function was devised to operate not only on the material level of the Atlantic cable but also to determine comprehensible telephone communication, the aim of which is mutual minding.

I propose, therefore, that at the level of processing in the connection web, a *structural* identity (such as the identify between machine language based on a binary code and the operations of computer hardware based on on/off switches) is an accurate and productive philosophical approach that describes this process. Identity becomes "isonomic" when the levels of programming languages which maintain access to the same information are taken as a metaphor for higher-level processes. But the actual procedures are instantiations (as programs) of the process, not just linguistic descriptions (Pribram 1970, 1971). *Isonomy* is defined as obeying a set of laws that are related to one another by a change in coordinates. Isonomy is akin to an identity position but takes account of levels of instantiation and thus avoids the problem of category errors such as those entailed in the liar's paradox (I am a liar). Furthermore, isonomy is framed in terms of algebraic rather than geometric homomorphisms. The procedures involved bind together the various scales of operation by way of reciprocal processes that lead to self-organizing structures. At the same time, because of their *mathematical* structure defining information-processing procedures, isonomy avoids the pitfalls of a promissory materialism and, as well, those of an evanescent unspecifiable mentalistic process.

Conclusion

There is thus good evidence that a class of orders lies behind the classical level of organization we ordinarily perceive and which can be described in Euclidean and Newtonian terms and mapped in Cartesian space-time coordinates (see also Clarke, 1995). This other class of orders is constituted of distributed organizations described as potential because of their impalpability until radical changes in appearance are realized in the transformational process. When a potential is realized, information (the form within) becomes unfolded into its ordinary space-time appearance; in the other direction, the transformation enfolds and distributes the information as this is done by the holographic process. Because work is involved in transforming, descriptions in terms of energy are suitable, and as the structure of information is what is transformed, descriptions in terms of entropy (and negentropy) are also suitable. Thus, on the one hand, there are enfolded potential orders; on the other, there are unfolded orders manifested in space-time.

Dualism of mental vs. material holds only for the ordinary world of appearances—the world described in Euclidean geometry and Newtonian mechanics. I gave an explanation of dualism (Pribram, 1965) in terms of procedural difference in approaching the hierarchy of systems that can be discerned in this world of appearances. This explanation was developed into an identity theory, a constructional realism. But it was also stated that certain questions raised by a more classical dualistic position were left unanswered by the explanations given in terms of an identity position.

Two issues can be discerned: (1) What is it that remains identical in the various levels of the hierarchy of programs or compositions? and (2) Is the correspondence between machine language (program or, see below, musical notation) and the machine or instrument's operation an identity or a duality? I believe the answer to both questions hinges on whether one concentrates on the order (form, organization) or the embodiments in which these orders become instantiated (Pribram, 1996).

There is a difference between surface structures which become transformed and the deeper isonomy which in-forms the transformations (Pribram, 1996). In brain processing, this is a difference between what transpires in the connection web and what is handled by the level of neural circuitry. In psychology, it is the difference between experiencing and behaving. Transformations are necessary to material and mental "instantiations"—Plato's particular appearances—of the ideal in-forms: the instantiation of Beethoven's Ninth Symphony is transformed from composition (a mental operation), to score (a material embodiment), to performance (more mental than material), to recording on compact disc (more material than mental), to the sensory and brain processes (material) that make for appreciative listening (mental). But the symphony as symphony remains recognizably "identical" to Beethoven's creative composition over the centuries of performances, recordings, and listenings.

Instantiations depend on transformations among orders. What remains invariant across all instantiations is "in-formation," the form within. As noted, the measure of information in Gabor's terms applies both to the organization of the material wetware of the brain and the cable hardware in telecommunication on the one hand, and on the other hand, to the organization of the mindful communication itself. Thus the "in-formation" is neutral to the material/mental dichotomy. Surprisingly, according to this analysis, it is a Platonic "idealism" that motivates the information revolution (e.g., "information-processing" approaches in cognitive science) and distinguishes it from the materialism of the industrial revolution. Further, according to my perspective, as in-formation is neither material nor mental, a scientific pragmatism akin to that practiced by Pythagoreans will displace mentalism and dualism as well as materialism as central philosophical concerns.

Thus, by temperament, I need to be grounded in the nitty-gritty of experimental and observational results as much as I am moved by the beauty of theoretical formulations expressed mathematically. Therefore, in my opinion, in the 21st century the tension between idealism (the potential), and realism (the appearance) which characterized the dialogue between Plato and Aristotle, will replace that between mentalism and materialism, a tension which, at its most productive, will lead to new directions in experimentation, observation, and mathematical theory construction in the spirit of a Pythagorean pragmaticism.

These considerations suggest that these new directions in experimentation will change the venue of science. Currently our emphasis is on what Aristotle called efficient causes, the "this causes that." According to the proposals presented in this chapter, 21st-century science will supplement searches guided by efficient causation with research guided by Aristotle's final causes. Searches guided by final causation ask how things and events are put together to be what they are and what they tend to become. This type of research, which is by no means new (especially in thermodynamics and psychophysics), emphasizes transfer functions, transformations that occur as we search for ways to understand relations among patterns at different scales of observation. The finding that atomic numbers "explain" the periodic table of elements is an example of research guided by this kind of causality.

Pythagoras examined by experiment and mathematical (thoughtful) description orders at all scales of observations available to him. These scales ranged from universal (spiritual) to those composing musical tones produced by vibrating material objects. There is every evidence, from what has occurred in the second half of the 20th century, that in the coming millennium a similar range of experience will be the grist of our explorations. At the very center of

such endeavors is humankind's understanding of its relation to the universe—
and at the center of this understanding lies the relation between the orders
invented or discovered by the operations of that "three-pound universe," the
brain, and those in which it is embedded.

As of now, these are speculative but historically well-grounded proposals
that are set forth to provoke 21st-century dialogue, research, and theorizing.
Anyone interested?

Appendix

The intracellular spread of dendritic polarizations can be accounted for by microtubular structures that act as wave guides and provide additional surface upon which
the polarizations can act (Hagen et al., 1994; Hameroff, 1987; Penrose, 1994). The
extracellular spread may be aided by a similar process taking place in the glia which
show a tremendous increase in the metabolism of RNA when excited by the neurons
which they envelope. But these mechanisms, by themselves, do not account for the
initial relative isolation of the spine head polarizations, nor the related saltatory aspects
of the process.

To account for these properties we turn to the dendritic membrane and its
immediate surround. Dendritic membranes are composed of two oppositely oriented
phospholipid molecules. The interior of the membrane is hydrophobic, as it is formed
by "lipids which form a fluid matrix within which protein molecules are embedded—
the lipids can move laterally at rates of 2 μm/sec; protein molecules move about 40
times more slowly (50 nm/sec or 3 μm/min)" (Shepherd, 1988, p. 44). Some of the
intrinsic membrane proteins provide channels for ion movement across the membrane.

The outer layer of the membrane "fairly bristles with carbohydrate molecules
attached to the membrane protein molecules: glycoproteins. The carbohydrate may
constitute 95 percent of these molecules [which form a] long-branching structure [that
resembles] a long test tube brush, or a centipede wiggling its way through the extracellular space. It attracts water, imparting a spongy torpor to the extracellular space"
(Shepherd, 1988, pp. 45–46).

On the basis of these considerations, Jibu, Yasue, and I (1994, 1996) propose that
a perimembranous process occurs within dendritic compartments during which boson
condensation produces a dynamically ordered state in water. We have gone on to speculate that each pattern of signals exciting the dendritic arborization produces a macroscopic, ionically produced change of the charge distribution in the dendritic network,
altering the water molecular field in the immediately adjacent perimembranous region.
A macroscopic domain of the dynamically ordered structure of water is created in
which the electric dipole density is aligned in one and the same direction. It is this

domain of dynamically ordered water that is postulated to provide the extracellular perimembranous substrate of the interactions among polarizations occurring in dendritic spine heads.

The transformation of the distributed saltatory dendritic process into storage depends on the existence of "impurity," that is, ions in the dynamically ordered structure of water in the perimembranous region. Among several kinds of ions typical for the extracellular and intracellular fluid are Na^+, K^+, Ca^{2+}, Cl^-, etc. The effect of the presence of such ions in the dynamically ordered structure of water is due to the electromagnetic interaction of the coulomb type, and so its strength depends highly on the distance between each water molecule and the ion in question. Thus, patches of dendritic membrane become the site of memory storage. According to Alkon (1989), the interaction is communicated intracellularly (dromically) to the cell body which, in turn, generates factors that return (antidromically) to the site of the interaction and hard-wire it. The intracellular processes are triggered by a reduction in K^+ ion flow (which results only when the conditional and unconditional stimuli are paired).

Both the extracellular and the intracellular processes need a physical substrate, a medium, within which to accomplish the molecular transformations that lead to reduction of K^+ ion flow that accompanies conditioning. The extracellular spongy torpor produced by glycoproteins provides the necessary structure for holding perimembranous-ordered water to which ions can adhere. Internally, the dynamically ordered water can provide the substrate for dromic and antidromic conductivity in the dendritic compartment activated by the temporal association of a conditional with an unconditional input signal. The deep structure of memory storage can thus become implemented.

References

Alkon, D. L. (1989). Memory storage and neural systems. *Scientific American*, *261*(1), 42–50.

Alkon, D. L., & Rasmussen, H. (1988). A spatial-temporal model of cell activation. *Science*, *239*, 998–1005.

Bolster, B., & Pribram, K. H. (1993). Cortical involvement in visual scan in the monkey. *Perception and Psychophysics*, *53*(5) 505–518.

Chomsky, N. (1965). *Aspects of the theory of syntax*. Cambridge, MA: MIT Press.

Clarke, C. J. S. (1995). The nonlocality of mind. *Journal of Consciousness Studies*, *2*(3), 231–240.

Dirac, P. A. M. (1930). *The principles of quantum mechanics*. Oxford: Oxford University Press.

Dirac, P. A. M. (1951). Is there an aether? *Nature, 168*, 906.

Douglas, R. J., Barrett, T. W., Pribram, K. H., & Cerny, M. C. (1969). Limbic lesions and error reduction. *Journal of Comparative and Physiological Psychology, 68*, 437–441.

Douglas, R. J., & Pribram, K. H. (1969). Distraction and habituation in monkeys with limbic lesions. *Journal of Comparative and Physiological Psychology, 69*, 473–480.

Efron, R. (1989) *The decline and fall of hemispheric specialization* (MachEachran Lectures). Hillsdale, NJ: Erlbaum.

Einstein, A. (1961) *Relativity: The special and the general theory*. New York: Random House.

Feynman, R. P., Leighton, R. B., & Sands, M. (1963). *The Feynman lectures on physics*. Reading, MA: Addison-Wesley.

Freud, S. (1895/1953). *Project for a scientific psychology*. In *Standard Edition of the Complete Psychological Works of Sigmund Freud* (vol. 1, pp. 281–397). Trans. and ed. J. Strachey. London: Hogarth.

Gabor, D. (1946). Theory of communication. *Journal of the Institute of Electrical Engineers, 93*, 429–441.

Gabor, D. (1948). A new microscopic principle. *Nature, 161*, 777–778.

Gallistel, C. R. (1990). *The organization of learning*. Cambridge, MA: MIT Press.

Hagan, S., Jibu, M., & Yasue, K. (1994). Consciousness and anesthesia: An hypothesis involving biophoton emission in the microtubular cytoskeleton of the brain. In K. H. Pribram (Ed.), *Origins: Brain and self organization*. Hillsdale, NJ: Erlbaum.

Hameroff, S. R. (1987). *Ultimate computing: Biomolecular consciousness and nano technology*. Amsterdam: North-Holland.

Hameroff, S. R., & Penrose, R. (1995). Orchestrated reduction of quantum coherence in brain microtubules: A model for consciousness. In J. S. King & K. H. Pribram (Eds.), *Scale in consciousness experience: Is the brain too important to be left to specialists to study?* (pp. 241–246). Hillsdale, NJ: Erlbaum.

Harth, E., Unnikrishnan, P., & Pandya, A. S. (1987). The inversion of sensory processing by feedback pathways: Model of visual cognitive functions. *Science, 237*, 184–187.

Hebb, D. O. (1949/1961). *The organization of behavior, a neuropsychological theory.* New York: Wiley.

Heisenberg, W. (1969). *Physics and beyond.* Munich: Piper.

Herrnstein, R. J., & Loveland, D. H. (1975). Maximizing and matching on concurrent ratio-schedules. *Journal of the Experimental Analysis of Behavior, 24*, 107–116.

Hoagland, H. (1935). *Pacemakers in relation to aspects of behavior.* New York: Macmillan.

Jibu, M., Hagan, S., Hameroff, S. R., Pribram, K. H., & Yasue, K. (1994). Quantum optical coherence in cytoskeletal microtubules: Implications for brain function. *Biosystems, 32*, 195–209.

Jibu, M., Pribram, K. H., & Yasue, K. (1996). From conscious experience to memory storage and retrieval: The role of quantum brain dynamics and boson condensation of evanescent photons. *International Journal of Modern Physics B,*

Killeen, P. R. (1994). Mathematical principles of reinforcement. *Behavioral and Brain Sciences, 17*, 105–172.

Killeen, P. R., & Fetterman, J. G. (1988). A behavioral theory of timing. *Psychological Review, 95*(2), 274–295.

Killeen, P. R, Hansen, S. J., & Osborn, S. R. (1978). Arousal: Its genesis and manifestation as response rate. *Psychological Review, 85*, 571–581.

Landfield, P. W. (1976). Synchronous EEG rhythms: Their nature and their possible functions in memory, information transmission and behaviour. In E. H. Gispen (Ed.), *Molecular and functional neurobiology.* Amsterdam: Elsevier.

Lassonde, M. C., Ptito, M., & Pribram, K. H. (1981). Intracerebral influences on the microstructure of visual cortex. *Experimental Brain Research, 43*, 131–144.

O'Keefe, J. (1986). Is consciousness the gateway to the hippocampal cognitive map? A speculative essay on the neural basis of mind. *Brain and Mind, 10*, 59–98.

O'Keefe, J. & Conway, D. H. (1978). Hippocampal place units in the freely moving rat: Why they fire where they fire. *Experimental Brain Research, 31*, 573–590.

Penrose, R. (1989). *The emperor's new mind.* Oxford: Oxford University Press.

Penrose, R. (1994). *Shadows of the mind.* Oxford: Oxford University Press.

Petsche, H., Gogolak, G. & van Zweiten, P. A. (1965). Rhythmicity of septal cell discharges at various levels of reticular excitation. *Electroencephalography and Clinical Neurophysiology, 19*, 25–33.

Pöppel, E. (1972). Oscillations as possible basis for time perception. In J. T. Fraser, F. C. Haber, & G. H. Muller (Eds.), *The study of time* (pp. 219–241). New York: Springer-Verlag.

Premack, D. (1965). Reinforcement theory. In D. Levine (Ed.), *Nebraska symposium on motivation* (pp. 123–188). Lincoln: University of Nebraska Press.

Pribram, K. H. (1960). The intrinsic systems of the forebrain. In J. Field, H. W. Magoun, & V. E. Hall (Eds.), *Handbook of physiology, neurophysiology* (vol. 2, pp. 1323–1324). Washington, DC: American Physiological Society.

Pribram, K. H. (1963). Discussion of Young's paper. In V. B. Mountcastle (Ed.), *Interhemispheric relations and cerebral dominance* (p. 107). Baltimore: Johns Hopkins University Press.

Pribram, K. H. (1965). Proposal for a structural pragmatism: Some neuropsychological considerations of problems in philosophy. In B. Wolman & E. Nagle (Eds.), *Scientific psychology: Principles and approaches* (pp. 426–459). New York: Basic Books.

Pribram, K. H. (1970). The biology of mind: Neurobehavioral foundations. In A. Gilgen (Ed.), *Scientific psychology: Some perspectives* (pp. 45–70). New York: Academic Press.

Pribram, K. H. (1971). *Languages of the brain: Experimental paradoxes and principles in neuropsychology*. Hillsdale, NJ: Erlbaum.

Pribram, K. H. (1986). The hippocampal system and recombinant processing. In R. Isaacson & K. H. Pribram (Eds.), *The hippocampus* (vol. 4, pp. 329–370). New York: Plenum Press.

Pribram, K. H. (1991). *Brain and perception: Holonomy and structure in figural processing*. Hillsdale, NJ: Erlbaum.

Pribram, K. H. (1996). What is mind that the brain may order it? In P. R. Masani (Ed.), *Proceedings of the Norbert Wiener Centenary Congress*.

Pribram, K. H. (in preparation). *The work in working memory, development of the prefrontal cortex: Evolution, neurobiology, and behavior*.

Pribram, K. H, & Carlton, E. H. (1986). Holonomic brain theory in imaging and object perception. *Acta Psychologica, 63*, 175–210.

Pribram, K. H., Douglas, R. J., & Pribram, B. J. (1969). The nature of nonlimbic learning. *Journal of comparative and Physiological Psychology, 69*, 765–772.

Pribram, K. H., & McGuinness, D. (1975). Commentary on Jeffrey Gray's The neuropsychology of anxiety: An enquiry into the functions of the septohippocampal system. *Behavioral and Brain Sciences, 5*, 496–498.

Pribram, K. H., & McGuinness, D. (1992). Attention and para-attentional processing: Event related brain potentials as tests of a model. *Annals of the New York Academy of Sciences, 658*, 65–92.

Psaltis, D., & Mok, F. (1995). Holographic memories. *Scientific American, 273*(5), 70–76.

Shepherd, G. M. (1988). *Neurobiology* (2nd ed.). New York: Oxford University Press.

Shepherd, G. M., Brayton, R. K., Miller, J. P., Segey, I., Rindsel, J., & Rall, W. (1985). Signal enhancement in distal cortical dendrites by means of interactions between active dendritic spines. *Proceedings of the National Academy of Science, 82*, 2192–2195.

Sherrington, C. (1911/1947). *The integrative action of the nervous system*. New Haven, CT: Yale University Press.

Shiffrin, R. M., & Schneider, W. (1984). Automatic and controlled processing revisited. *Psychological Review, 91*, 269–276.

Schrödinger, E. (1944). *What is life? Mind and matter*. Cambridge, England: Cambridge University Press.

Smolensky, P. (1986). Information processing in dynamical systems: Foundations of harmony theory. In D. E. Rumelhart, J. L. McClelland, & the PDP Research Group (Eds.), *Paralle distributed processing: Explorations in the microstructure of cognition*. Vol. 1, *Foundations* (pp. 194–281). Cambridge, MA: MIT Press.

Spinelli, D. N., & Pribram, K. H. (1967). Changes in visual recovery function and unit activity produced by frontal cortex stimulation. *Electroencepholography and Clinical Neurophysiology, 22*, 143–149.

Schacter, D. L., & Tulving, E. (1994). What are the memory systems of 1994? In D. L. Schacter & E. Tulving (Eds.), *Memory Systems 1994* (pp. 1–38). Cambridge, MA: MIT Press.

Stumpf, C. (1965). Drug action on the electrical activity of the hippocampus. *International Review of Neurobiology, 8*, 77–138.

Szentagothai, J. (1985). Functional anatomy of the visual centes as cues for pattern recognition concepts. In D. Chagas, R. Gattass, & C. Gross (Eds.), *Pattern recognition mechanisms* (pp. 39–52). Berlin: Springer-Verlag.

Treisman, A. M. (1969). Strategies and models of selective attention. *Psychological Review, 76*, 282–299.

Van Heerden, P. J. (1968). *The foundation of empirical knowledge*. Netherlands: N.V. Uitgeverij Wistik-Wassenaar.

Wigner, E. P. (1939). On unitary representations of the inhomogeneous Lorentz group. *Annals of Mathematics, 40*, 149–204.

Yasue, K., Jibu, M., & Pribram, K. H. (1991). Appendices: A theory of nonlocal cortical processing in the brain. In K. H. Pribram (Ed.), *Brain and perception: Holonomy and perception in firgural processing* (pp. 275–330). Hillsdale, NJ: Erlbaum.

Young, J. Z. (1962). Why do we have two brains? In V. B. Mountcastle (Ed.), *Inter-hemispheric relations and cerebral dominance* (pp. 7–24). Baltimore: The John Hopkins University Press.

Zeigarnick, B. V. (1972). *Experimental abnormal psychology.* New York: Plenum Press.

9 What Are Brains For?

MICHAEL S. GAZZANIGA

Sex. Indeed, I would argue that the cathedrals we build, the books we read and write, the science we create, the cars we drive, the stocks we buy and sell, all of the mergers, the politics, and the wars we wage—in short, everything that constitutes the intricate web of life that we have constructed around ourselves with our amazingly large brains—serves a very simple purpose. Sex.

The question of what brains are for is quite different from the question, What do brains do? Evolution constructs brains that make decisions that will enhance reproductive success. Such decision systems, however, can do many other things as well. Frequently, psychologists and neuroscientists study what brains do, make suggestions about the atomization of the processes they study, and forget that what they are studying may be epiphenomenal.

Is this distinction important? So what if brains were built to do X, but now serve Y functions? It is the Y functions about which modern scientists are interested. If the brain accomplishes these functions incidentally to what it was constructed for, so be it. Unfortunately, modern scientists want to study only these incidental mechanisms. If the evolutionary perspective is simply set aside, the data collected by psychologists and neuroscientists alike are likely to be grossly misinterpreted. The far-reaching implication of the evolutionary view is that models built to explain various psychological and behavioral processes are examining the "noise" of the honed and highly efficient neural system that is devoted to making decisions about survival. Many psychological models, for example, assume that information is gathered, organized, and processed in something vaguely reminiscent of a computer (i.e., a kind of associative mechanism), that such devices are universal in the brain, and that with the right environmental contingencies, perceptual and cognitive processes can be explained.

Nowhere is this view more prevalent than in the area of human language. For instance, those of us old enough to have suffered the heyday of behaviorism and rank empiricism will remember being instructed that language was acquired through stimulus and response experiences. It was not until Chomsky's pioneering work in linguistics that it was realized that language reflected a biological event unique to our species. Steve Pinker's subsequent extension of Chomsky's thesis allowed us to appreciate the fact that language is an instinct, just like any other adaptation an animal possesses. Thus, language is not learned by Skinnerian-type associative systems. Rather, the ability to communicate through a language system exists because all members of our species possess an innate capacity to manipulate symbols in a spatio-temporal code that maps sounds onto meanings. Although we "learn" different sounds for those meanings, the laws of syntax are universal. Thus, if an evolutionary perspective were not invoked to interpret the work of Chomsky and Pinker, it is likely that more convoluted psychological theories of learning and development would be generated to explain the human language adaptation.

Another example of variant interpretations of a simple biological phenomenon is to be found among the many explanations for drug abuse. It is commonly believed that our brains were adapted to deal with the Stone Age environment. The adaptations that have accrued in the human brain were well suited to the environmental challenges occurring at that time. Thus, our body metabolism was engineered by natural selection to deal with the kinds of foods available at that time; our capacity for social contracts were similarly built up in the context of one-on-one interactions. Even our capacity to regulate the pleasure-pain continuum of felt sensation was built into our brains at a time when there was a limited supply of environmental goods that could trigger such responses.

Mind-altering drugs work because there are brain receptors that respond to those chemicals. Most such chemicals are also self-generated in small doses by the body in response to exercise and stress. There are opiate receptors that react to body-generated opiates that help to reduce pain after exertion. There are receptors for diazepam that respond to body-generated chemicals similar to the pharmaceutical. Natural selection has built these systems because they serve a survival function. Such systems can calm the body during stress, for instance, enabling an animal to respond to a given situation in an appropriate manner.

An alternative interpretation, which neglects to view drug abuse from an evolutionary perspective, states that drug intake results in addictions, and those addictions reflect a distorted psychological state. Hence, the "science" of the psychology of addictions emerges. In one sense, Western 20th-century society distorts and overloads a biological system and triggers in some people a psychological situation that can be maladaptive. Studying addiction as if it reflected such a psychological state may be profitable in some situations, but in most cases, it overlooks how an underlying adaptation has simply been abused.

The portrait I have sketched here suggests that many psychological evaluations are only superficial analyses that explain the noise in a biological system rather than how the system actually works and what it is capable of doing. In the last decade, we have begun to appreciate that the brain is not a big, freewheeling network that carries out associations built upon simple conditional relations and constructs complex perceptual and cognitive functions out of them. Work in animal psychology, evolutionary psychology, linguistics, and neuroscience has directed our attention to a more fruitful approach to understanding how the brain is built and how it generates mental functions.

This approach builds upon the fundamental notion that brains accrue specialized systems (adaptations, e.g., syntax, upright facial recognition, stress reduction mechanisms, etc.), through the process of natural selection. These systems are highly specific and are best understood in the context of the function they serve. Errors in analysis occur when a basic, complex system proves capable of handling a modern-day task, and in that capacity appears to have a different set of properties. These proximate properties may be so tangible in our modern culture that they become accepted as the fundamental mechanism involved in the behavior or cognitive function in question. Such mistaken emphasis easily leads to misinterpretation of phenomena.

From Associationism to Circuitry

One of the great challenges for future neuroscientists will be to understand how the brain accommodates and instantiates adaptations. As William James stated, the human brain has more instincts, not fewer, than other animals. How does the beautifully adapted human brain represent these instincts, and how does it incorporate them into the dynamic activities that constitute consciousness? Moreover, what can these processes tell us about the nature of consciousness itself? This chapter outlines my own work on hemispheric specialization and employs an evolutionary perspective to interpret this work. In it, I attempt to indicate something of the nature of functional distribution between the hemispheres, culminating in a model of the mechanisms that underlie human consciousness.

Neuropsychological examinations have demonstrated that focal lesions of the cerebral cortex produce specific perceptual and cognitive disorders. My colleagues and I have addressed questions regarding localization of function in the brain by testing each disconnected hemisphere in split-brain patients. While some of the claims made by these studies have become exaggerated, especially in the popular press, there are, nevertheless, certain marked differences between the two half-brains.

Following disconnection of the human cerebral hemispheres, the verbal IQ of the patient remains intact (Nass & Gazzaniga, 1987; Zaidel 1990) and problem-solving capacity, as demonstrated in hypothesis-formation tasks, remains unchanged for the left hemisphere (LeDoux et al., 1977). While there can be deficits in free recall and in some other performance measures, the overall capacity for problem solving appears to be unaffected. In other words, isolating the right half of the cortex from the dominant left half causes no major change in cognitive functions. Thus, the left hemisphere remains unchanged from its preoperative capacity, while the disconnected right hemisphere, which is equal in size, is seriously impoverished on a variety of cognitive tasks.

Although the largely isolated right hemisphere remains superior to the isolated left hemisphere for some activities, such as the recognition of upright faces, some attention skills, and (perhaps) emotional processes, it is poor at problem solving and many other mental activities. Again, a brain system (the right hemisphere) with roughly the same number of neurons as the one that easily cognates (the left hemisphere) is not capable of higher-order cognition. This is compelling evidence that simple cortical cell number by itself cannot fully explain human intelligence. There must be specialized circuits within the left hemisphere that provide unique support for higher-level cognitive activity.

In the perceptual domain, it appears that the right hemisphere possesses special structures that are dedicated to the efficient detection of upright faces (Gazzaniga, 1989). Although the left hemisphere can also perceive and recognize faces, and demonstrates superior capabilities when the faces are familiar, the right hemisphere appears specialized for unfamiliar facial stimuli (Levy et al., 1972; Gazzaniga & Smylie, 1983). This pattern of asymmetry has also been shown for the rhesus monkey (Hamilton & Vermiere, 1988). Since the right hemisphere is superior for perception of faces, it would be reasonable to suppose that it is also specialized for the management of facial expressions. While both hemispheres can generate spontaneous facial expressions, however, only the dominant left hemisphere can generate voluntary facial expressions (Gazzaniga & Smylie, 1990).

Taken together, these brief illustrations suggest the sort of functional distribution that exists between the human cerebral hemispheres. Before I discuss the actual neural representations of those functions, it is necessary to consider the cortical entity that integrates and coordinates them into the seemingly coherent whole that enables consciousness. This entity exists in the left hemisphere, and we have dubbed it the "interpreter." The left hemisphere interpreter possesses a unique capacity to interpret behavior and unconsciously driven emotional states. We have shown how the left, dominant-speaking hemisphere deals with the behaviors we know we can elicit from the disconnected right hemisphere.

We first revealed the phenomenon using a simultaneous concept test, in which a patient is shown two pictures, one exclusively to the left hemisphere and one exclusively to the right, and is asked to choose from an array of pictures placed in full view in front of him the ones associated with the pictures lateralized to the left and right sides of the brain. In one example, a picture of a chicken claw was flashed to the left hemisphere and a picture of a snow scene to the right hemisphere. Of the array of pictures placed in front of the subject, the obviously correct association was a chicken for the chicken claw and a shovel for the snow scene. Case P. S. responded by choosing the shovel with the left hand and the chicken with the right. When asked why he chose these items, his left hemisphere replied, "Oh, that's simple. The chicken claw goes with the chicken, and you need a shovel to clean out the chicken shed." In this case, the left brain, observing the left hand's response, interprets that response into a context consistent with its sphere of knowledge—one that does not include information about the left-hemifield snow scene.

This same general concept has been observed when the left brain struggles to deal with mood shifts that have been produced in an experimental situation by manipulating the disconnected right hemisphere. A positive mood shift triggered by the right hemisphere causes the left hemisphere to interpret its current experience in a positive way, regardless of the seeming logic of such an interpretation. Similarly, when the right triggers a negative mood state, the left interprets a previously neutral situation in negative terms.

It has been appreciated for some time that inference and interpretation are important aspects of normal memory functioning (Bartlett, 1932), and the notion of the left-hemisphere interpreter would predict that the two hemispheres might respond differently in some mnemonic tasks. Phelps and Gazzaniga (1992) showed that when split-brain patients were shown pictures representing a common scene, the two hemispheres responded differently when tested 2 hours later. Their memory was tested with a lateralized yes/no recognition test, where the distracter pictures were either consistent or inconsistent with the original scene. The left hemisphere performed below chance on consistent distracter pictures, whereas the right hemisphere was above chance on these pictures and performed at the same level of accuracy as the pictures originally presented. In short, the right hemisphere, which has no interpretive mechanism, rejected pictures that could have been part of the story. The left hemisphere, on the other hand, with its capacity for making inferences and interpretations, was more strongly influenced by the expectations for actions common to a scene. Similar results have recently been reported by Metcalfe et al. (1995).

In short, the view argued here is that we should consider the human brain as a collection of specialized, often very complex systems, each engineered by natural selection to aid our species in making better decisions about how to enhance reproductive success. The neuropsychological evaluation of the human brain-damaged patient has time and again revealed the dramatic nature of these specializations. Possessing a deficit in one domain seems to little influence complex capacities in other domains. How could that be other than by recognizing that our psychological nature is composed, in part, of a collection of specialized systems?

For those of us interested in how the brain accomplishes the physical representation of these specializations, it is instructive to consider how neuroscientists have come to think about this problem. In the following we shall see that the field is only beginning to ask the relevant questions.

The Neuron as a Computational Unit

Armed with the insight that organisms are a collection of specialized, highly adaptive systems designed to solve particular challenges, the neuroscientist's chore is to attempt to understand how the brain carries out these specific functions. This is an enormous task, of course, and simply raising the question of how the nervous system functions from an evolutional perspective reveals a lack of agreement about fundamental issues. On the other hand there is a prevalent belief that complexity and specific capacities are due to the development of new cortical areas. This view holds that bigger is better, and that additional cortical area is what is responsible for new adaptive functions.

In this regard, between-species comparisons reveal that some features of cortical organization are highly conserved across mammals (Krubitzer, 1995). There is great deal of variation in the specifics of cortical organization, however, and these variations exist both between and within species. For example, Krubitzer asserts that the variations seen in rodents and their behavior are easily detected in their brain maps. The highly visual arboreal squirrel has a cone-rich retina, a large lateral geniculate, and a relatively large visual cortex, whereas the terrestrial muroid rodents, such as the rat, have a relatively small visual cortex but large somatosensory cortices. She concludes that if an animal has a particular sensorimotor style that requires the dominant use of a particular sense or motoric system, the cortex involved with managing those activities will be expanded, relative to other regions of sensory cortex, and contain more subdivisions and interconnections of those subdivisions within the specialized region. How these differences relate to increases in perceptual and cognitive abilities in different mammalian species, however, is unclear.

The notion that simply expanding the cortex increases psychological complexity is an inadequate explanation for the behavioral, perceptual, and cognitive complexity observed in a number of extant species. Modern analysis of animal behavior, by both ethologists and animal learning theorists, supports the view that the brain of any species is a collection of *specific* learning systems, each one honed to deal with particular environmental challenges (Gallistel, 1995). According to this view, learning task A does not necessarily prepare an animal to learn task B of seemingly similar complexity. In other words, the brain is *not* a general problem solver, nor can neuronal number alone, as reflected in cortical surface size or more cortical columns, account for the addition of these specialized systems in different mammalian lineages.

This view flies in the face of the common belief that bigger is better that has been so prevalent in the history of neuroscience (see Finger, 1994). For example, it has been suggested that the gross lateral asymmetry of the temporoparietal region underlies left-hemisphere specialization for language.

Lesion studies demonstrate that this brain area is involved in language processes, and it has been argued that this is the case because it is bigger. There are several lines of evidence that dispute such a claim. First, a number of great apes possess an enlarged planum temporale that is reported to be lateralized to the left hemisphere. Although the issue of whether other species possess language systems is controversial, it is clear that no other primates, including those with this enlargement, possess the degree and quality of language skills that humans do.

Second, we recently reexamined this issue using three-dimensional surface area measurements of the posterior infrasylvian cortical surface from magnetic resonance images. This region extends from the posterior ridge of Heschl's gyrus to the sylvian point, and compsises the planum temporale plus the inferior wall of the terminal ascending sylvian ramus. Three-dimensional computer models were constructed by tracing contours of this region as it appeared in successive coronal scans and then interpolating a three-dimensional triangular mesh between each pair of adjacent contours. No significant directional asymmetry was found (Loftus et al., 1993). In order to determine whether distortion artifacts of other projection methods could account for earlier findings of asymmetry in this region, the same set of contours were used to compute another set of measurements with a more conventional algorithm. The results obtained with the second, more traditional method showed a striking leftward asymmetry. These findings suggest that even in humans, directional asymmetry of cortical surface area in language areas is contentious. In sum, it is not clear that bigger is actually better, and even if it were, that it accounts for the increase in complexity of language systems is a problematic claim at best.

Possible Nature of Cellular Specializations

Because increases in the size of the brain or brain area alone cannot account for increases in specialized systems acquired during evolution, one must look for other mechanisms that can account for the changes observed in mammals. It is at this point that a deep conundrum for neuroscience is apparent. If one is to assume that it is not total cell number (i.e., brain size) that explains specific adaptations, then perhaps there are microcircuitry differences that do. If this were so, how might they be expressed in the nervous system? Are individual neurons in the cortex of monkeys either more complicated in their morphology or more diverse across the population than, say, those of a rodent or large reptile? Or, should one simply look at the complexity of connections that exist between cortical areas? Or, is the complexity to be found in the biochemical processes of the neuron?

Holloway (1968) argues that the main factor accounting for large behavioral differences among primates is neuronal complexity, not neuron number. Most measures of pyramidal cell complexity (absolute numbers of spines, number of basal dendrites, maximum branching order, percent neuropil, etc.) demonstrate that primates, especially humans, have the most complex and varied types of pyramidal cells.

E. G. Jones, one of the world's leading neuroanatomists, has demonstrated that, although the relative size and distribution of pyramidal cells by layer is conserved across species, and the targeting of pyramidal cell projections appears to be conserved as well (i.e., those in layer V always project to subcortical sites and those in layer VI to thalamus and claustrum), there may be more branching of single axons to multiple subcortical sites in rodents and other small mammals than in humans. Jones believes that the real differences are localized in the nonpyramidal cells.

Although nonpyramidal cells have a basic uniformity in all mammals examined, axonal arborizations seem to be more stereotyped in monkeys and cats than in rats. For example, a chandelier cell is unmistakable in those species but has not been identified conclusively in rats. In terms of physiological properties of neurons, Jones feels that there is a limited variety of non-P cells that behave the same in rats as in monkeys. The data, however, are limited, and more work is called for in a wider variety of mammals. For Jones, the unresolved question is whether the relative proportions of the different types of non-P cells change, or whether their numbers simply increase in primates.

Contrasting with the view that cell morphology is more complex and can account for differences in mammals is the belief that there are more types of neurons. In David Amaral's view, the fact that there are more types of neurons means that more computations can be done in parallel, and the brain works faster. He believes that one can begin to understand the issues regarding specialized brain systems by determining why there are more types of neurons in animals with more complexly organized brains (like primates). In his view, neurons have not evolved to be generalized "computational units" that are capable of handling all brain computations, but rather they have evolved as structurally and pharmacologically differentiated units to carry out specific jobs and specific computations. Even in the hippocampus of a single species, pyramidal cells in different parts of the hippocampus (CA3 vs. CA1) look different and express different complements of receptors, presumably because they are carrying out different computations. For example, interneurons in the mammalian cortex can be differentiated by the types of synapses they make (basket cells vs. chandelier cells), the chemicals they contain (γ-aminobutyric acid [GABA] plus somatostatin vs. GABA plus parvalbumin), or the kinds of inputs they receive.

Amaral hypothesizes, "If we think in terms of computer design, the fastest computers do not use generalized chips for all operations, but an assortment of chips that carry out specialized functions very well and very fast. My guess is that the primate brain must process greater amounts of information faster and more subtly than the lizard brain. Thus, the greater diversity of neurons in the monkey and human brain leads to greater efficiency of processing. Diversity of activity must be an important design feature of the brain if you consider how many variants of the glutamate receptor (and every other receptor) there are in the brain."

Others take a different view. Floyd Bloom and John Morrison believe that morphology has been given too much weight in distinguishing cell types. They prefer a definition of cell type that takes connectivity, biochemical phenotype, and location into consideration as well. They find morphology to be a relatively bad predictor of neurochemical phenotype and connectivity— two sets of characteristics that are probably closer to functional organization than is morphology. In short, they believe that the biochemical specializations in primate cortical neurons may be a much better reflection of differences between cells than morphology.

These sentiments are also held by Ira Black. One of the clear messages emerging from the growth or trophic factor field is that cell context is critical to determining the responses of a neuron or glial cell to the very same stimulus. The same factor may be mitogenic for one cell, survival-promoting for another, neuritogenic for another, and so forth. These differences derive, at least in part, from the use of different intracellular signal-transduction cascades, many of which activate and repress unique suites of genes in different cells. In Black's view, the cells and the systems in which they are located have been exquisitely selected to perform incredibly diverse functions, from motor to memory. Black asks, "Is it surprising that different tasks demanded the use of different molecular mechanisms for survival? Is it surprising that these differences have morphologic correlates in many instances? Just as the brain is not an all-purpose thinking machine, there doesn't seem to be a single all-purpose neuron for all seasons."

Clearly, after a hundred years of looking at the brains of dozens if not hundreds of species, each living in its own niche, and each having its own specializations, there really is no clue to how the brain builds specific functions from neuronal elements. There is no agreement that cell complexity, cell number, cell metabolism, cell connections, or cell milieu is the key factor. Perhaps the question needs to be addressed from a completely different perspective. E. O. Wilson describes with great clarity how the ant has adapted to different environments in radically different ways (Holldobler & Wilson, 1990). Ants found in the tropics build huge mounds in which they live. Ants in the Sahara possess radically different strategies to survive the arid environment. There are literally dozens of different strategies that different species of ants have developed to deal with the problems posed by their environment. Perhaps a fruitful approach to gain insight into how neural circuit organization might support different kinds of solutions would be to study variations of brain organization within a species, or to examine brains in closely related species with radically different behaviors.

The Overarching Nightmare: The Answer Is in the Spike Pattern

Having said all of the above and having reviewed the difficulties in determining how neuroscience might unlock some of the secrets of the evolution of the brain and mind, we should realize that there is a totally different way to consider what it is we are looking for. Instead of looking for physical substrates that are unique and support specific computational capacities, we might discover the answers to how the brain generates complex capabilities in informational terms. Nowhere is this insight more succinctly stated than in John Tooby and Leda Cosmides' observations about the task of cognitive neuroscience:

> Understanding the neural organization of the brain depends on understanding the functional organization of its cognitive devices. The brain originally came into existence, and accumulated its particular set of design features, only because these features functionally contributed to the organism's propagation. This contribution—that is, the evolutionary function of the

brain—is obviously the adaptive regulation of behavior and physiology on the basis of information derived from the body and from the environment. The brain performs no significant mechanical, metabolic, or chemical service for the organism; its function is purely informational, computational, and regulatory in nature. Because the function of the brain is informational in nature, its precise functional organization can be described accurately only in a language that is capable of expressing its informational functions—that is, in cognitive terms, rather than in cellular, anatomical, or chemical terms. Cognitive investigations are not some soft, optional activity that goes on only until the "real" neural analysis can be performed. Instead, the mapping of the computational adaptations of the brain is an unavoidable and indispensable step in the neuroscience research enterprise; it must proceed in tandem with neural investigations, and indeed will provide one of the primary frameworks necessary for organizing the body of neuroscience results. (Tooby & Cosmides, 1995, p. 1190)

Tooby and Cosmides' message as to which level we need to examine when trying to understand how the brain does its job is clear. It is the ebb and flow of neuronal patterns of firing that holds the key to understanding how the brain makes its decisions. The physical substrates allow certain kinds of computations to be carried out, but once they are expressed it is the pattern of the neuronal code that represents the neural code for function. Evolutionary theory has generated the notion that we are a collection of domain-specific systems. The neuroscientific understanding of this notion is the greatest challenge that the student of mind-brain research faces in the next century. One surely does not want to appeal to the few neurotransmitters that are most active to explain thousands of specific systems. The brain must solve new challenges in a highly complex and probably distributed way. Let's quickly recall how it all works.

The neural system of any given animal at any given time is in a state that is more or less specific, but in fact through time, there are changes in the microarchitecture of the neural system. If a mutated change or random change, which occurs as a result of simple variations in growth dynamics, enhances the probability of reproductive success, then there is a higher probability that the mutation will be inherited by future generations. In no way does an organism construct a solution to a problem de novo. Only by chance is a new network generated and additional characteristics and abilities added. Thus, brain mechanisms evolved to meet new challenges and perform specific tasks that enhance reproductive success.

Unfortunately, this ad hoc fashion of building a brain makes it very difficult for neuroscientists to tease out what types of tasks a system has actually evolved to accomplish. This is surely the reason why it is so difficult to find localized circuits that are *wholly* responsible for a perceptual or cognitive capacity. The experienced neuropsychologist will study patients with focal lesions who might well exhibit a rather specific disorder. Yet it is also common to study a patient with an amazingly focal disorder that suffers from a large diffuse lesion.

Even the appearance of ever-more-advanced brain–imaging techniques has not helped us understand localization in a better or different way. Positron emission tomography (PET) and functional magnetic resonance imaging (fMRI) can yield reliable and reproducible images of the brain at work, solving particular kinds of cognitive and perceptual tasks. Yet those images only reveal particular brain areas that are more active on a given task. They do not include other areas that may also be active on the task but simply less so.

In conclusion, our journey through the profoundly fascinating but young area of how the brain represents adaptive changes, not only within but also between species, finds modern knowledge wanting. While most observers would grant that the human brain is a complex web of adaptations that are somehow built into the nervous system, no one knows how. Upon reflection, it is probably also the case that the neural specificity that underlies specific adaptations constitutes a specific network that may be widely distributed throughout the brain. Since evolutionary changes work in ad hoc and efficient ways, commandeering systems to assist in a particular chore by chance, the probability of finding a circuit that underlies a particular task may well be impossible.

And yet that is the assignment of the thinking neuroscientist. While work continues at the level of informational descriptions, a level that may well be the one on which we will understand brain function, those of us committed to studying what the nervous system can do may find inspiration by also recognizing what the brain is for.

Acknowledgments

In this modern day and age, one can solicit the opinions of some of the world's leading scientists via e-mail. My thanks to Ted Jones, David Amaral, John Morrison, Floyd Bloom, and Ira Black for providing me with their insights and thoughts on these critical issues. This work was aided by NIH grants NINDS 5 R01, NS22626-09, and NINDS 5 P01 NS17778-014 and by the James S. McDonnell Foundation.

References

Bartlett, F. C. (1932). *Remembering: A study in experimental and social psychology*. Cambridge, England: Cambridge University Press.

Finger, S. (1994). *Origins of neuroscience*. Oxford: Oxford University Press.

Gallistel, C. R. (1995). The replacement of general-purpose theories with adaptive specializations. In *The cognitive neurosciences*. M. S. Gazzaniga (Ed.), Cambridge, MA: MIT Press.

Gazzaniga, M. S. (1989). Organization of the human brain. *Science, 245*, 947–952.

Gazzaniga, M. S., & Smylie, C. S. (1983). Facial recognition and brain asymmetries: Clues to underlying mechanisms. *Annals of Neurology, 13*, 536–540.

Gazzaniga, M. S., & Smylie, C. S. (1990). Hemispheric mechanisms controlling voluntary and spontaneous facial expressions. *Journal of Cognitive Neuroscience, 2*, 239–245.

Hamilton, C. R., & Vermiere, B. S. (1988). Complementary lateralization in monkeys. *Science, 242*, 1961–1964.

Holldobler, B., & Wilson, E. O. (1990). *The ants*. Cambridge, MA: Harvard University Press.

Holloway, R. L., Jr. (1968). The evolution of the primate brain: Some aspects of quantitative relations. *Brain Research, 7*(2), 121–172.

Krubitzer, L. (1995). The organization of neocortex in mammals: Are species differences really so different? *Trends in Neuroscience, 18*(9), 408–417.

LeDoux, J. E., Wilson, D., & Gazzaniga, M. S. (1977). Cognition and commissurotomy. *Brain, 100*, 87–104.

Levy, J., Trevarthen, C., & Sperry, R. W. (1972). Perception of bilateral chimeric figures following hemispheric disconnection. *Brain, 95*, 61–78.

Loftus, W. C., Tramo, M. J., Thomas, C. E., Green, R. L., Nordgren, R. A., & Gazzaniga, M. S. (1993). Three-dimensional quantitative analysis of hemispheric asymmetry in the human superior temporal region. *Cerebral Cortex, 3*, 348–355.

Metcalfe, J., Funnell, M., & Gazzaniga, M. S. (1995). Right-hemisphere memory superiority: Studies of a split-brain patient. *Psychological Science, 6*, 157–164.

Nass, R., & Gazzaniga, M. S. (1987). Cerebral lateralization and specialization of the human nervous system. In V. B. Mountcastle, F. Plum, and S. R. Geiger (Eds.), *Handbook of Physiology: The Nervous System* (vol. 5, pp. 701–761). Bethesda MD: American Physiological Society.

Phelps, E. A., & Gazzaniga, M. S. (1992). Hemispheric differences in mnemonic processing: The effects of left-hemisphere interpretation. *Neuropsychologia, 30*, 293–297.

Tooby, J., & Cosmides, L. (1995). Mapping the evolved functional organization of mind and brain. In M. S. Gazzaniga (Ed.), *The cognitive neurosciences*, pp. 1185–1197. Cambridge, MA: MIT Press.

Zaidel, E. (1990). Language functions in the two hemispheres following complete cerebral commissurotomy and hemispherectomy. In R. Nebes & S. Corkin (Eds.), *Handbook of neuropsychology* (vol. 4). Amsterdam: Elsevier.

III PSYCHOLOGY (MEMORY, THEORY, AND COGNITION) IN THE 21ST CENTURY

10   The Future of Cognitive Psychology?

Henry L. Roediger III

My task in this chapter is admirably straightforward: to predict the future. Actually, the authors were given three interwoven tasks: (1) to predict the future of science as a whole, (2) to predict the future of psychology, and (3) to predict the future of our own discipline (which in my case is cognitive psychology, and more particularly human learning and memory). The agenda is ambitious, and the fact that I don't have the foggiest specific idea about the future of any of these three topics will not deter me in the least. After all, it is easier to write science fiction than to write science. In the latter case one is usually constrained by such mundane features as data, theory, the plausibility of one's statements, and so on. For an essay like the present one, these normal moorings on reality can be untied; we are permitted to speculate freely. The fact that most of us probably had given the distant future little thought before being set this task will also not deter us, although it might give pause to the reader. I am reminded of what P. B. Medawar (1969) wrote about scientists' approach to method: "Ask any scientist what he conceives the scientific method to be, and he will adopt an expression that is at once solemn and shifty-eyed; solemn, because he feels he ought to declare an opinion, shifty-eyed because he is wondering how to conceal the fact that he has no opinion to declare. If taunted he would probably mumble something about 'Induction' and 'Establishing the Laws of Nature,' but if anyone working in a laboratory professed to be trying to establish the Laws of Nature by induction we should begin to think he is overdue for leave."

So I begin my essay here in a shifty-eyed, but not particularly solemn, mood. We may be solemn about the scientific method, but there is no reason to be so when contemplating the future. The history of attempts to predict the future is comical, at best, and there is no reason to think that the writers of this volume will do better than those in the past. The future is as unpredictable as it is unknowable, so we may as well enjoy ourselves when thinking about it. Attempts to predict the future with a solemn mien would only make our efforts look more pathetic in the future, should anyone dip back into this book and its predecessor to see how far off the mark we were.

My aim here is to take a look back and then a look forward. I will first ask how well I (or a scholar of the time) might have predicted the future had I been alive and asked to do so at various periods in the past. Then, with the thoughts aroused by this exercise firmly in mind, I venture to write about the future.

A Look Backward in Time

The title of this book provides grand ambition, as it includes the millenarian theme already being overused in contemplating the year 2000. (This overuse is apparent already, even though I write at the end of 1995.) What does the 21st century hold for us? Before contemplating possible answers to this question, let us consider, briefly, what possibility there would have been to predict where we are today from the past. I will consider three epochs: 1000 years, 100 years, and 25 years.

Of course, the biases of hindsight are well known. As the saying goes, hindsight is 20/20 and we all are great experts in telling why, after the fact, some event must have occurred. Experimental psychologists have repeatedly documented that people can easily explain, after the fact, the occurrence of events and then believe that they would have predicted them. However, controlled studies show they could not predict the events, even the ones whose outcomes seem obvious in retrospect (Fischoff, 1975; Wood, 1978). Because of this knowledge, I doubt that anyone today could have accurately predicted the course of the future in my field—the cognitive psychology of learning and memory—at any point even in the relatively near past (say 25 years ago or more), even in broad terms. But let us first consider longer periods of time, in keeping with the millenarian theme of this book.

Imagine a European scholar, probably a monk or another ecclesiastical scholar, who had some interest in how the mind learns and remembers, writing in A.D. 1000 to predict where scholarship may lie in 1000 years. Who can imagine what this mythical scholar may have thought? If we are charitable, we can imagine that, at best, he (and it probably would have been a male) may have thought that the future would lie in the art of perfecting memory. Because medieval scholars knew of mnemonic systems, he would probably have bet on their perfection as a main topic for future scholars. That prediction would have been partly right, had it been made. The art of memory did occupy some scholars of at least the Middle Ages with many techniques handed down from Greek and Roman writers and other new ones created (Yates, 1966). (The study of mnemonic systems still occurs, but this topic is not now hotly discussed in cognitive psychology.) Our hypothetical scholar's other probable thoughts may have concerned arguments of free will and determinism, of how God's will and method were unveiled in the human mind. (When reading intellectual history, I am always struck by how religious beliefs permeated all thought on every topic in the past, because the situation is so different in the academy today.) Surely the scholar of a thousand years ago would have been certain that today's thinkers would have been similarly influenced by religious questions and issues. In this he would have been wrong, for the most part. We do occasionally hear scientists referring to discovering the secrets of Mother Nature, who seems to take on (at least metaphorically) some trappings of a knowable and kindly, but elusive, deity. She is the closest most scientists come to making religious statements today.

Could the scholar of a thousand years ago have predicted the rise of modern science beginning in the 1500s, the development of so many specialized branches of knowledge, and the remarkable intellectual achievement in the late 19th century of experimental and scientific methods being applied to the study of mind? Even with our wisdom of hindsight, the answer would have to be no. The scholar a millennium ago would have no chance of even coming close, no matter how well informed and perspicacious he might have been. And change during most of the last millennium was, relative to today's pace, much slower. Therefore, for any authority today to write seriously about the future of his or her field a thousand years hence is surely sheer folly. I won't even try.

Let us move to a more modest unit of time, the century. Could a scholar 100 years ago predict where we are today? As I see it, the task now becomes more manageable; I can even imagine a scenario where the predictions could, in a general sense, be accurate. However, my real belief is that the answer is still no; an experimental psychologist writing in 1900 could not have predicted where we are today. Experimental psychology had begun only in the 1860s and 1870s, mostly by physicists and physiologists who branched into new regions. Progress was uneven in the early years and few universities opened psychology departments until much later, after the discipline was securely established. (Rice University, where I write these words, did not establish a separate psychology department until the early 1970s, but that was partly because Rice was founded as a science and engineering institute. The California Institute of Technology still does not have a psychology department.) Although our contemporary knowledge of the growth and development of psychology may make us think that this course was inevitable, the path doubtless could have been quite different.

Certainly it would have been difficult a century ago to predict accurately the multifaceted nature of contemporary psychology. Experimental methods had been applied to problems of sensation and perception, but Wilhelm Wundt, one of the early champions of the experimental approach, did not believe that these methods could be extended to higher reaches of cognition—to remembering, or thinking, for example. Rather, he believed that one must study (as he did) the products of cultures, much as a cultural anthropologist or sociologist would, to gain evidence about the more creative aspects of mind. Ebbinghaus's (1885/1964) great experiments on memory showed that at least this topic could be submitted to experimental inquiry, but to extrapolate from his experiments to modern cognitive science (much less modern psychological science) in all its manifestations would have too great a leap for even the brightest minds of 1900.

William James's (1890) monumental two-volume work, *Principles of Psychology*, captured wonderfully what was known at that point, but even James had his doubts about the field he so beautifully ratified in his writings, at one time remarking that psychology was "a nasty little science" as he turned back to philosophy late in his career. Careful experimentation often seemed to bore him. The philosophers were then, as now, asking grand questions about mind. Experimental psychologists were probably seen as providing answers to only some rather lower-level questions. Could anyone have then foretold how creatively experimental methods could be extended to study all manner of perceiving, reading, speaking, remembering, and thinking, to mention just some main topics in cognitive psychology? If we added the startling methods and insights provided by those studying cognitive development, social cognition, and other related fields, we would certainly overpower the ability of any scholar in 1900 to predict the current scene.

If a scholar could not have predicted the future of the field 1000 or even 100 years ago, what about 25 years ago? That seems a manageable number, so let's take 1970 as a convenient point. Could a cognitive psychologist of 1970 have predicted where the field would be in 1995 or 2000? Even here I think the answer is no, at least in anything less than general form. I am in a bit better position to analyze this scenario, because I began graduate school at Yale University in the 1969–1970 academic year. Most of my undergraduate background had been in what was then called human experimental psychology. However, I applied to Yale to study social psychology (never having taken a course in the topic, but having read Brown's [1965] wonderful textbook). My first semester I took Robert Crowder's excellent course in human learning and memory and decided that my interests lay more in that direction, so I switched programs, which was remarkably easy to do. Wendell Garner, Ruth Day, Rowell Huesmann, and Alex Wearing were also on the faculty in the newly christened program in cognitive psychology, Endel Tulving was soon to arrive (in 1971), and John Anderson was hired the following year. Ulric Neisser's textbook, *Cognitive Psychology*, was used in Crowder's course, along with many articles, and it defined the new field and gave everyone a rallying cry.

If you had asked me in the early 1970s what the future would hold in 25 years, I would doubtless have projected the current topics that were being enthusiastically investigated into the future. What were these topics? I will mention the terms without trying to explain them: sensory memories (iconic and echoic memory, and particularly the study of modality and suffix effects in serial recall, at least in Crowder's laboratory at Yale); the role of imagery in memory, and the study of mnemonic devices by Paivio, Bower, and others; the distinction between primary (or short-term) and secondary (or long-term) memory, especially as studied through serial position analyses of single-trial free recall by Glanzer, Murdock and Craik, and as captured in Atkinson and Shiffrin's [1968] model; the topic of intentional or directed forgetting also received considerable attention and was the focus of my first major project at Yale (Roediger & Crowder, 1972); organization in memory (especially in multitrial free recall, where Tulving [1962] studied how subjective organization developed and Mandler [1967] had people directly sort and form organizational units); experiments I conducted both as an undergraduate and graduate student asked about Tulving's (1966) discovery of part/whole negative transfer in free recall (then a hot topic) and were part of the study of organizational processes; the role of retrieval processes in memory (in Tulving's work on encoding specificity and the recognition failure of recallable words, which was just being published; relatedly, I conducted my dissertation on Slamecka's

[1968] finding of retrieval inhibition from part-list cues); the study of word perception and reading was booming, with the lexical decision task becoming a popular topic of study in the 1970s and the Reicher-Wheeler word superiority effect occupying the interest of many researchers; relatedly, the study of the structure of knowledge, or semantic memory, was coming into focus in Collins and Quillian's (1969) model and the experiments designed to test it were widely discussed; the role of attention, as studied by Posner and Garner, among many others, continued a line of research begun in the 1950s and 1960s; and the elegant item recognition paradigm, developed by Sternberg (1966) and often called the Sternberg paradigm, was being applied to ask many questions. There were many other topics of interest, too, but those mentioned above were some of the most popular in my corner of the world at Yale in the early 1970s.

If you had asked me then to project into the future, I would have doubtless placed the study of sensory memories, the relation among memory stores, the organization of memory, retrieval processes in memory, imagery, and all the rest as secure bets for the next 25 years. I would have been wrong on most counts. All the topics mentioned above enjoyed at least 5 years of intense interest after 1970, but most of these topics are not being studied so enthusiastically today and some hardly receive any attention in contemporary literature (e.g., the organization of memory, as indexed by experimental interest in such topics as part/whole negative transfer).[1]

It seemed clear in the early 1970s that other topics were on the way out. To mention but two, the interference theory of forgetting was at a high-water mark, with many publications in the late 1960s. I think I could have foretold (or, more accurately, I could have expressed the opinions of my mentors) that the conflicting findings and unwieldiness of the theory would make it less attractive as a future topic of research (even though the theory did then and does still address critically important problems). Therefore, I and others might have predicted (correctly) that research on interference theory was due for a decline. (Of course, this belief may only reflect hindsight bias; research related to interference theory was still lively in 1970.) The rapidity and completeness of the decline in studies of traditional interference theory probably stunned everyone.[2] On the other hand, I would have also predicted a decline for the study of associative theories of memory in general, had I been asked in 1970 or so, and there I would have been dead wrong. Associationism in the form of John Anderson's theories (e.g., Anderson, 1972; Anderson & Bower, 1973) and in connectionism (McClelland & Rumelhart, 1986) was about to rise triumphant.

How well could someone in my field have predicted, in 1970, the research topics that were to excite and occupy researchers for the next 25 or 30 years? I believe the answer is "very poorly," though perhaps not quite so badly as for someone in 1995 or 2000 trying to predict the scene in 2020–2025. Here I list five important topics that arose in the study of learning and memory and discuss why I think they would not have been predicted in 1970, drawing some general conclusions at the end about how new topics emerge.

1. *The levels-of-processing approach to memory.* In 1972 Fergus Craik and Robert Lockhart published one of the most-cited papers in the history of cognitive psychology, announcing their levels-of-processing approach to human memory. Rather than conceiving of a flow of information through the cognitive system, with box-and-arrow diagrams, they argued that people normally go about the world trying to perceive and comprehend it as well as possible and that memory for events is a byproduct, reflecting the level or depth of processing of the original events. Many of the ideas they proposed were similar to those growing out of the attention literature of the 1950s and 1960s and most of the experimental facts about memory that they marshaled were ones developed from incidental learning experiments already published (Hyde & Jenkins, 1969).[3] I can recall reading their paper for the first time and thinking "So what else is new?," thereby causing myself to miss out on one of the most important sets of ideas for the next decade, which many other researchers eagerly embraced. The levels-of-processing approach is clearly one of the main currents in the psychology of learning and memory over the past 25 years (Roediger, 1993; see Lockhart & Craik, 1990, for a review of this area).

2. *The rise of neuroscientific approaches.* In 1970 the study of the mind and study of the brain were separate enterprises. I remember happening upon George Talland's (1965) book, *Deranged Memory*, while I was looking for books to read to satisfy Yale's (rather minimal) requirements prior to embarking on the dissertation. I asked if I should add it to my reading list and was told that it would be all right, but many others should appear ahead of it. The general attitude, often stated quite explicitly, was that nothing important would ever be learned about normal memory functioning from studying the pathological cases arising from injury to the brain. What could we learn from studying freaks of nature? Within 15 years that attitude had changed completely and the neuropsychology of memory was at the forefront of the field. But nobody I

knew would have predicted that in 1970. When reviewing evidence about the two-store memory theories in his *Annual Review of Psychology* paper, Postman (1975) wrote "We have not considered the results obtained with brain-damaged patients which continue to be cited as evidence for dual-process theory. . . . The existing data do not strike us as unequivocal; more important, extrapolations from pathological deficits to the structure of normal memory are of uncertain validity" (p. 517), and nearly everybody in the field then would likely have agreed with him. In fairness, there was an active research community studying the neuropsychology of memory in 1970, but no one in (what we perceived to be) the mainstream was paying attention. Most of the neuropsychological research then was derived from applying standard paradigms developed with normal subjects to see how various patient groups performed on them. This pattern of research activity was soon to change, as happened in the study of the next topic.

3. *The rise of implicit memory research.*   The standard measures of retention for the experimental analyses of learning and memory had been measures of recall (free, serial, or cued) and recognition. In each instance, subjects were asked to remember events, usually from the recent past, which had occurred in a particular time and place. Tulving (1972) referred to this as the study of event memory or episodic memory and contrasted its study with that of semantic memory, or general knowledge. In the late 1970s and early 1980s a new endeavor began, the study of implicit (or indirect) measures of memory. These measures were driven partly by techniques used to study semantic memory (the lexical decision task and some others), but more important in this development were studies from neuropsychology. Patients rendered amnesic from brain damage, who were seemingly incapable of learning and retaining new information, were suddenly shown to behave perfectly normally on these new types of memory measures that indexed retention indirectly. Interestingly, the initial studies of this phenomenon were published during the late 1960s and early 1970s by Warrington and Weiskrantz (1968, 1970), but no one in the mainstream paid attention until years later (and the early attention was usually to claim that their experiments could not be replicated). However, the Warrington and Weiskrantz experiments were replicated when subjects were given the appropriate instructional set, and these techniques were later modified and applied to the study of normal subjects in new and interesting ways (e.g., Jacoby & Dallas, 1981; Graf et al., 1982; Tulving et al., 1982). The three papers just cited reported experiments with normal subjects showing that

variables known to have systematic and powerful effects on explicit memory tests (recall and recognition) could have no effect or even opposite effects (e.g., Jacoby, 1983) on these new implicit (or indirect) measures. This set the field off on a new path that, I would argue, no one could have anticipated in 1970 (even though the seminal studies had already been published).

4. *Metacognition.* In 1970 Tulving and Madigan wrote in the *Annual Review of Psychology* that psychologists had made little true progress in understanding memory. They asked: "What is the solution to the problem of lack of genuine progress in understanding memory? It is not for us to say because we do not know. But one possibility does suggest itself: why not start looking for ways of experimentally studying, and incorporating into theories and models of memory, one of the truly unique characteristics of human memory: its knowledge of its own knowledge." (1970, p. 477). Except for early studies on the tip-of-the-tongue effect (Brown & McNeill, 1966) and the feeling-of-knowing effect (Hart, 1965), largely treated then as isolated curiosities, Tulving and Madigan were correct that no one much worried about the problem of how people assessed and regulated their own memories. But many rose to the challenge and studies of metacognition (of how people know about their own cognitive processes) came soon afterward. They were initiated by Flavell and Wellman's (1977) experiments with children, asking how the ability to monitor memory changes with age. Other types of experiments using techniques of metacognition began to boom later. Subjects were asked to make feeling-of-knowing judgments, judgments of learning, reality monitoring judgments (did I do it or imagine doing it?), judgments of the source of information (who said the information? did I read it?), remember/know judgments, and many others (see Nelson, 1992, for a sample of articles). In 1970 memory was thought to be best measured "objectively," with subjects' intuitions about what they might be accomplishing during a test playing little role in the analysis (except for occasional measures of confidence on recognition tests). There was some analysis of the strategies subjects applied while learning, but these were sporadic. In the 1970s and 1980s these experimental practices changed and the study of metacognition remains a hot topic to this day (Metcalfe & Shimamura, 1994).

5. *Memory errors and confusions.* The history of experimental analysis of learning and memory has largely been about how much people could accurately remember. The analysis of errors was mostly restricted to correcting measures of veridical performance for guessing, in attempting to arrive at a

more accurate assessment (or a truer measure) of memory. The idea of systematically studying errors to gain an understanding of how remembering occurred was not much in favor, despite important precursors (Bartlett, 1932). Several different analyses changed this state of affairs in the late 1960s and early 1970s (see Roediger, 1996; Schacter, 1995). To mention a few, Neisser's (1967) important text, *Cognitive Psychology*, resurrected Bartlett's (1932) approach to remembering, and important experiments in the early 1970s showed how this approach could be melded with more modern experimental analyses (e.g., Bransford & Franks, 1971). Loftus and Palmer (1974) initiated the first experiments examining how later misinformation provided about an event could systematically alter retention of the event. Combined with assessments using metamemory techniques, we can now conclude that misinformation can alter one's recollection of the event and that often the rememberer cannot distinguish the "new" recollection that is false from one that is true. Later, Johnson and Raye (1981) began their pioneering series of experiments on reality monitoring, or the ability to distinguish fact from fantasy (and confusions of one with the other).

All these experiments and many more (see Roediger, 1996) brought the study of memory errors to the forefront. This trend might have been predicted by some in 1970—many of the pieces were there but no one was yet working on the puzzle—but I certainly would not have been a prognosticator with that prediction. (One lesson from this line of research on memory errors and illusions is that it is hard enough to know the past accurately; how much harder must it then be to know the future?)

I have described five main trends in the study of human memory dating since 1970 whose occurrence, I maintain, most observers would have been unlikely to predict in 1970. (I do not think it was my being a graduate student that leads me to conclude that I could not foresee these trends.) A few commonalities exist among these five cases. First, in each case the initial studies that were later to become celebrated existed well before the topic became an important general thrust of research. The early experiments were truly ahead of their time. They were published, but had to be combined later with insights by others to have an impact. Some of the ideas, such as those leading to the levels-of-processing framework, were very much in the air, albeit more in the study of attention than memory. Others, such as the neuropsychological influence and the study of implicit memory, were further removed from the mainstream, and it would have been harder to predict the power with which such studies gripped the field later on. In short, even when the early hints of new trends were before the eyes of anyone who cared to gaze at them, they were missed. And these case studies illustrate why predicting the future of research, even in a relatively circumscribed area, is so difficult.

A Look Forward in Time

My lessons from the past are intended to give us pause. Surely we cannot predict the fate of science, psychology, or even the study of learning and memory, in the next millennium. Even attempting to discuss what might transpire in the next thousand years is folly (apologies to my coauthors in this volume who may be attempting this feat). Predicting, concretely, for even the next 100 years would be fraught with difficulty. I will try my hand at predicting some trends in my field for the next 25 years. Even though I have just argued that I would have failed if I had done this 25 years ago, and failed badly, I did not try then. I will try here along with the cowriters of this book. Who knows? Perhaps we will succeed. Another good reason to pick 25 years is that I have a reasonable chance of living through them and can see if any of my predicted trends come to pass. (Predicting the next 5 years would be too easy—just predict that the research on the hot topics of the present will continue and usually one will be right over the short term. It takes topics time to die just as it takes them time to build).

Because I am writing at the end of December 1995, newspapers and radios are treating readers and listeners to astrologers' predictions of the future and, less often, looking back to their feeble attempts to predict the past year's events. I do derive some guidance from their efforts, however. Those claiming the best record make the most general predictions, along the lines of "There will be civil wars around the world," or "The President of the United States will face an international crisis," or "Terrorist acts will upset international relations." These are all safe bets for next year, and the following year, and so on. Astrologers often predict assassinations, too, but the form is usually "The leader of an important power will be assassinated in 1996." Some made that prediction last year and, sadly enough, Yitzak Rabin of Israel was assassinated. But no one predicted that specific event. The iron law for making predictions is that the more general the prediction, the more likely it is to be verified by some event in the future. But the truth of the prediction is no cause to believe the predictor truly prescient; with general predictions, many events can be interpreted as fulfilling the prediction. Conversely, specific predictions (in futurology as in science) are more easily falsified. With this rule in mind, my first prediction:

1. *Most of the specific predictions in this volume will be wrong.* (Let's define *most* as 80%, to be specific here.) Specific predictions include ones that set times—such as my own 25-year limit, or even more refined figures (such as "by the year 2013"). I would thereby exclude from considerations such platitudes as my next two predictions, which sound reasonable and almost certainly have to be true, but are good predictions only because of their generality. My second and third predictions are:

2. *New discoveries will lead research in the psychology of learning and memory (or any other field) in new and unexpected directions.* This has happened in every previous 25-year epoch, so can be confidently predicted for the next quarter century. Specific predictions would state what these directions might be, but I doubt anyone knows. (Some speculations exist below in other predictions.)

3. *New discoveries will undermine currently cherished findings, theories, and assumptions.* Again, this pattern happens in every 25-year period, so seems a certainty. Besides, we would not want to live through the next 25 years of research if it were not true. Once again, the trick would be in specifying which findings, theories, and assumptions would be overthrown, but I cannot confidently do that.

Next I turn to predictions that are more concrete and might actually be falsified.

4. *The psychology of learning and memory will become (even more) interdisciplinary.* This seems another safe bet. The main problem clouding interpretation of the outcome would be a ceiling effect—is the field already as interdisciplinary as it can be? Currently, learning and memory are studied from a dizzying variety of perspectives, from molecular, to cellular, to synaptic, to neural systems, to artificial networks, to behavioral analyses with animals, to ethological analyses, to experimental analyses of humans, to metaphorical models, to mathematical models, to social-psychological concerns, and recently even to social, cultural, and historical analyses. After all, everyone from neurobiologists and animal learning psychologists on the one hand, to cultural anthropologists and historians on the other, worry for one reason or another about how people (and other animals) retain past experiences. The same is true of collections of people, from the passing down of legends in preliterate societies to the writing of recent history, such as about the assassination of John F.

Kennedy and the fall of the Nixon presidency (to pick two events that seem open to multiple historical re-creations). One can imagine a future in which historians team with experimental psychologists to ask how (say) the records and reporting of different events become transfigured as they are passed from one generation (of scholars in history, or subjects in psychology) to the next. Factors such as the scholars' or subjects' interests and beliefs in the topic at hand could be manipulated, along with many others.

Although many disciplines currently worry about the problems of learning and memory in their own domain, with their particular field's own assumptions, viewpoints, and theories, there is great room for cross-fertilization of thought. Not long ago I was asked to review a paper for the *Journal of Southern History* on the topic of what could be learned about the institution of slavery from accounts provided by slaves themselves. Briefly, most current accounts of slavery in the American South have come from records and reminiscences of the slave owners, using their interpretations of events. This fact might account for the relatively benign picture of slavery that appears in some history books: yes, slaves led a hard life, but generally they were well treated because they were valuable personal property. Recently, some historians have tried to systematically evaluate the relatively infrequent narratives of the slaves themselves, but these are quite scattered by region, by the gender and age of the writer, and so on. These historians sometimes consult with psychologists, asking questions that most psychologists are unprepared to answer. How accurately might memory for an episode from, early in a slave's life (e.g., the family being sold at auction and broken up when the rememberer was 6 years old) be retained, if it were not retold or written down until the person was 75 and asked to do so by an historian? How might the tale change? This question and many others like it are common among historians studying this issue, because it was mainly between 1915 and 1935 that historians began to collect reminiscences from former slaves, who were then quite old. How good might such evidence be as history?

Psychologists cannot answer this question now, but future longitudinal research could conceivably provide some information that would aid historians. In general, one profitable future development in the psychology of learning and memory would be to take a life-span approach through longitudinal research. This type of research would doubtless have to be carried out by teams of researchers, over generations, much like the famous studies of gifted children initiated by Lewis Terman in the 1920s and still ongoing today. But such studies would open up the field to many fascinating questions that have not yet even been raised, much less answered. Many other interdisciplinary collaborations would probably address similarly new questions, ones not even being considered now.

5. To become more specific, *I predict that at least a fledgling program of life-span memory research will begin in the next quarter century.* At the moment there is, even among experimentally oriented psychologists, a rather sharp division of labor. Many researchers such as myself study learning and memory in young adults, largely college students. Other researchers study learning and memory in children; another group of investigators studies learning and memory in older adults. Still others are interested in learning and memory in various specialized populations: patients with specific patterns of brain injury, people with Alzheimer's disease, people diagnosed as schizophrenic or clinically depressed, and so on. Although researchers interested in the populations mentioned above overlap a bit and to some degree a e informed of one another's findings, none really examines the person over the life span.

A few researchers have worried about retention of specific bodies of knowledge over long periods of time (such as Bahrick's [1984; Bahrick et al., 1975] studies of the retention function of names and faces and Spanish vocabulary learned in college), but these studies were conducted long after the fact, when there could be no control or manipulation of conditions of learning or of the intervening experiences. In the future, I predict that a true life-span psychology of learning and memory will develop, wherein research participants will be recruited as infants (with permission of their parents), given various experiences under controlled conditions, and then tested at various periods during their lives. Intervening events could be manipulated to some degree, too. In addition, parents may be induced to record important events accurately at the time of their occurrence (accidents, birthday parties, deaths of relatives, first dates) and the knowledge about these events can be assessed later under varying retrieval conditions. If records of textbooks and school grades are maintained, this would represent another rich source of information to be tested in later life. A true life-span approach to learning and memory, through longitudinal studies, might serve to increase our knowledge of many important properties of memory. Although such a field is only a dream now, it could (and should) become a reality in the future.

6. *The "everyday memory movement" will pay important scientific dividends, by being combined with the traditional experimental logic of cognitive psychology to*

lead to important new insights.   Neisser (1976, 1978) critiqued the psychology of learning and memory and found it sadly wanting, too tied to sterile laboratory paradigms. He advocated abandoning laboratory methods for a more ecologically valid psychology of memory, using ethological observational methods and the like. Many psychologists rallied to his cry and began studies of ecological memory or everyday memory. Banaji and Crowder (1989) surveyed the scene some years later and found little to cheer about; they announced the ecological or everyday memory approach "bankrupt." Their article, in conjunction with those of Neisser, ignited a debate that continues today. The essence of Banaji and Crowder's (1989) argument is that without experimental control over conditions of learning and testing, no firm conclusions about memory (inside or outside the laboratory) can be made. Any attempt to favor external validity over internal validity is a mistake; one must first achieve internal validity to have any hope of producing generalizable (externally valid) knowledge. Yet the ecological movement eschewed experimental control for a purely observational approach. I weighed in on the side of Banaji and Crowder (1989) in this little debate (Roediger, 1991), noting that the studies claimed as the best of the everyday memory movement (such as Loftus and Palmer's [1974] study of eyewitness memory) actually used traditional laboratory methods, experimental control, and the usual logic of experimental, cognitive psychology. The triumphs of a true observational approach were relatively few (although I would certainly include Neisser's [1981] fascinating study of John Dean's memory in this group).

So why do I now think the everyday memory movement will lead to great insights? Although I think the methods advocated by this approach were generally wrong-headed, the beneficial effect is to open the study of learning and memory to new topics, ones not previously in its purview. The everyday memory movement had a liberating influence on the topics and content considered legitimate areas of inquiry in the psychology of learning and memory. This influence, and the emphasis on applied problems (such as the current focus of psychologists on the accuracy or inaccuracy of memories recovered during therapy) will have an important impact in the future. Because one group of researchers now keeps its sights focused outside the laboratory, new phenomena may be identified and, initially, described through observational study. However, such identification and description should not be an end in itself (as the original proponents of this movement seemed to imply), but rather a beginning to careful experimental study. In the most satisfying case laboratory methods can help unravel paradoxes arising between what psychologists have learned from laboratory research and what everyday memory researchers have found. The recent work by Koriat and Goldsmith (in press) represents an excellent example. I predict we shall see many more like it in the future.

7. *Neuroscientific approaches to learning and memory, already prevalent, will become even more dominant.* Cognitive psychologists have tended to live in relative ignorance of advances in neuroscience, at least until lately. Their experimental analyses have been conduced largely on intact adult subjects, with normal working brains, and their theoretical analyses have been tn the form of verbal descriptions of assumptions, ideas, and hypotheses (e.g., the levels-of-processing framework), metaphorical models (likening semantic memory to a giant dictionary, for example), or to mathematical models with numerous parameters and explanatory constructs. Until lately, cognitive psychologists have rarely considered neural underpinnings of their constructs or sought explanations of phenomena in brain mechanisms. All this will change dramatically in the future, continuing a trend already in evidence.

Cognitive psychologists have often defended their abstract level and mode of explanation by appealing to the computer metaphor of mind: electrical engineers and other physical scientists may be interested in the hardware that runs computers, whereas computer scientists, designers, and programmers develop and understand the software. Yes, the software may have to operate within the constraints of the hardware, but the rules programmed into the computer can be studied and understood at their own level of analysis, without a programmer needing to know much about the hardware Correspondingly, the argument goes, cognitive scientists may operate at the behavioral level of analysis in trying to discover the programs that run the mind while (in parallel) neuroscientists learn about the brain's hardware that supports the program. I first heard this defense of the cognitive level of analysis in graduate school and it has become something of an article of faith among cognitive psychologists, but it is now clear to me that we should (and must) give up this idea that the study of cognition can be (and maybe even should be) divorced from the study of the brain. We give up too much and get little in return.

Robert Bjork (1989) argued not long ago that the computer metaphor is all but dead in cognitive psychology. He wrote:

> At the current stage of research on human memory, we are poorly served by the computer metaphor. Thirty years ago, as an alternative to the stimulus-response approach, the information-processing approach was invaluable.... We have come to realize, however, that in virtually every important respect, the human information processor is functionally nothing like the standard digital computer. From the standpoint of a computer scientist, there appears to be considerable value in drawing upon modern cognitive neuroscience and cognitive science to reconfigure the processing architecture of the next generation of computers. From the standpoint of a cognitive psychologist, there is no remaining value in the standard computer metaphor (p. 310).

Later in the same chapter, which was on inhibitory processes in memory, Bjork commented that "A new metaphor has emerged to influence the thinking of memory researchers: the brain metaphor.... Ideas about memory are being shaped by the accelerating knowledge of the possible functions of certain brain structures in human memory" (p. 328). Bjork was clearly right in 1989, although not everyone seems to have gotten on board the new band-wagon. There even seems to be stiff resistance in some quarters. But I predict that the future holds great promise for alliance of traditional cognitive psychologists and others with the prefix *neuro-* in their disciplinary description: neuropsychologists, neurologists, neuroradiologists, neuroscientists, etc. Some corollary predictions flow from assuming this one is true.

   8. *Neuroimaging techniques will assume increased importance and many great discoveries of the future will result from the marriage of cognitive, experimental techniques applied to subjects whose brains are being imaged.* This trend is already apparent, especially in the work concerned with positron emission tomographic (PET) analyses of cognitive function (Posner & Raichle, 1994). Many studies have already appeared that have tentatively identified brain areas responsible for perceiving words, faces, and music and for studies of encoding and retrieval processes in remembering. In some instances, the results confirm findings obtained from neuropsychological work with brain-damaged patients, but in other cases novel findings have emerged which were unanticipated by patient findings. An example of the last outcome is the relatively consistent finding from PET and MRI (magnetic resonance imaging) studies that the right frontal

lobe plays an important role in episodic memory retrieval (Nyberg et al., 1996), although other memorial functions are subserved by the frontal lobes, too (Buckner, 1996). Neuroimaging techniques will, I predict, gain in ascendancy in the cognitive neuroscientists' methodological armamentarium. These techniques may overshadow, but not replace, the typical strategy used in cognitive neuropsychology of studying single cases or studying patient groups (such as patients with Korsakoff's syndrome or diseases of the Alzheimer's type). Although steady advances in technology are responsible in part for these exciting developments, equally important (in my opinion) is the application of well-developed techniques and methods employed by cognitive psychologists over the years. The best work in the future will probably come from technically sophisticated imaging facilities (PET, functional MRI, event-related potentials, and others) combined with the experimental logic and methods of cognitive psychologists, who can adapt their methods to the needs of the imagers to ask interesting and important questions.

9. *The greater influence of cognitive neuroscience will change the theoretical landscape of psychologists interested in learning and memory.* Metaphorical models of memory, those likening memory to a storehouse, or to a library, or to other concrete storage devices (see Roediger, 1980, for a review), will decrease in importance and will seem even more misleading (or beside the point) than they do now. Why speculate about metaphors that might work like the mind, when we can root our theoretical understanding of behavior in the neural mechanisms that are responsible? There will still be much room for controversy, competing theories, and so on. Witness the controversy that has occupied researchers in neuroscience over the past 15 to 20 years over the role of the hippocampus and surrounding structures in modulating memory.

10. This next prediction for the future of theory flows from the prior one and can be stated succinctly: *Cognitive psychologists will begin pursuing a reductionist theoretical approach, in collaboration with neuroscientists.* Reductionism has been mostly regarded as a wrong approach in cognitive psychology during the past 25 years, and for good reason: many neurological discussions attempted in the past (such as some of those by the Gestalt psychologists in the 1930s and 1940s) seem not just wrong but completely far-fetched today. Nonetheless, reductionist approaches help constrain speculation and provide theories with a firm foundation. Now that relatively noninvasive techniques for the study of brains of intact people have become available, reductionism—

explaining behavior in neuroscientific terms—seems both inevitable and desirable.

11. I end with a surprise prediction: *Some form of behaviorism will return and be reintroduced into psychology as a strong force to be reckoned with.* This will occur grudgingly a first, but then enthusiastically. I do not mean the Skinnerian form of behaviorism that eschews all talk of mental constructs and all reference to internal workings of the mind or brain (although I think this approach also has its place). But, for cognitive psychology, I mean the behaviorism of Hull or Spence or Tolman, in which theoretical constructs had to be grounded in observable behavior. Those theorists did propose constructs rooted in concrete observations, a practice that has been all but eliminated in contemporary cognitive psychology, as I have noted before (Roediger, 1980, 1993). Currently, theorists are literally permitted to propose nonsense constructs—models of mind have many constructs that are not moored to observable behavior. Rather, the entire model produces predictions that can be checked against aggregate behavior, but the individual constructs that compose the model have no external markers. I predict (or imagine) a world in the future in which psychology returns to the idea that hypothetical constructs should make contact with observable behavior, even if indirectly. The trend toward neuroscientific explanation may hasten the return of this form of behaviorism. The study of observable behavior should always be central to psychology, even cognitive psychology. (On the other hand. I made a prediction similar to this in my 1980 paper on memory metaphors and the theoretical scene is unchanged 15 years later, except perhaps to be worse on this dimension.)

Conclusions

In this chapter I cast a backward glance at where we have been and argued that even the most prescient scholar, whose knowledge encompassed the field of psychology, could not have predicted the future course of the field at various vantage points in the past (even from the relatively short distance of a quarter century). Next I made 11 predictions for our progress for the next 25 years. Two were generic predictions—ones true for every 25-year epoch—but the others can be tested against the future. I hope Professor Solso will arrange another volume in 25 years to assess how well we predicted the future of our disciplines. Perhaps some of us will even be there to write for him.

Acknowledgments

I appreciate comments by Robert L. Solso and Kathleen B. McDermott.

Notes

1. Many of these topics may simply have been mined (experimentally and theoretically) for all they were worth at the time. They will lie dormant until a new generation of researchers has creative insights to renew their investigation.

2. An interesting challenge that might be set today's researchers is to predict which of the current hot topics will last the longest, which will fade, and which will lead (whether fading or not) to enduring contributions to our understanding.

3. Similar observations were made by a revision psychologist, P. I. Zinchenko, in 1962, but his work was generally unknown in the West until it was translated into English and published in a 1981 volume edited by J. V. Wertsch. Solso (1995) provided an accessible summary.

References

Anderson, J. R. (1972). FRAN: A simulation model of free recall. In G. H. Bower (Ed.), *The psychology of learning and motivation* (vol. 5). New York: Academic Press.

Anderson, J. R., & Bower, G. H. (1973). *Human associative memory*. Washington, DC: V.H. Winston & Sons.

Atkinson, R. C., & Shiffrin, R. M. (1968). Human memory: A proposed system and its control processes. In K. W. Spence & J. T. Spence (Eds.), *The psychology of learning and motivation: Advances in research and theory* (vol. 2). New York: Academic Press.

Bahrick, H. P. (1984). Semantic memory content in permastore: Fifty years of memory for Spanish learned in school. *Journal of Experimental Psychology: General, 113*, 1–47.

Bahrick, H. P., Bahrick, P. O., & Wittlinger, R. P. (1975). Fifty years of memories for names and faces: A cross-sectional approach. *Journal of Experimental Psychology: General, 104*, 54–75.

Banaji, M. R., & Crowder, R. G. (1989). The bankruptcy of everyday memory. *American Psychologist, 44,* 1185–1193.

Bartlett, F. C. (1932). *Remembering: A study in experimental and social psychology.* Cambridge, England: Cambridge University Press.

Bjork, R. A. (1989). Retrieval inhibition as an adaptive mechanism in human memory. In H. L. Roediger, III and F. I. M. Craik (Eds.), *Varieties of memory and consciousness: Essays in honour of Endel Tulving* (pp. 309–330). Hillsdale, NJ: Erlbaum.

Bransford, J. D., & Franks, J. J. (1971). The abstraction of linguistic ideas. *Cognitive Psychology, 2,* 331–350.

Brown, R. (1965). *Social psychology.* New York: Free Press.

Brown, R., & McNeill, D. (1966). The tip-of-the-tongue phenomenon. *Journal of Verbal Learning and Verbal Behavior, 5,* 325–337.

Buckner, R. (1996). Beyond HERA: Contributions of specific prefrontal brain areas to long-term memory retrieval. *Psychonomic Bulletin & Review, 3,* 135–148.

Collins, A. M., & Quillian, M. R. (1969). Retrieval time from semantic memory. *Journal of Verbal Learning and Verbal Behavior, 8,* 240–248.

Craik, F. I. M., & Lockhart, R. S. (1972). Levels of processing: A framework for memory research. *Journal of Verbal Learning and Verbal Behavior, 11,* 671–684.

Ebbinghaus, H. (1885/1964). Memory: *A contribution to experimental psychology.* New York: Dover.

Fischoff, B. (1975). Hindsight foresight: The effects of outcome knowledge on judgment of uncertainty. *Journal of Experimental Psychology: Human Perception and Performance, 1,* 288–299.

Flavell, J. H., & Wellman, H. M. (1977). Metamemory. In R. V. Kail & J. W. Hogen (Eds.), *Perspectives on the development of memory and cognition.* Hillsdale, NJ: Erlbaum.

Graf, P., Mandler, G., & Haden, P. (1982). Simulating amnesic symptoms in normal subjects. *Science, 218,* 1243–1244.

Hart, J. T. (1965). Memory and the feeling-of-knowing experience. *Journal of Educational Psychology, 56*, 208–216.

Hyde, T. S., & Jenkins, J. J. (1969). Differential effects of incidental tasks on the organization of recall of a list of highly associated words. *Journal of Experimental Psychology, 82*, 472–481.

Jacoby, L. L. (1983). Remembering the data: Analyzing interactive processes in reading. *Journal of Verbal Learning and Verbal Behavior, 22*, 485–508.

Jacoby, L. L., & Dallas, M. (1981). On the relationship between autobiographical memory and perceptual learning. *Journal of Experimental Psychology: General, 3*, 306–340.

Johnson, M. K., & Raye, C. L. (1981). Reality monitoring. *Psychological Review, 88*, 67–85.

James, W. (1890). *Principles of psychology*. New York: Holt.

Koriat, A., & Goldsmith, M. (in press). Memory metaphors and the laboratory/real life controversy: Correspondence versus storehouse views of memory. *Behavioral and Brain Sciences,*

Lockhart, R. S., & Craik, F. I. M. (1990). Levels of processing: A retrospective commentary on a framework for memory research. *Canadian Journal of Psychology, 44*, 87–112.

Loftus, E. F., & Palmer, J. C. (1974). Reconstruction of automobile destruction: An example of interaction between language and memory. *Journal of Verbal Learning and Verbal Behavior, 13*, 585–589.

Mandler, G. (1967). Organization and memory. In K. W. Spence, & J. T. Spence (Eds.), *The psychology of learning and motivation* (vol. 1, pp. 327–372). New York: Academic Press.

McClelland, J. L., & Rumelhart, D. E. (Eds.). (1986). *Parallel distributed processing: Explorations in the microstructure of cognition*. Cambridge, MA: MIT Press.

Medawar, P. B. (1969). *Induction and intuition in scientific thought*. London: Methuen.

Metcalfe, J., & Shimamura, A. P. (1994). *Metacognition: Knowing about knowing*. Cambridge, MA: MIT Press.

Neisser, U. (1967). *Cognitive psychology*. New York: Appleton-Century-Crofts.

Neisser, U. (1976). *Cognition and reality*. San Francisco: Freeman.

Neisser, U. (1978). Memory: What are the important questions? In M. M. Gruneberg, P. E. Morris, & R. N. Sykes (Eds.), *Practical aspects of memory* (pp. 3–24). San Diego: Academic Press.

Neisser, U. (1981). John Dean's memory: A case study. *Cognition, 9*, 1–22.

Nelson, T. O. (1992). *Metacognition: Core readings*. Boston, MA: Allyn & Bacon.

Nyberg. L., Cabeza, R., & Tulving, E. (1996). PET studies of encoding and retrieval: The HERA model. *Psychonomic Bulletin and Review, 3*, 135–148.

Posner, M. I., & Raichle, M. E. (1994). *Images of mind*. New York: Freeman.

Postman, L. (1975). Verbal learning and memory. *Annual Review of Psychology, 26*, 291–335.

Roediger, H. L. (1980). Memory metaphors in cognitive psychology. *Memory and Cognition, 8*, 231–246.

Roediger, H. L. (1991). They read an article? A commentary on the everyday memory controversy. *American Psychologist, 46*, 37–40.

Roediger, H. L. (1993). Learning and memory: Progress and challenge. In D. E. Meyers & S. Kornblum (Eds.), *Attention and Performance XIV: A Silver Jubilee* (pp. 509–528). Cambridge, MA: MIT Press.

Roediger, H. L. (1996). Memory illusions. *Journal of Memory and Language, 35*, 76–100.

Roediger, H. L., & Crowder, R. G. (1972). Instructed forgetting: Rehearsal control of retrieval inhibition (repression)? *Cognitive Psychology, 3*, 244–254.

Schacter, D. L. (1995). Memory distortion: History and current status. In D. L. Schacter, J. T. Coyle, M. M. Fischbach, L. E. Mesulam, & L. E. Sullivan (Eds.), *Memory distortion*. Cambridge, MA: Harvard University Press.

Solso, R. L. (1995). *Cognitive Psychology*, (4th ed.). Boston: Allyn & Bacon.

Slamecka, N. J. (1968). An examination of trace storage in free recall. *Journal of Experimental Psychology, 76,* 504–513.

Sternberg, S. (1966). High-speed scanning in human memory. *Science, 153,* 652–654.

Talland, G. (1965). *Deranged memory: A psychonomic study of the amnesic syndrome.* New York: Academic Press.

Tulving, E. (1962). Subjective organization in the free recall of "unrelated" words. *Psychological Review, 69,* 344–354.

Tulving, E. (1966). Subjective organization and effects of repetition in multi-trial free-recall learning. *Journal of Verbal Learning and Verbal Behavior, 5,* 193–197.

Tulving, E. (1972). Episodic and semantic memory. In E. Tulving & W. Donaldson (Eds.), *Organization and memory* (pp. 381–403). New York: Academic Press.

Tulving, E., & Madigan, S. A. (1970). Memory and verbal learning. *Annual Review of Psychology, 21,* 437–484.

Tulving, E., Schacter, D. L., & Stark, H. A. (1982). Priming effects in word-fragment completion are independent of recognition memory. *Journal of Experimental Psychology: Learning, Memory, and Cognition, 8,* 336–342.

Warrington, E. K., & Weiskrantz, L. (1968). New method of treating long-term retention with special reference to amnesic patients. *Nature, 217,* 972–974.

Warrington, E. K., & Weiskrantz, L. (1970). Amnesic syndrome: Consolidation or retrieval? *Nature, 228,* 628–630.

Wood, G. (1978). The knew-it-all-along effect. *Journal of Verbal Learning and Verbal Behavior, 4,* 345–353.

Yates, F. (1966). *The art of memory.* Chicago: University of Chicago Press.

Zinchenko, P. I. (1981). Involuntary memory and the good-directed nature of activity. In J. V. Wertsch (Ed.), *The concept of activities in Soviet psychology.* Armonk, NY: Sharpe.

11 The Memory Trainers

GAY SNODGRASS

Preface

In the 21st century, basic science funding has been drastically cut, thereby leaving many trained cognitive scientists unemployed in basic research. At the same time, there has been an increased demand by the public in general, and in particular by the elderly, for a widely available system of memory assessment and memory training. It is commonly accepted in the 21st century that just as physical training is an important adjunct to physical health, so mental training is important to mental health, defined broadly as maintenance and improvement in all cognitive capacities, not just the emotional ones. Memory training in particular has become very popular both because it is believed to help maintain memory function and because it provides a way to chart the decline of memory function. Charting the decline of memory function is important for the effective use of the suicide pact which many elderly clients now choose as a way of ending life with grace and dignity. The drastic cuts in funding for long-term medical care coupled with the legalization of physician-assisted suicide has led to many elderly choosing suicide over a prolonged, painful, and financially ruinous decline. The plight of the elderly plagued with mental decline, such as Alzheimer's dementia, is particularly poignant because at the point where the decline in mental capacity may make life no longer worth living to them, they are incapable of choosing suicide as a way out. This has led to the use of the pre-suicide agreement in which the patient early in his mental decline chooses a state of deterioration beyond which he is not willing to go and at which point he wishes his life to be terminated. Determining such a condition requires, of course, that cognitive capacity be monitored both before and during the course of the disease. Enter the memory trainers.

Memory trainers are recruited from the ranks of Ph.D.'s in cognitive psychology and cognitive science. One of the most distinguished of such training centers is the Institute for Memory Training at Empire State University. Following is a transcript of a speech delivered at the Worldwide Conference on Memory Training by the director of the institute, Dr. Joy Smoothlawn.

TRAINING THE MEMORY TRAINERS—A VIEW FROM THE PAST

JOY SMOOTHLAWN, PH.D.
EMPIRE STATE UNIVERSITY

Thank you for inviting me to address this distinguished group in this historic year 2050 at the midpoint of the 21st century. In this talk, I will describe both our techniques for training memory, and our techniques for training the memory trainers. Before I do so, however, I think it is important to describe the history behind these memory training techniques. I know that in today's climate we tend to take a narrow view of training techniques, asking only Do they work?, not What is the theory on which they are based?, or What is their history? But I firmly believe that to make continued progress in our science we need to continue to carry out basic research and to speculate about the why as well as the how. As you may know, our institute is funded by our memory training centers. Our students, who still earn a Ph.D. rather than an M.I.T. (master of instruction and training), receive both practical experience as interns in one of the memory training centers, and theoretical experience in conducting basic research.

It is now fairly well established that memory, like intelligence, is based upon several partially separable abilities. The reason they are only partially separable is that memory, like intelligence, shares a common ability. In research on intelligence, this common ability has been called g since Spearman's time. In memory research, this general ability has come to be called m. Like g, m has come to be treated as a theoretical construct which cannot be uniquely measured by a single test, although in memory research many investigators believe that m can be identified with working memory capacity. But I am getting ahead of my story. Before I can describe how our training techniques work, I must first take a little detour back over the history of memory research.

History of Memory Research

Our present situation, in which we postulate about 15 memory abilities, should be understood against the backdrop of a history of memory research in which a minimum of two memory systems have always been assumed. We begin our story in the late 1960s, when the state of memory theory at the time was well described in a famous paper by Atkinson and Shiffrin.[1] They described two memory systems. The short-term memory (STM) system held information in temporary storage while a "control process" operated on its contents. The effects of that control process, which was assumed to be subvocal rehearsal, determined whether the contents of STM would be transferred to the second memory system, long-term memory (LTM), or would be lost from STM by entry of new information. Long-term memory was viewed as a permanent repository of potentially unlimited capacity which stored information in terms of its meaning or significance to the individual. This contrasted with STM, which was a temporary repository of very limited capacity that stored items of information in a very shallow or nonmeaningful format such as the item's sound or articulation.

The capacity of STM is generally acknowledged to be on the order of seven plus or minus two "chunks" to use the terminology of George Miller's famous paper.[2] A chunk is a piece of information that has a unitary representation in memory. So a seven-digit telephone number consists of seven chunks, but a well-known date such as 1492 consists of only one chunk. Miller suggested in his paper that the only way the capacity of STM could be increased is by increasing the size of a chunk. He described the case of the psychologist Sidney Smith who trained himself to quickly recode binary digits (i.e., sequences of 0's and 1's) into varying chunk sizes, from two to five (a chunk size of three corresponds to recoding binary digits into octal digits). His memory span was roughly constant at 12 octal digits, which meant that when he was recoding binary digits into five-digit chunks, he could repeat back a total of 40 binary digits!

Miller argues that much of our most sophisticated learning corresponds to such recoding. A child learning to read is learning how to turn five unrelated letters into a whole word with a unitary meaning. A student of psychology who is learning about experimental paradigms can recode several paragraphs of procedural explanation into a few-word description of a well-known experimental paradigm. So the power of recoding is obviously of great value.

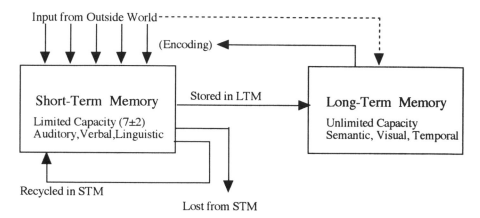

Figure 11.1   The two-store memory model of Atkinson and Schiffrin (1968).

Interestingly, however, we today are in the same situation as Miller was in 1956. There seems no way to increase the capacity of STM beyond its limit of several chunks, and so this bottleneck between the outside world of sensation and the inside world of memory continues to restrict the rate and efficiency with which we can encode information.

Figure 11.1 shows this early two-store model of memory. Input from the outside world enters STM (and may also enter LTM directly—the uncertainly of this option is indicated by the dashed line from the outside world to the LTM store). Items are encoded into STM from either the perceptual field or a short-term visual memory (which will not concern us here). The encoding process is heavily dependent upon LTM, as indicated by the arrow from LTM to the encoding process. The exact process whereby this encoding takes place has long been of intense interest, particularly for linguistic stimuli such as words, and we are still pondering some of its mysteries. However, from the standpoint of memory, what is important is that the material does get encoded into the chunks of Miller, and these chunks are then cycled through STM in a verbal, acoustic, articulatory form via the process of subvocal rehearsal. Items then may enter LTM or may be lost. As indicated in figure 11.1, the format of storage in LTM is more likely to be semantic, temporal, spatial, and pictorial in nature.

Up until the early 1960s, students of memory had been resolutely and single-mindedly concerned with verbal materials. Following the 19th-century pioneering studies of Ebbinghaus, who introduced the nonsense syllable (a pronounceable but nonmeaningful string of letters such as "BEX") in order to avoid meaning in memory, researchers had used lists of words or nonsense syllables as materials with which to study memory. One of the leading journals of that day, entitled the *Journal of Verbal Learning and Verbal Behavior* (and since renamed the *Journal of Memory and Language*), represents that trend. However, we receive information from the outside world in a variety of formats, including pictorial and spatial representations, motor movements, smells, touches, tastes, etc. So some pioneering psychologists, of whom the most famous was Allan Paivio, sought to extend the scope of memory research from words to pictures, and to correspondingly extend the scope of LTM from an exclusively verbal system to one that encompassed both verbal and pictorial information.

Paivio proposed that LTM could be divided into two parts. One, the pictorial system, stored images, and the second, the verbal system, stored verbal codes. The two systems were independent but interrelated and some types of inputs, such as easily nameable pictures and concrete words, could be encoded into both systems. The possibility of this dual coding for these commonly used materials is referred to as the dual-coding theory of memory storage. Note, however, that some pictorial materials that are inherently indescribable, such as people's faces and abstract paintings, are encoded only in the pictorial system, whereas some verbal materials that are inherently nonimageable, such as abstract words and phrases, are encoded only in the verbal system.[3]

Figure 11.2 illustrates Paivio's dual coding model. When a picture is presented for study, it is always encoded into the pictorial code system (indicated by the solid line) and it may be encoded into the verbal system (indicated by the dotted line). Similarly, when a word is presented for study, it is always encoded into the verbal code system and only sometimes encoded into the pictorial system. The relative strengths of the two codes are indicated by the thickness of the solid lines (so the pictorial code is stronger than the verbal code) and the relative probabilities of the alternative codes are indicated by the thickness of the dashed lines (so the probability of encoding a picture verbally is higher than the probability of encoding a word pictorially). Similar differences in strengths and probabilities are shown at the bottom of figure 11.2 in which picture recognition and recall is better than word recognition and recall both because of differences in strength of codes and in probabilities of dual-coding. In Paivio's system, meaning is incorporated into the two symbolic systems. Thus, the meaning of an object (or its depiction) can be found in its

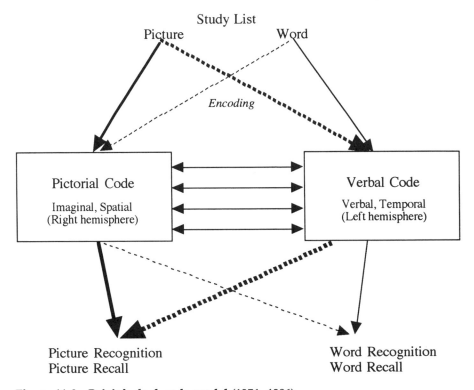

Figure 11.2 Paivio's dual-code model (1971, 1986).

association with other pictorial codes, and to their associations with verbal codes (as indicated in the bidirectional arrows connecting the two systems). A similar way of constructing meaning is assumed for verbal codes.

Critics of the dual-coding position argued that meaning cannot be represented as simple associations among codes; rather, it is necessary to postulate a separate representational store, common to both pictures and words, which represents their meaning. Meaning is represented in these models as networks of nodes connected by labeled links representing relationships. This representational store is also known as semantic memory. The first model of semantic memory (indeed, the first use of the term) was proposed by Quillian in his master's thesis; subsequent developments of the structure and operation of semantic memory were made by Collins and Quillian in 1969 and by Collins and Loftus in 1975.[4]

Although these semantic memory models are important in their own right, for the purposes of the present discussion we will only consider them as they have been grafted onto the dual-code model of Paivio. In these "common code" models of how verbal and pictorial information is represented in LTM, there are separate verbal and visual stores which preserve the surface characteristics of words and pictures, but these are both connected to a common representational system. This common representational system acts to integrate information from visual and verbal sources. So, for example, seeing a movie and reading the novel of the movie produce identical representations at this deeper level. Pictorial and verbal code systems retain surface information about pictures and words such as how they appear, how they sound, and how they are spelled, but the common conceptual store serves to unite the two representations so that the same meaning (represented by a node and its associates) is contacted by both a picture and its name. Figure 11.3 shows a schematic representation of the common code model, adapted from one proposed by Snodgrass.[5] The major difference between the common code model and Paivio's model is that visual and verbal code stores access a common semantic memory, and that communication between the two stores is normally made via connections in the semantic store. Thus to translate a picture to a word, as in a picture-naming task, subjects first access the visual image store, then the semantic store, then the verbal store.

The possibility of pictures being encoded into pictorial codes, and in general the possibility of spatially organized information being remembered without translation into verbal codes posed difficulties for the notion that the format of storage in STM is strictly verbal. Certainly when we write, attempt to attend to the last few words of a sentence, or look up a telephone number, our consciousness appears to be filled with acoustic or articulatory images (i.e., internal speech). However, when we count the number of windows in our apartment or house, try to visualize how a new sofa will look in our living room, or listen to a baseball game on the radio and try to keep track of who's on first, second, and third base, our consciousness appears to be filled with visual and spatial images.

The reality and operation of a visuospatial STM was elegantly demonstrated in the early 1970s by Roger Shepard and his colleagues. They carried out a series of innovative experiments on mental rotation, in which subjects were presented with pairs of three-dimensional shapes that were in different orientations and asked to decide as quickly as possible whether they were

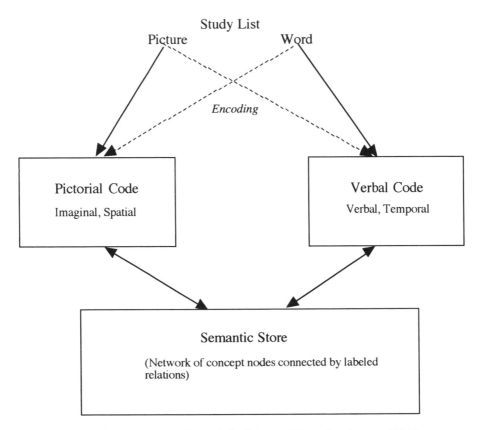

Figure 11.3 The common code model. (Adapted from Snodgrass, 1984.)

identical or not. Their results indicated that in order to perform the task, subjects imagine one object rigidly rotated into the other, that the rate of rotation is fixed at about 60 degrees per second, and that in the process of rotation they mentally pass through representations of intermediate orientations, just as would happen in real-life rotation.[6] These studies showed decisively that subjects were able to use visuospatial operations in STM in order to solve the task.

In the 1980s, Alan Baddeley proposed a reworking of the notion of STM which he called "working memory." In his theory of working memory, there is a central executive which operates at least two "slave systems," a verbal or articulatory loop much like the original STM memory of Atkinson and Shiffrin's model, and a visuospatial sketchpad of the sort that would be required for the mental rotation operations of Shepard's subjects.[7] As we shall see, we incorporate these two functions of working memory into our battery of tests.

In the meantime, another development catapulted LTM into yet another dichotomy of systems. In order to understand this development, the audience needs to understand how experiments in memory were conducted in those days. A subject in a typical memory experiment might be shown a list of words or pictures. Sometime after this list was presented, subjects would then be asked to remember which of the words or pictures occurred in the study list. This test of memory usually took one of two forms: In a recall test, subjects would be asked to list all of the items in the study list. In a recognition test, subjects would be shown possible examples of study list items, only some of which actually occurred in the list, and asked to discriminate old or studied items from new or distracter items. The subject's task is thus to remember whether or not a particular item occurred at a particular time, rather than to remember what the item meant, whether he or she liked the item, and so forth. Yet, as we noted above, it is well known that in order to remember something well, the subject needs to access its meaning. This meaning is not contained in the item itself as it is presented during the study list, but rather is information that has accumulated gradually over the subject's life span. To a bilingual English–French speaker, the words "apple" and "pomme" mean the same things and access the same meanings, while to a monolingual English speaker, the word "pomme" is a meaningless nonsense syllable. We know that meaningful material is much better retained than nonmeaningful material, so an important component of remembering the occurrence of an item in a memory test is accessing its meaning. The meaning of an item also resides in memory, but this seems to be a different type of memory than memory for an item's occurrence on a list.

In 1972, Endel Tulving noted that researchers had used the term "memory" to refer to both of these types of information—occurrence information and meaning information—and proposed that the two types of LTM systems were different and should be called by different names. He proposed the term "episodic memory" to refer to the first type, occurrence information, and the term "semantic memory" to refer to the second type, meaning information.[8] So, for example, a question such as "What did you eat for dinner last night?" is a question which relies on retrieval from episodic memory, whereas a question such as "What kind of pizza do you prefer?" relies on retrieval from semantic memory. The two memory systems differ in many kinds of ways.

Perhaps the most striking difference is in the speed of learning. Information in the episodic system is often entered in one trial (a single presentation of an item on a study list, or a single encounter with a stranger may be remembered forever). In contrast, information about the meaning of a word is built up in semantic memory over numerous encounters with the word. A second difference between the two memory systems is that retrieval from episodic memory changes the memory (a once-recalled word will be better recalled on the second attempt), whereas retrieval from semantic memory leaves it unaffected. A third difference is that context influences retrieval from episodic memory much more than retrieval from semantic memory. We are able to use the same word with the same meaning in a variety of contexts, whereas we may be unable to remember an episode in our past life if we change our retrieval environment (e.g., we may fail to recognize a friend in a foreign country).

In 1985, Tulving introduced a third system in addition to episodic and semantic memory—procedural memory.[9] Procedural memory is memory for perceptual, motor, and cognitive skills; semantic memory is encyclopedic knowledge about the world which need not be associated with autobiographical time and place of acquisition to be expressed; and episodic memory is knowledge about the occurrence of events that are tied to the rememberer's past and thus autobiographical. We can illustrate this trichotomy with an example from typing. Knowing how to type is procedural; knowing where the letter r is on the keyboard is semantic; and remembering that one typed a letter to ABC Company yesterday is episodic. Tulving viewed these three systems as hierarchical, with episodic memory a specialized subsystem of semantic memory, and semantic memory a specialized subsystem of procedural memory, as shown in figure 11.4.

SYSTEMS VS. PROCESSES

Before continuing with our history of memory research, it will be useful to digress a moment and discuss what people mean when they speak of different memory systems. This issue has reemerged from time to time, although even in the 21st century we have still not resolved the controversy (more exactly, agreement has been reached that the controversy is incapable of resolution). Everyone agrees that there is a visual system and an auditory system. The two systems can be distinguished by the following three criteria: (1) distinct sense organs (eyes vs. ears); (2) distinct representations in the brain; (3) distinct causes

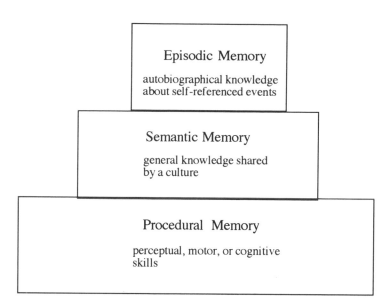

Figure 11.4   Tulving's (1985) proposal for a tripartite memory system.

resulting from damage to the two systems (blindness vs. deafness). These are clear cases against which the use of the term *system* in memory research can be compared.

Consider the two systems of episodic and semantic memory proposed by Tulving. They clearly do not satisfy criterion (1) above. Sense organs for both types of memory include all of the perceptual ones (vision, audition, smell, taste, and somatesthesia) as well as internal ones such as thought and remembrance itself. Thus you can remember seeing something, you can remember imagining something, and you can remember that you remembered seeing or imagining something. However, Tulving and other investigators have argued forcefully that both of the remaining two criteria are met by the two memory systems. Consider criterion (2), distinct representations in the brain. A hypothesis now firmly supported by both behavioral and physiological data is that episodic and semantic memory systems are subsumed by different memory structures—the hippocampal system for episodic memories and the neocortex for semantic memories. To be more precise, episodic memories are initially stored in both the hippocampus and neocortex, with the hippocampus involved in conscious recollection of the memories and the neocortex involved in unconscious or involuntary registration. In contrast, semantic memories, which represent accumulated episodic memories from which common elements are extracted, come to be stored exclusively in the neocortex. Because of the dual representation of episodic memories, it was sometimes difficult to show that these two systems were in fact dissociated from one another, as should be the case if there were separate and independent storage of the two types of memories.

Finally, consider criterion (3), distinct causes resulting from damage to the two systems. It should be possible to find patient groups in whom semantic memory is unimpaired but in whom episodic memory is impaired (but not vice versa insofar as episodic memories move from hippocampal to neocortical representations). Of course, a great deal of research into memory disorders has shown that both amnesia and dementia are characterized primarily by deficits in episodic memory and not by deficits in semantic memory.

IMPLICIT VS. EXPLICIT MEMORY

A related dichotomy between systems of LTM was developed by Daniel Schacter, a student of Endel Tulving.[10] *Implicit memory* can be defined as retention without awareness, as exhibited by enhanced processing of a stimulus that has been presented before in the absence of recovery of information about its prior occurrence. So, for example, a subject may be able to more easily perceive a word when he or she has seen the word previously on a study list. This type of retention is also known as priming or repetition priming. A related type of priming, semantic priming, refers to enhanced retrieval of the item in response to a related cue, as when, in response to a free association task, a subject might respond "swan" to the stimulus term "white" rather than the more common response "black" because the subject had previously been exposed to the word "swan" in a prior study list.

This type of retrieval is often termed unconscious, automatic, or indirect, and its most striking feature is that subjects whose episodic or explicit memory is markedly deficient, such as patients with anterograde amnesia, show normal implicit memory in that their priming scores are comparable to those of control subjects. Figure 11.5 shows a schematic representation of the two memory systems.

Implicit memory tasks can be divided into those that are perceptual in nature, and those that are conceptual in nature. In both, subjects are exposed

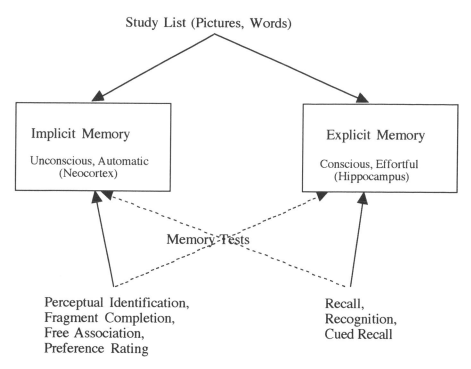

Figure 11.5   The implicit vs. explicit memory systems.

to a study list of intact words or pictures. In perceptual implicit tasks, subjects are given a test that is perceptual in nature, such as completing the word fragment A____A____IN (the correct completion is ASSASSIN) or filling in missing fragments of a picture and naming it. The first type of task is called word fragment completion and the second is called picture fragment completion. Another type of task is perceptual identification in which a word or picture is shown very briefly and then masked, and the subject is asked to identify it.

Figure 11.6 shows examples of stimuli shown during the study phase and during the test phase of word and picture fragment completion experiments. During study, subjects are either told to study the items for a subsequent task, or are given an orienting task such as rating their pleasantness or complexity. At test, subjects are shown fragmented words or pictures which are taken from the study list such as fragments of the words ASSASSIN and TOBOGGAN

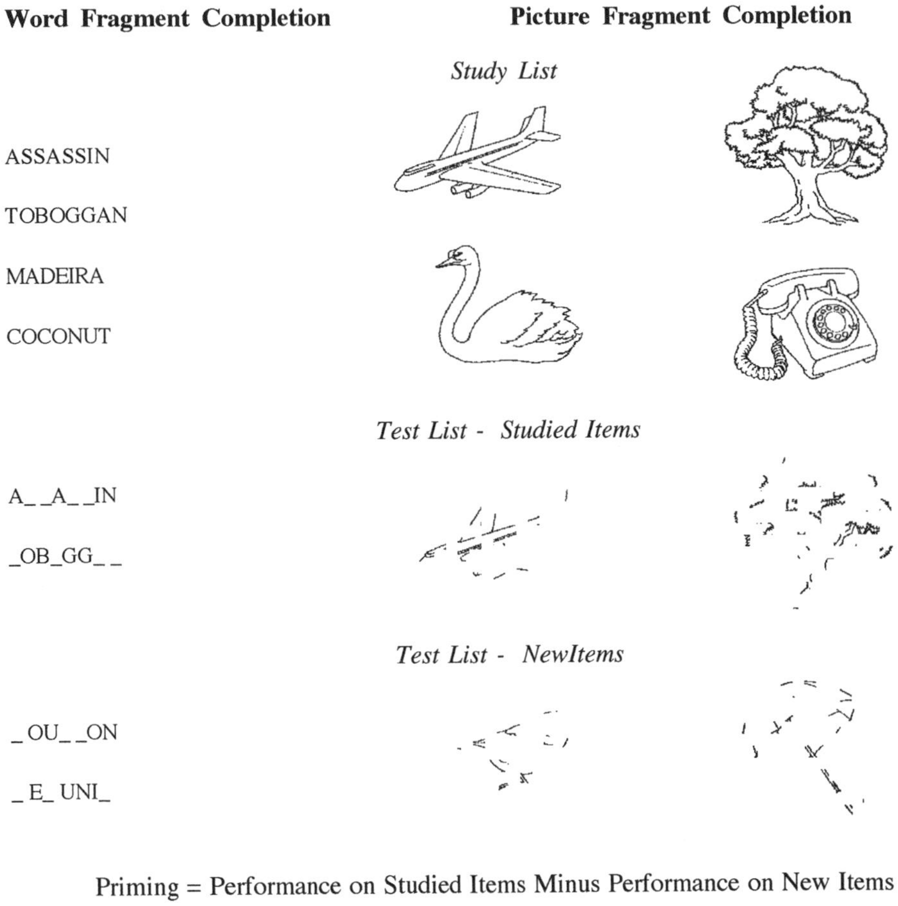

Word Fragment Completion   **Picture Fragment Completion**

Study List

ASSASSIN

TOBOGGAN

MADEIRA

COCONUT

Test List - Studied Items

A_ _A_ _IN

_OB_GG_ _

Test List - NewItems

_ OU_ _ON

_ E_ UNI_

Priming = Performance on Studied Items Minus Performance on New Items

Figure 11.6   Illustration of two implicit tasks: word fragment completion and picture fragment completion.

and fragmented pictures of an airplane and a tree. In addition they are shown fragmented words or pictures which had not been shown on the study list such as fragments of the words BOURBON and PETUNIA and fragmented pictures of a bird and an umbrella. Subjects are usually better able to identify the studied items than the new items, and the measure of this effect, called priming, is the difference in performance between studied and new items. Specifically, we compute the proportion of old items correctly identified and subtract from that the proportion of new items correctly identified to measure the amount of priming.

As far as the subject is concerned, this is not a memory test at all, rather it is a test of perceptual acuity or closure abilities. In fact, under our previous dichotomy between episodic and semantic memory systems, we would call all of these semantic memory tasks because the subject is asked to call upon his or her knowledge of language and of the appearance of objects to do the task. If the subject did not have the word "assassin" in his or her vocabulary, it would be far harder to fill in the fragment above. However, it becomes an implicit memory task because the effect of prior exposure to the word or picture is evaluated by whether perceptual performance on words or pictures that have been studied is better than on those that have not been studied.

The initial interest in implicit memory tasks was the finding that learning or priming in such tasks seemed to be independent of explicit or episodic memory performance. In particular, amnesic patients who showed disastrous episodic memory performance on such tasks as recall and recognition, and elderly subjects who showed performance below that of young normals on episodic tasks, both showed normal implicit learning when measured by priming scores.[11] This seemed to implicate a different system of memory, and indeed it is now generally accepted that priming occurs in the neocortical system rather than in the hippocampal system, so that people with damage to the hippocampus can nonetheless show normal priming in implicit memory tasks.

WHY TWO SYSTEMS FOR EPISODIC MEMORY?

You can probably empathize with the people of the last century who wondered why nature designed the brain in such a puzzling way. Why should episodic memories (memories of events which are tagged with the time and place of occurrence) be stored in each of two places? The major proponent of the hippocampal hypothesis, as it came to be called, was the neuroscientist Larry Squire, whose groundbreaking work with both animals and amnesic patients established the hippocampal thesis.[12]

Squire suggested that both retrograde and anterograde amnesia in human amnesic patients could be understood by assuming that episodic memories were first stored in the hippocampus and then after a variable length of time moved to the neocortex. Retrograde amnesia is a graded loss of memories which were acquired prior to the damage; the loss is most severe for memories just prior to the time of damage and lessens for earlier memories. Anterograde amnesia is an inability to learn new episodic information. Damage to the hippocampus would thus obliterate memories which had not yet migrated to the neocortex, causing retrograde amnesia. It would also prevent new episodic memories from being stored, causing anterograde amnesia. Amnesics can, of course, learn anything that is stored in the neocortex such as primed or activated information. A famous anecdote will make this difference clear. The French neurologist Claparède was treating a female patient with Korsakoff's syndrome (an amnesic syndrome caused by alcoholism) over a period of several years. The patient never gave any sign of recognizing the doctor even after meeting with him multiple times. Each time she would meet him and shake his hand as if he were a new acquaintance. One day he secreted a pin in his hand which pricked her when they shook hands. The next day she refused to shake hands with him. When questioned why, she first replied, "But surely I have the right to hold back my hand," and when pressed she added, "Perhaps there is a pin hidden in your hand." When Claparède asked her what made her suspect that he wanted to prick her, she would respond, "It's an idea which came into my head," or she would say, "Sometimes there are pins hidden in hands." However, she never recognized that the association between shaking hands and pain originated from her past experience.[13]

Here, then, is a case in which the patient was able to make a generalized semantic association between shaking hands and being pricked, but was unable to localize that experience to a specific time and place of occurrence. In other words, she apparently was able to store into semantic memory the general fact that there is danger in shaking hands without having stored the specific episode in episodic memory.[14]

In the mid-1990s, a rather ingenious explanation for the hippocampal hypothesis was proposed by James McClelland and his collaborators.[15] McClelland, along with his colleague David Rumelhart, were two of the major proponents of the neural network approach to modeling human cognition (a.k.a. connectionism or parallel distributed processing). In the mid-1980s, Rumelhart and McClelland published a two-volume work on connectionist modeling which became the bible to a new generation of mathematically sophisticated and neurologically educated researchers.[16]

Connectionism was quite successful at modeling what we have been calling semantic memory learning. This included learning how to pronounce words, learning how to categorize objects, and learning how to use the past tense correctly. However, one of the much-vaunted failures of connectionism was its failure to model episodic learning. Connectionist models showed so-called catastrophic interference, in which new learning interfered so with old learning that the model showed virtually no memory of a prior list. Now, of course, people also show interference in that new learning does interfere with old learning, but the magnitude of the interference is much smaller in people than the magnitude of the interference showed by the models.[17] This failure of connectionist models was what caused McClelland and his collaborators to develop an explanation of why the brain had evolved as it had to learn new information. In order to avoid catastrophic interference, connectionist models must incorporate very slow learning parameters. This corresponds to the operation of semantic memory, which slowly accumulates experiences so as to extract the common elements and discard accidental properties. Learning in semantic memory is accomplished by the neocortex. In contrast, the rapid one-trial learning shown by subjects in episodic memory is accomplished by the hippocampus. Here connections are sparse because they do not need to encode the encyclopedic information known by a subject, so hippocampal systems can show the rapid learning characteristic of the episodic system.

This, then, is the explanation of why episodic memories are stored in two places. In order to remember recent events, such as where you left your keys this morning (as opposed to where you habitually leave your keys), and what you had for dinner last night (as opposed to what you normally eat), you need a fast active system that will encode recent events and permit rapid retrieval of this information. However, you also need a system to slowly build up semantic information of the sort Where do I habitually leave my keys or What do I habitually eat for dinner in order to establish that encyclopedic or semantic memory which records repeated events and extracts from them their common elements.

How Many Types of Memory Are There?

So here we were at the end of the 20th century with a rather bewildering array of dichotomous and even trichotomous memory systems. It was at this point—in the late 1990s and early 2010s—that students of memory began to become interested in individual differences in memory abilities and the possibility that some of these abilities could be trained. Of course, the very existence of various types of memories—particularly the distinction between explicit and implicit memory—was based upon differences between groups. And at one time Tulving had suggested that subject-based dissociations could be the basis for evidence of separate systems. That is, if separate systems underlie episodic, semantic, and procedural memory, then people might be relatively good in all episodic tasks and relatively poor in all procedural tasks, or vice versa. Correlations between subjects' performance within a set of tasks subserved by one system should be higher than correlations across tasks between systems.

Until the turn of the century, most research focused on group, rather than individual differences. A great deal of research was directed toward questions such as the nature of memory deficits in amnesia, dementia, and aging. Up until the late 1990s, it was generally held that implicit learning was based upon sensory rather than conceptual properties of the studied stimulus, whereas explicit learning was based upon conceptual rather than sensory properties of the studied stimulus. Implicit learning was said to be "data-driven" whereas explicit learning was said to be "conceptually driven" to use the terms of Larry Jacoby and Henry Roediger.[18] Thus when elderly subjects showed deficits in explicit memory but no deficits in implicit memory, a reasonable inference was that they were not processing the stimulus at the conceptual or "deep" level but were only attending to the surface or "shallow" level aspects of the stimulus—they were attending to appearance but not to meaning. This corresponded well with another prevailing view of memory introduced in the early 1970s called levels of processing.

In 1972, Fergus Craik and his colleague Robert Lockhart proposed a theory of memory which they termed "levels of processing." The levels-of-processing approach sought to replace the old two-store model of Atkinson and Shiffrin with a single memory system in which the strength and durability of a memory trace of a studied item was determined by the type (or level) of processing the subject applied to that item.[19] Although their theory has not fared well, the experimental paradigm they used to test their theory, by directing the subject to different levels of processing, was adopted by many researchers and is still in use today. In this paradigm, the subject during the study phase of a memory experiment is given some orienting task to do which focuses his or her attention on different aspects of the stimulus. For example, the subject may be asked to decide whether a word is in upper- or lowercase letters which only requires attention to the word's graphemic aspects; or the subject may be asked whether the word rhymes with a target word, which only requires attention to its phonemic aspects; or the subject may be asked whether the word fits into a sentence frame, which requires attention to its conceptual or meaning aspects. These tasks illustrate a continuum of processing from shallow to deep, and when memory for items studied with such orienting tasks is evaluated by explicit memory tests such as recall or recognition, subjects show correspondingly better memory as the depth of the processing task increases. However, when memory is evaluated by implicit memory tests, these depth effects are normally absent or at least markedly attenuated, thereby supporting the notion that explicit tasks are primarily based upon conceptual processing (of the deep sort), whereas implicit tasks are primarily based upon perceptual processing (of the shallow sort).

However, this neat and tidy dichotomy was questioned by several developments during the 1990s. First, a number of investigators found that, contrary to common wisdom, explicit memory showed a greater decrement than implicit memory when perceptual changes were introduced to studied stimuli at test. For example, Gay Snodgrass and her collaborators manipulated whether a fragmented picture was shown with the same or different fragments from study to test. Figure 11.7 shows examples of this manipulation.

During the study phase, subjects attempted to identify fragmented pictures and were told whether they were correct or wrong and what the name of the picture was. During test, they were shown either the same or a different fragmented image of the same object (as illustrated in figure 11.7). Now this constitutes a very subtle manipulation of surface characteristics of the studied object. Snodgrass looked at two types of tests—the implicit test of picture fragment completion, in which priming was measured, and the explicit test of picture recognition. According to the data-driven vs. conceptually driven hypothesis, the change in fragments should affect priming in picture fragment completion, which is sensitive to surface characteristics, but not memory, in picture recognition, which is sensitive to conceptual characteristics. Instead, however, just the opposite pattern was obtained. Picture fragment completion

Study Phase

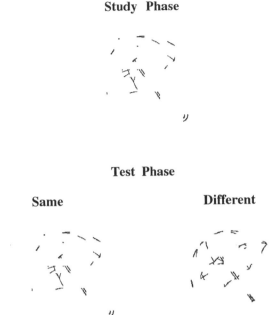

Test Phase

Same   **Different**

Figure 11.7 Example of a fragmented picture at study tested with the same or different fragments at test.

was unaffected by whether the fragments were the same or different, whereas recognition memory showed a decrement for different fragments. That is, subjects were less able to *recognize as old* a fragmented image that was different from that studied, but they were equally able to identify by name this different fragment.[20]

The second development concerns a well-known phenomenon in explicit memory known as the picture superiority effect. The picture superiority effect refers to the fact that pictures are better remembered in both recall and recognition tests than their names. A variety of explanations have been proposed for the picture advantage. Paivio has argued that pictures are better than words for two reasons: first, pictures are more likely to be dually encoded than words, and second the image code is a superior memory code to the verbal code. Douglas Nelson and his colleagues suggested in the late 1970s that pictures benefited from their more elaborate sensory code.[21] Others, however, suggested that pictures benefited from superior access to semantic memory, and thus were superior on conceptual rather than perceptual grounds. In the mid-1990s Mary Sue Weldon and her colleagues showed that the picture superiority effect did not extend to a semantic priming task (i.e., an implicit memory task), thereby supporting the original Nelson and Paivio positions that it is the superior sensory or image code of pictures which accounts for their better memory.[22] The fact that the picture superiority effect in explicit memory is due to sensory rather than conceptual factors again highlights the importance of the sensory code in explicit memory tasks. From an evolutionary point of view, this superior memory for sensory-rich stimuli like pictures and spatial locations appears like a rational design choice for an evolving central nervous system: it was more important for early man to recognize edible fruits and the route back home than to remember words written on a memory drum or computer screen.

Finally, and not surprisingly given the developments described above, recent studies with elderly people and demented patients showed that their memory difficulties stem from their inability to store a coherent image of a scene and to notice sensory details that would serve to anchor the scene to a particular time and place (a necessary step for the operation of explicit memory). In one of our surveys of everyday memory performance, we asked people questions such as "What did you have for dinner last night?" The vast majority reported that they searched a stored memory image for evidence of what they had eaten, and this tendency was much greater in the younger than in the older subjects. In contrast, when people were asked an everyday semantic memory question such as "What is your favorite dinner?," they reported much less imagery, and there was no difference between young and elderly subjects on reported imagery.

Implications for the Development of a Memory Test Battery and Memory Training

Here, then, is where we were at the turn of the century when the memory establishment decided to turn to more practical applications of our knowledge about memory. This development came about for several reasons. First, because of cutbacks in research support, we no longer had grant funds to support either basic research or research training. Second, with the aging of America, we had a population of elderly people who were increasingly eager to learn more about their own memory capabilities and to have access to a resource that would enable them to chart any decline in abilities. And with the development of well-standardized memory test batteries, it was possible to evaluate a variety of memory training techniques by their effect on performance on the test battery.

Of course, components of each aspect of this enterprise already existed. Research in aging was fueled by the belief that more knowledge about differences between young and old memory could help us with remediation. England in particular was well advanced in memory training techniques, and conferences on practical aspects of memory, although they did not take place very often, invariably called for more and better research on how we could "give away psychology" to the public. And parts of existing intelligence test batteries already tested various components of the memory system.

A person reading this chapter from the vantage point of the end of the 20th century might wonder why tests of memory weren't developed using the then popular brain imaging techniques such as PET, MRI, or even ERP. This alphabet soup of techniques to study the activation of different brain regions appeared to offer hope for diagnosis and remediation of memory and other types of difficulties, such as problems in critical thinking, problem solving, and impulse inhibition. However, in hindsight it is easy to see why these techniques proved inadequate for evaluating a person's memory functioning. The reason is that successful memory operates by successful behavior, not successful brain activation patterns. To use your memory to remember where you left your keys, to remember to turn off the stove, or to remember to take your pills, you need to actually find your keys, turn off the stove, and take your pills: Success is defined by behavior, not by activation patterns in the hippocampus. And we know from decades of research on prediction and evaluation that the best predictor of future behavior is past behavior, so the best predictor of future memory performance is past memory performance, as evaluated either by day-to-day activities, or by behavior on a memory battery. This is why both our evaluation and remediation activities are based upon behavioral measures rather than physiological measures.

The Memory Battery

Here, then, are the components of the memory battery. These are an amalgam of all of the theories about the structure of memory which we have reviewed in our history. In addition, however, we have needed to test each memory system with several subtests; for example, to test episodic memory with tests for sensory as well as conceptual properties of studied objects. All of these tests are computerized with sufficiently numerous study materials so that our clients can repeatedly test themselves on each component from the privacy and confidentiality of their home computers. When the client feels confident that he or she understands the requirements of a particular test and wishes to have the test results recorded in the national data bank, the client so indicates.

Short-Term or Working Memory (Generally Considered to Be Basic to All Other Memory Skills) These tests measure the capacity of a subject's short-term or working memory. Recall that this capacity tends to be very small, on of the order of seven plus or minus two items. Subjects are presented with the to-be-remembered items and then asked to recall them immediately, so the immediate recall coupled with the small number of items presented makes it an STM test. Two kinds of STM tests are used: memory span for digits, which measures the capacity of the verbal or articulatory loop, which is generally assumed necessary to encode verbal material into LTM, and memory span for spatial location, which measures the capacity of spatial STM generally assumed necessary to encode pictorially and spatially organized material into LTM.

1. Memory span for digits (measured by the number of digits which can be correctly recalled in the correct serial order)
2. Memory for spatial location (measured as the number of blackened cells within a 6 × 6 matrix which can be correctly reproduced)

Both of these tests are carried out using the staircase procedure of threshold determination common in sensory psychophysics. In the staircase procedure, each time the subject is correct, the number of items to be remembered is increased by one, and each time the subject is incorrect, the number of items to be remembered is decreased by one. The subject's span is defined as the average number of items presented across trials, and thus tracks the moment-to-moment fluctuations in memory span produced by fluctuations in attention or a particularly difficult or easy sequence. Typically 20 trials are run in each of the STM tests.

Episodic Long-Term Memory   These tests measure the ability of subjects to encode episodes of experience into LTM and retrieve them with respect to their time and place of occurrence. Because these tests are concerned with LTM we present a larger number of items than can be held in STM. Because we want to eliminate as far as possible *any* contribution from STM we also use a brief distracter task so as to empty the contents of STM before asking the subject to retrieve the information. In order to encode information into and retrieve information from episodic LTM, the rememberer typically has to encode not only what happened but where it happened, when it happened, with whom it happened, how he or she felt about it, and so on. These correspond to the what, where, when, who, how, and so what of the typical newspaper story. Accordingly, our episodic memory tests are designed to separately measure aspects of each of these features of the episode. In addition, as we noted above, it has become clear that memory for what (or item memory as we like to call it) should be broken into conceptual or meaning information about the item as well as the item's sensory characteristics. In order to evaluate performance on these different aspects of episodic memory, we have developed a battery of seven tests.

1. *Conceptual item memory* is tested by free recall of a list of unrelated abstract words. Each list consists of 16 items, and after each list subjects are given a distracter task in which they count backward by threes from a random three-digit number. This procedure is generally assumed to clear out the contents of STM by eliminating the recency portion of the serial position curve. A total of five lists is presented (of which the first is practice) and the subject's score is total number recalled regardless of order. Because the number of abstract words is quite large, this is a test that is capable of multiple repetitions without exhausting the stock of words.

2. *Sensory item memory* is tested by a faces recognition test, in which subjects are shown lists of random unfamiliar faces and then given a two-alternative forced-choice recognition test to distinguish old or studied faces from new or unstudied faces. The faces are selected randomly from the national database's supply of digitized photographs of citizens of the country. These constitute a virtually limitless supply of testing materials, so clients can be tested repeatedly on this test.

3. *Temporal memory* is tested by presenting unrelated pairs of words auditorily to the subject, one after the other, and then giving the subject a temporal order recognition test. In this test, the same pair of words is presented again, in

either the same or a reversed order, and the subject's task is to classify each pair as to whether it is in the same or different order. Here, two kinds of word pairs are used—pairs of abstract words and pairs of concrete words. This provides us with two scores, one for the more easily remembered concrete words and one for the harder-to-remember abstract words. Again, several lists are presented, and STM is cleared by a backward counting task, this time with auditory presentation and vocal responding.

4. *Spatial memory* is tested in an exactly analogous way to that used for temporal memory. Unrelated pairs of pictures are presented side by side in a visual display. The subject's task is to remember their spatial order. Memory is tested by presenting the same pairs again, but this time half of them are in reversed spatial order and the other half are in the same spatial order, and thee subject's task is to decide which are same and which are reversed.

Of course, both temporal and spatial memory are correlated with item conceptual and item sensory memory because in order to remember a spatial or temporal order correctly, it is necessary to remember the items themselves.

5. *Contextual memory* is the ability of a subject to remember the context within which a particular item occurred. In the intelligence testing literature, this is called associative memory. In this test, subjects are presented with pairs of words (again, both abstract and concrete words) and asked to learn the right-hand word as a response to the left-hand word. After a list of 20 pairs is presented, and STM is cleared, the client is given the left-hand (stimulus) word from the study list and asked to recall its response word. This is also known as paired-associate learning in the experimental literature.

6. *Source memory.* Source memory is memory for the origin of a remembered experience. Here is an example. How did you hear of a particular fact or event? Did you see it on television, hear it from a friend, or read it in a newspaper? Marcia Johnson invented the paradigm of source memory, and used it for the particular situation of distinguishing imagined events from perceived events.[23] However, in this test, we concentrate on remembering who told you what (this is a particular problem for our memory-impaired clients). The study sequence consists of a series of trials in which "talking heads" give fictional facts (e.g., Bob Smith was promoted to general manager of ABC Corporation). The talking heads are photographs of faces from the national register given the capability of simulating speech. Speech patterns are selected to be as distinctive as possible. The memory test for source memory consists of presenting the fact again (e.g., Bob Smith was promoted to general manager of

ABC Corporation) along with a pair of two faces. One face is the source of the information and the other face had been on the list but said something different. In this test, we have attempted to simulate real-life experience in which the two possible sources of a message might very well be familiar people.

7. *Memory for past emotions.* One of the most potent determinants of whether something is remembered is the amount of emotion that accompanies the event. A demented or amnesic patient may often remember an emotion-laden event such as the death of a spouse. It is, of course, difficult to devise a test of remembered emotion as each individual patient has his or her own hierarchy of emotional events. In order to test the ability of clients to associate an event with an emotion (and thereby to either retrieve the event by the retrieval of the emotion or to retrieve the emotion by the retrieval of the event) we designed the following test (one which owes a great deal to the Thematic Apperception Test or TAT). Clients are shown a scene with several elements, any one of which might be noticed and given an appropriate emotion. For example, the scene might show a couple embracing on a beach against a backdrop of a beautiful sunset. Each scene is capable of being associated with each of two disparate emotions. In this case, sadness can be evoked by describing the scene as one in which two lovers must part, and happiness can be evoked by describing the scene as one in which the viewer experiences great joy by looking at the sunset. After a series of such scenes, the client is given the scene again and asked to indicate which emotion he or she is experiencing: happiness, sadness, anger, fear, frustration, or neutral. The ability of clients to retrieve the emotion associated with the scene is evaluated by whether their judgment of emotion corresponds to the particular experience they were assigned during the study phase.

Semantic Long-Term Memory Semantic LTM is encyclopedic knowledge about the world which a person has built up over the course of his or her life. In the intelligence testing literature, this kind of knowledge has often been referred to as "crystallized intelligence" and many of the tests we describe below were adapted from those already in use in intelligence testing.

1. *Vocabulary or lexical knowledge.* This is a test of a person's vocabulary, and is conducted much like the vocabulary subtests of the Wechsler Adult Intelligence Scale (WAIS). The client is given a word along with four or five definitions, and must select the correct definition. The technological advance that computers make possible is a procedure similar to the staircase method

of memory span testing described earlier. Specifically, the vocabulary test has been graded by difficulty, and once subjects have exceeded a criterion number of correct responses at one difficulty level they are moved to the next highest level; conversely, once subjects have exceeded a criterion number of error responses at one difficulty level they are moved to the next lowest level. Their level of vocabulary knowledge can thereby be more accurately gauged because more definitions at that level can be tested. This is one of the few tests which is not amenable to multiple tests by clients. There are only about 10 forms for this test, and because clients are thought to be able to look up and memorize definitions, we cannot let our clients practice on this test.

2. *Object knowledge or knowledge of names.* In this task, subjects are shown pictures of common objects and asked to name them as quickly as possible. Because picture-naming difficulty has been shown to be highly related to age of acquisition of the object's name, this test too has been ordered from easiest to most difficult in terms of the picture's age of acquisition. Prior research has shown us that one of the best predictors of subsequent development of Alzheimer's and the best test for staging severity of Alzheimer's is this test. The client's naming times and naming errors are monitored by the computer, and the test is terminated once the difficulty level of the pictures has clearly exceeded the client's capabilities.

3. *Semantic fluency.* Semantic fluency tests evaluate the speed and efficiency with which information can be retrieved from semantic memory. Clients are given a cue or category and asked to generate as many examples fulfilling the cue or category as they can. For example, they might be asked to list as many animals as they can in 1 minute, or as many words beginning with the letter T as they can in 1 minute. Production is vocal, and the computer times and records the responses, using the voice recognition programs specific to the particular client. Because these tests need to be given repeatedly, we have expanded the number of categories used from the usual semantic ones (e.g., animals, tools, household objects, plants, and so on) to more unusual categories such as things you might pack in your suitcase or things you prefer.

Implicit Long-Term Memory Implicit LTM tests evaluate the efficiency with which information in the semantic system can be activated or primed. Because such effects depend upon an intact semantic system, implicit learning is generally not observed in people without intact semantic memory systems, such as advanced-stage Alzheimer's patients.

1. *Priming in word and picture fragment completion.* Subjects are shown a series of word and picture fragments and try to identify them. After each attempt, they are told what the object is. After lags varying from a single intervening trial to 20 intervening trials, subjects are shown the fragmented word or picture again and asked to identify it again. The degree to which previous exposure to the fragment helps with present identification is a measure of priming. The priming effect is graded, being largest for the shortest lags and smallest for the longest lags, so the test is sensitive to rather large individual differences in implicit memory performance.

2. *Priming in word and picture naming.* The same paradigm is used as before except that intact pictures and words are shown and the subject's task is to name the picture and to pronounce the word. Priming is evidenced by a decrease in naming or pronunciation latencies from the first to the second presentation and again, the priming effect is graded by lag, so large individual differences can be detected.

3. *Implicit learning of a motor sequence.* This test is one of the few which implicates motor learning as a process. Using a paradigm first invented by Art Reber and his student Axel Cleeremans, subjects are asked to try to press the correct key out of four after a series of four lights have gone on.[24] The pattern is very difficult to figure out, and the phenomenon called implicit learning is the one in which subjects can do better than the chance outcome of 25% correct without being able to articulate a rule about what governs the sequence. This kind of implicit learning is probably one of the last memory functions to go, and may underlie intact performance of severely impaired demented patients who nonetheless can still learn to perform some activities on the basis of just such implicit learning.

Justification of the Memory Battery

Initially, the memory tests were developed on the basis of all of the theories about differences in memory systems outlined at the beginning of my talk. So we have short-term vs. long-term memory; visual vs. verbal memory; explicit vs. implicit memory; and even procedural memory as evaluated by the implicit learning test.

However, as you well know, the typical way in which standardized tests are evaluated as measuring separate abilities is by factor-analyzing the battery of tests and determining whether two tests load on the same factors. We have also followed this procedure in developing and testing the present battery. We have found that, consistent with our fourfold classification scheme, tests within each system are more highly correlated than tests across systems. And STM tests correlate highly with each of the episodic tests.

In addition, we have found that, consistent with clinical reports and prior results of testing, the time course of dementia follows the expected decline. The first set of tests to show deterioration are the episodic long-term tests, followed by the implicit tests (with the exception of implicit learning), followed by the semantic tests, and finally both the STM and implicit learning tests show deterioration (at that point, in fact, the patient is usually so disoriented and impaired as to be unable to sit for any tests at all).

You might at this point be curious about how these tests are used to fulfill the suicide pact which many clients with beginning stages of dementia wish to establish. These clients have been monitoring their own memory performance over the years, and know that the first signs of dementia will show up in the episodic tests. They make their own decision about how impaired they are willing to become before wishing to terminate their lives. Many patients feel that without episodic memory—without the ability to register information about events in day-to-day life in memory—they would rather be dead, and so they set that as their criterion for carrying out the suicide pact with their physician. When all of their episodic memory test scores become indistinguishable from chance scores, the pact is initiated. This option is taken by approximately 20% of the clients who opt for the suicide pact.

Almost all of the remaining clients are happy to remain alive as long as their semantic and implicit memory systems are intact. This would let them carry on conversations, find their way around a sheltered environment, and recognize the faces and voices of loved ones, so for them, these are sufficient cognitive resources to continue to make life worth living. However, as soon as they show deterioration on semantic memory tests such as picture naming, vocabulary, and semantic fluency, they wish to have the pact initiated. Exactly how much deterioration is to be tolerated is personally set by each client prior to signing the pact, and we err on the conservative side in deciding when that criterion has been met.

What Can Be Trained?

Finally, what can we say about memory training? As we noted earlier, STM capacity can only be trained by recoding so as to make larger chunks. There does not seem to be any way to increase the number of chunks which can be held in STM. Thus, in our memory training classes, we do not emphasize STM training. Rather, we concentrate on techniques for encoding information more efficiently into long-term episodic memory. When we question clients about what their concerns and fears are about their memory, they most often list the following six problems, shown below in their order of importance:

1. I can't remember the names of new people I meet.
2. I can't remember the names of people I already know.
3. I can't remember who told me what.
4. I can't remember whether I told someone this.
5. I can't remember whether I took my pills.
6. I can't remember when something happened.

Let's go through techniques for dealing with these memory problems one by one. As we will see, virtually all of these problems are problems in episodic memory, and the techniques which we train are often well-known mnemonic devices which have been known about for centuries.

1. *I can't remember the names of new people I meet.* People's names are notoriously difficult to remember. The major reason for this is that people's names are arbitrary. Two people named Carol are no more similar to one another than a person named Carol and a person named Jessica. So you cannot use your knowledge of the person as good or bad, extroverted or introverted, beautiful or ugly, old or young, as an indication of what his or her name is. Because people are social, and care about what other people think of them, this inability to remember people's names looms particularly large in people's concern about their memory. We have found that remembering people's names is trainable. We recommend the following techniques to our memory training classes:

First, when you are meeting someone new, concentrate on their first names, as you will often not be required to remember their last names. Try to make an association between their first name and somebody you already know with that name. To take an obvious example, if your sister's name is Carol, and you meet someone whose first name is Carol, make the association "She has the same name as my sister." Elaborate this as much as you can. For example, imagine similarities and differences between the two people so that when you see the new Carol, you will immediately make the association "Carol" and be able to greet her by name. This technique has become so popular that many people give a new acquaintance their own particular mnemonic for remembering their name. One of our memory trainers introduces herself to her clients as "Mabel on the table," and I introduce myself as "Joy to the World." We encourage our clients to develop their own mnemonics for their own names to help others remember them.

2. *I can't remember the names of people I already know.*   Problem 2 can also be helped by your solution to problem 1. First, if you think about people you already know in associating to the name of someone you have just met, you will have already rehearsed the name of a person you know. Second, try to rehearse the association between their name and their face. If you are attending a meeting or a party where you know there will be people whose names you sometimes forget, imagine them sitting around the table and form a visual memory image of their face and retrieve their name in your imagination every time you see their face. This helps you to perform fast and effortless retrieval when you greet them or want to address them in some way.

3. *I can't remember who told me what.*   Problem 3 is a problem in what we call source amnesia. You remember a fact or episode but you forget the source of that fact or episode. This can be very embarrassing. You may find yourself recounting a funny story to the same person who told you that story. The phenomenon of source amnesia is particularly acute when you get information over a telephone, because the only sensory quality you have to associate to the fact is the person's voice. Even more difficult is when you obtain the information over e-mail, because now there is no cue as to the source of the information except the person's name at the end of the message and perhaps the person's own peculiar writing style.

How can we solve this problem? Again, creative imagery can come to the rescue. When you are speaking to someone on the telephone, try to visualize that person speaking to you. Cover the person with clothes, put him or her in a chair, in a room, with background scenery. This will make a phone conversation more like an actual conversation, and will produce less source confusion. The same technique can be applied to e-mail messages. Try to visualize the person as he or she is writing the message so that you can remember what its source is.

4. *I can't remember whether I told someone this.*   Problem 4 is the reverse problem of source amnesia—it's target amnesia. You can't remember whether

you have told someone something. And, as we all know, nothing is more annoying than being told something 20 times. Again, this problem surfaces much more when people communicate via the intermediary of voice or e-mail. Dealing with this problem is similar to that of problem 3, in that you need to imagine the person as you are communicating the information to him or her, so as to avoid doing it more than once.

5. *I can't remember whether I took my pills.*   Problem 5 can be solved by a simple physical memory aid. You can acquire a 7-day pill case in which you or your helpmate fills each day's supply with the appropriate pills. Then, given that you can remember what day of the week it is, you can remember whether you took your pills or not by whether that day's supply is empty. An alternative solution would be to mark a calendar each time you take your pills.

6. *I can't remember when something happened.*   Temporally dating events is probably the most difficult thing we do. Particularly as we get older, the more recent memories often get confused with the older memories. When we speak of temporal dating, we don't mean assigning a particular date of the year to an event, but rather knowing that event 1 occurred after event 2, and knowing roughly how long ago event 1 occurred.

How can we train people to relate an autobiographical event to a particular time in their life? We train our students with the following technique. We ask them to establish a "time line" for their life, in which a salient event is associated with each month of the year. This is a fairly easy task for active people who work or are involved in many activities, but it is more difficult for the older retired person. We give them suggestions for selecting an event. This could include a birthday of a beloved one, a public event which catches their interest, or some event in their life which is of significance. These events are recorded in a diary of monthly events. Then when some event occurs, the person is encouraged to try to relate its time of occurrence to the closest monthly event. Did it occur prior to or after October's salient event, for example.

Notice that we train people on those problems which they find most relevant to their day-to-day lives, not problems which are tested by our memory battery. Nonetheless, after such training, we often find that our clients score higher on the test battery, particularly those tests concerned with episodic memory. So we feel that the history of memory research which produced the memory battery, and its use in evaluating people's memory abilities, their ability to profit by training, and their ability to use the outcome to make informed life-

and-death decisions, reflects well on these past pioneers of memory research. Thank you, and please don't forget my name.

Notes

1. Atkinson, R. C., & Shiffrin, R. M. (1968). Human memory: A proposed system and its control processes. In K. W. Spence & J. T. Spence (Eds.), *The psychology of learning and motivation* (vol. 2, pp. 89–122). New York: Academic Press.

2. Miller, G. A. (1956). The magical number seven, plus or minus two: Some limits on our capacity for processing information. *Psychological Review, 63,* 81–97.

3. Paivio's work is summarized in two books, Paivio, A. (1971). *Imagery and verbal processes.* New York: Holt, and Paivio, A. (1986). *Mental representations: A dual coding approach.* New York: Oxford University Press.

4. See Quillian, M. R. (1968). Semantic memory. In M. Minsky (Ed.), *Semantic information processing.* Cambridge, MA: MIT Press; Collins, A. M., & Quillian, M. R. (1969). Retrieval time from semantic memory. *Journal of Verbal Learning and Verbal Behavior, 8,* 240–247; and Collins, A. M., & Loftus, E. F. (1975). A spreading-activation theory of semantic processing. *Psychological Review, 82,* 407–428.

5. Snodgrass, J. G. (1984). Concepts and their surface representations. *Journal of Verbal Learning and Verbal Behavior, 23,* 3–22.

4. Shepard, R. N., & Metzler, J. (1971). Mental rotation of three-dimensional objects. *Science, 171,* 701–703. See also Cooper, L. A., & Shepard, R. N. (1984). Turning something over in the mind. *Scientific American, 251,* 106–114, and Shepard, R. N., & Cooper, L. A. (1982). *Mental images and their transformations.* Cambridge, MA: MIT Press/Bradford Books.

7. Baddeley, A. D. (1983). Working memory. *Philosophical Transactions of the Royal Society of London, 302,* 311–324.

8. Tulving, E. (1972). Episodic ,and semantic memory. In E. Tulving & W. Donaldson (Eds.), *Organization of memory* (pp. 381–403). New York: Academic Press.

9. Tulving, E. (1985). How many memory systems are there? *American Psychologist, 40,* 385–398.

10. See Schacter, D. L. (1987). Implicit memory: History and current status. *Journal of Experimental Psychology: Learning, Memory, and Cognition, 13*, 501–518.

11. See Cohen, N. J., & Squire, L. R. (1980). Preserved learning and retention of pattern-analyzing skill in amnesia: Dissociation of knowing how and knowing that. *Science, 210*, 207–210.; Graf, P., Squire, L. R., & Mandler, G. (1984). The information that amnesic patients do not forget. *Journal of Experimental Psychology: Learning, Memory, and Cognition, 10*, 164–178.; Parkin, A. J. (1982). Residual learning capability in organic amnesia. *Cortex, 18*, 417–440.; Schacter, D. L., & Graf, P. (1986). Preserved learning in amnesic patients: Perspectives from research on direct priming. *Journal of Clinical and Experimental Neuropsychology, 8*, 727–743; Warrington, E. K., & Weiskrantz, L. (1968). New method of testing long-term retention with special reference to amnesic patients. *Nature, 217*, 972–974.

12. See Squire, L. (1992). Memory and the hippocampus: A synthesis from findings with rats, monkeys. and humans. *Psychological Review, 99*, 195–231.

13. Claparède, E. (1911). Recognition et moitié. *Archives de Psychologie Genève, 11*, 79–90.

14. For a superb introduction to amnesia, see Parkin, A. J. (1987). *Memory and amnesia.* New York: Blackwell.

15. See McClelland, J. L., McNaughton, B. L., & O'Reilly, R. C. (1995). Why there are complementary learning systems in the hippocampus and neocortex: Insights from the successes and failures of connectionist models of learning and memory. *Psychological Review, 102*, 419–457.

16. Rumelhart, D. E., McClelland, J. L., & the PDP Research Group (Eds.). (1986). *Parallel distributed processing: Explorations in the microstructure of cognition* (2 vols.). Cambridge, MA: MIT Press.

17. See McCloskey, M., & Cohen, N. J. (1989). Catastrophic interference in connectionist networks: The sequential learning problem. *Psychology of Learning and Motivation, 24*, 109–165, and Ratcliff, R. (1990). Connectionist models of recognition memory: Constraints imposed by learning and forgetting functions. *Psychological Review, 97*, 285–308, for examples of failures of connectionist models; and Sloman, S., & Rumelhart, D. E. (1992). Reducing interference in distributed memory through episodic gating. In A. F. Healy, S. M. Kosslyn, & R. M. Shiffrin (Eds.), *From learning theory to cognitive processes: Essays in honor of William K. Estes.* Hillsdale, NJ: Erlbaum, for an example of how to reduce interference.

18. See Jacoby, L. L. (1983). Remembering the data: Analyzing interactive processes in reading. *Journal of Verbal Learning and Verbal Behavior, 22,* 485–508, and Roediger, H. L., & Blaxton, T. (1987). Effects of varying modality, surface features, and retention interval on priming in word-fragment completion. *Memory & Cognition, 15,* 379–388.

19. See Craik, F. I. M., & Lockhart, R. S. (1972). Levels of processing: A framework for memory research. *Journal of Verbal Learning and Verbal Behavior, 11,* 671–684, for the original statement of the theory; and Craik, F. I. M., & Tulving, E. (1975). Depth of processing and the retention of words in episodic memory. *Journal of Experimental Psychology, 104,* 268–294, for experimental tests of the technique.

20. Snodgrass, J. G., Hirshman, E., & Fan, J. (1995). The sensory match effect in recognition memory: Perceptual fluency or episodic trace? *Memory and cognition,* in press.

21. Nelson, D. L., Reed, V. S., & McEvoy, C. L. (1977). Learning to order pictures and words: A model of sensory and semantic encoding. *Journal of Experimental Psychology: Human Learning and Memory, 3,* 485–497.

22. Weldon, M. S., & Coyote, K. C. (1996). There is no picture superiority effect on implicit conceptual tests. *Journal of Experimental Psychology: Learning, Memory, and Cognition,* in press.

23. See Johnson, M. K., Hashtroudi, S., & Lindsay, S. (1993) Source monitoring. *Psychological Bulletin, 114,* 3–28, and Johnson, M. K., & Raye, C. L. (1981). Reality monitoring. *Psychological Review, 88,* 67–85.

24. See Cleeremans, A., & McClelland, J. L. (1991). Learning the structure of event sequences. *Journal of Experimental Psychology: General, 120,* 235–253.

12   On Future Psychological Categories

Jerome Kagan

Anyone reading the most respected psychological texts written 100 years ago would realize that accurate prediction of the future is impossible because even the most prescient prophets cannot anticipate the new machines, historical conditions, and theoretical conceptions that are presently unformed. Neither Wundt, Titchener, Jung, nor Freud imagined the invention of functional magnetic resonance imaging (MRI), the microelectrodes and amplifiers that permit study of single neurons, or the influence of the cognitive sciences, which gave memory, reasoning, and concept formation a primacy over the affective phenomena that dominated inquiry at the end of the last century. Thus, a student in 2096 will probably satirize the three predictions that appear reasonable to me at the present time. The first two ideas are argued briefly because they seem obvious; the last prophecy is elaborated because it seems less apparent.

Technical Discoveries

The most secure prediction is that the invention of new procedures that rely on technical advances will permit psychologists to study the brief, private, cognitive, and emotional events that, at present, must be inferred from coarse-grained overt behaviors, test performances, and self-reports. Most psychological inquiry is restricted to the quantification of events that are easily made public, as 18th-century botanists measured the color, shape, and size of leaves, because the hidden mechanisms that are at the foundation of the public events continue to remain impenetrable. Psychologists study emotions by coding facial expressions; they study memory through direct recall of information; they study anxiety by asking adults to describe their fears. These data will remain relevant, but the brief physiological and cognitive events that accompany the

molar phenomena, but denied access to consciousness, will yield their important secrets as new technical procedures are invented.

No one can know the form of these future inventions. Even I. I. Rabi,
whose discovery of the nuclear spin of sodium became the foundation for
MRI, was surprised by what he had discovered:

> The experiment was beautiful ... these atoms in spatially quan-
> tized states, analyze them in one field, turn your focus back and
> there it is. Count them! It was wonderful. ... I really believed in
> the spin, there are the states, count them! Each one, I suppose,
> seeks God in his own way. (cited in Rigden, 1987, p. 88)

One consequence of the novel information will be the replacement of
currently broad concepts with narrower ones that specify setting conditions
and form of response. The term "implicit memory," for example, implies very
particular procedures and test behaviors (Schacter, 1987). This prediction
supports Whitehead in his debate with Russell over whether one can excise
predicates-from the propositions in which they occur and generalize about
them, independent of their noun and object partners (Whitehead, 1928).
Future psychologists will not write sentences of the form, "Learning ... ",
without specifying the species, mode of acquisition, and response being
acquired.

The End of Infant Determinism

The second prediction, more relevant to the study of personality development,
is that the extraordinary influence that has been awarded to early experience
will be modulated by robust demonstrations of the influence of a child's temperament as well as the continued malleability of brain structures to experience. If the synapses of rats can be altered by enriching their cages with objects
(Greenough, 1987), it must be an error to claim that most of the products of
the first year of life are stable indefinitely. Many developmental psychologists
have been reluctant to acknowledge such capacities for change after the first
or second year because of a wish, almost religious in its zeal, to simplify the
extraordinarily complex phenomena of human personality development.
When adults are uncertain about an aspect of life that has great personal relevance, they become susceptible to a quick fix. Many European intellectuals in

the years between the two world wars, troubled by economic recession and social unrest, believed that Marxism was the cure for the world's woes—a decision regarded even by political liberals as naively innocent of social history and of human weaknesses.

The claim that an insecure (or secure) attachment in a 1-year-old infant sets the child's course for the next decade is seized upon with equal enthusiasm because the unpredictable variation in adolescent profiles, some of which is maladaptive, also generates considerable uncertainty (Ainsworth et al., 1978; Goosens & van IJzendoorn, 1990). Hence, parents are eager to learn that there is a process that can reduce the complexity to one broad, easily understood mechanism that is controllable in the infant nursery.

The return of temperamental ideas, which remained attractive from Hippocrates to the end of the 19th century, will also modify the power awarded to early experience and motivate developmental scientists to document the interaction of temperament and experience, as evolutionary biologists study how the interaction between the inherited characteristics of a species and its environmental niche affect reproductive success. The outcome variables for developmental psychologists are profiles that simultaneously minimize the agent's distress while maximizing civility in the individual and order in the society in which the agent functions.

Further, temperamental constructs represent a person's chronic state of preparedness for the evocation of a particular emotion, in contradistinction to the many brief, acute states that can be created in any person in a few moments. Because the neural circuits that mediate an acute state of fear to a conditioned stimulus are different from those that mediate a continued susceptibility to becoming fearful, scientists will be motivated to probe both classes of neural events and to give them different names.

Classification

The third prediction, which occupies the rest of this paper, is that advances in neuroscience and the longitudinal study of childhood temperaments will be accompanied by classifications of psychological phenomena that differ from those that are currently popular. The initial stage in all inquiry is a parsing of the phenomena of interest into theoretically useful categories. Obviously, the categories chosen affect not only the probability of discovering a valid functional relation but, in addition, the specific functional relation uncovered. The

Greek categories of air, water, fire, and earth were too gross to be fruitful. The developmental categories oral, anal, phallic, and genital have also been abandoned, although the categories paranoid and obsessive-compulsive, which were popular at the same time, remain useful. The categories used by brain scientists are sufficiently different from those of psychologists, even when both groups believe they are studying the same phenomenon. It is inevitable that each group of scholars will invent different theories for what is now regarded as the same event.

THE BASES FOR CLASSIFICATION

The assignment of events into categories is based on shared characteristics, either discrete features or continuous dimensions. Although the biochemists usually press primarily for continuously graded metrics, like concentration and rate, it remains a stubborn fact that structures, like neurons or the cerebellum, cannot be summarized in quantitative terms. "Form and structure are not natural subjects for biochemistry that deals with scalar quantities ... Building staggeringly complex organs by simply specifying the constituent protein components is unlikely. Such a strategy would be tantamount to trying to specify a bridge ... by merely giving a list of parts" (Penman, 1995, p. 5257).

Psychologists typically rely on five different bases for judging similarities in nature.

CONTEMPORARY FEATURES

The most frequent basis for classification in psychology is the presence of shared features, most often behaviors, test scores, and self-reports, but, increasingly, physiological profiles. In rare instances, Down syndrome, for example, similarity in a chromosomal feature is a critical basis for a category.

Piaget's classification of children into any one of his four major stages of intellectual development is based on a set of proscribed behaviors given to particular problems set by an examiner. Six-year-olds who gave the correct answer to the conservation and addition and multiplication of class problems would be categorized as concrete operational, regardless of their past history, genetic pedigree, emotional profile, or level of school achievement.

There has been a strong tendency to use performance on one procedure as the foundation for a broad category. Perhaps the most egregious error, often made in clinical settings, is to categorize a child as having "impaired memory functioning" because of a low score on the digit recall scale of the Wechsler Intelligence Scale. The correlations between declarative (recall) memory for numbers, recognition memory for scenes, and implicit memory for words is low. Hence, it is a mistake for clinicians to treat performance on the digit recall test as the basis for categorizing a child's memorial talents.

The "Big Five" personality types also rely only on similarity in contemporary features, in this case answers to self-report questionnaires (McRae & Costa, 1987). It is likely, however, that each of the five categories contains persons with very different histories, and, therefore, very different future behaviors.

A small number of scientists use similarity in contemporary biological qualities. Porges (1992), for example, categorizes infants and children on the basis of their vagal tone; Fox et al. (1994) and Davidson (1994) classify children and adults on the basis of differential desynchronization of alpha frequencies in the right or the left frontal areas; Gunnar (1994) classifies children on the basis of their cortisol profiles.

As with behavior, similarity in physiological features can result from different antecedent conditions. A high vagal tone measured in the laboratory, for example, can be the product of restlessness, a very relaxed mood, or an extreme degree of attentiveness to the stimulus events in the testing room. Greater electroencephalographic (EEG) activation of the right frontal area can be due to very low activation on the left side and normal activation on the right or normal activation on the left and high activation on the right, as Fox and Davidson have noted. These two mechanisms lead to similar asymmetry scores, but are associated with different psychological profiles. At present, classifications of children or adults based only on physiological variables, without the addition of any psychological characteristics, have generally not proved as useful as those that are based on a combination of both psychological and physiological qualities (Weiner, 1992).

In sum, although classification based only on contemporary features remains the most frequent strategy, the individuals that are placed in a particular group are usually heterogeneous with respect to other significant qualities. Hence, those additional qualities should be added to contemporary features. One of the most useful sources of supplementary information comes from the individual's past.

Past Qualities

The use of similarity in past characteristics, usually experiential but occasionally biological, has proved fruitful, especially when combined with contemporary features. Three-year-old children classified as shy because of quiet, withdrawn behavior with unfamiliar peers have at least two different histories. One group was easily aroused to motor activity and crying during infancy and is shy because of a temperamental predisposition to become uncertain with strangers. The other group acquired their shyness as a product of experience. The two groups differ in the frequency and intensity of fearful behavior to unfamiliar objects in nonsocial contexts, with the former, temperamental, group more fearful than the latter (Kagan, 1994).

Other examples include the use of prematurity to predict cognitive development; early (or late) appearance of pubertal changes to predict aspects of adult personality; and impaired control of impulsive behavior in the preschool child to predict delinquency during adolescence (Caspi & Silva, 1995). Although most examples rely on an early quality that places a child at risk for a later difficulty, only a minority of those in the risk category develop the expected profile. Hence, it is usually fruitful to combine past with contemporary features. For example, combining the categorization of a 4-month-old infant as minimally aroused by stimulation with the 4-year-old's contemporary sociability with unfamiliar adults permits unusually accurate prediction of a sociable, extroverted style when interacting with unfamiliar children of the same age and sex (Kagan, 1995).

The use of past biological features is not common in psychology, although Magnusson (1988) combined level of urinary epinephrine with behavior in school-age children to predict later occurrence of delinquency. However, most studies that used childhood measures of heart rate, blood pressure, or cortisol alone, without any behavioral features, failed to find strong relations to later psychological profiles. Peripheral physiological variables are subject to so many different influences, including local physiological conditions that render each target somewhat autonomous from central control, that failures are not surprising.

Immediate Consequences

The appeal of pragmatism made American psychologists friendly to the use of similarity in immediate behavioral and emotional consequences as a basis for categorization. The classification of emotions provides an example. Fear, sadness, and anger are classified as negative emotions, despite dramatic differences in their incentives and physiologies, simply because all three have undesirable consequences for a person's quality of work and social encounters. By contrast, Ekman (1980) and Izard (1977) classify human emotions on the basis of similarity in facial features, not behavioral consequences.

The category of events named reinforcements represents the clearest example of reliance on consequences as a distinguishing feature. The gaining of food, sex, warmth, escape from pain, or the sudden appearance of a colorful object can strengthen the response that preceded—or predicted—the event. Even though the features of the above events and their physiological correlates are different, all are categorized as reinforcements because of their similar immediate consequences.

Psychiatrists using the DSM (*Diagnostic and Statistical Manual of Mental Disorders*) rules to decide if a person should be classified as having *anxiety disorder* add a judgment of impairment in everyday function to the patient's reports of his or her symptoms. A patient with occasional insomnia and a concern with earthquakes who claimed that his work and family interactions did not suffer from these apprehensions would not be categorized as having an anxiety disorder.

However, similarity in immediate consequences, when used alone, has not proved useful in the more mature sciences and will become less important in psychology's future. Fatigue can follow a host of different diseases that should be treated in different ways. Perhaps that is why utilitarianism had a short life in Western moral philosophy. If, as a consequence of my jumping into an icy river to save a child, both the child and I drowned, few observers would claim that my action should be categorized as irrational or amoral.

LONG-TERM CONSEQUENCES

The criterion of long-term consequences is chosen less frequently by psychologists, although it is more popular among biologists. The concept of at-risk ecologies, whether based on PCBs in the water, lead particles in the air, or thinning of the ozone layer, share an undesirable outcome in the distant future.

The concept of insecure attachment, which combines avoidant and resistant behaviors in 1-year-olds observed in Ainsworth's Strange Situation, is an example from development (Ainsworth et al., 1978). Avoidant and resistant 1-year-olds share neither similar past histories nor contemporary behaviors in the assessment situation, yet both are placed in the category "insecurely attached" because of a hypothesis that they are at risk for anxiety and impaired social functioning in the distant future.

Werner (1993) proposed a category of "high-risk infants" that combined prematurity, perinatal trauma, poverty, low parental education, low birth weight, and an unpredictable family life because of the belief that these very different conditions had similar future consequences. Apparently, an aggregate index of these features does predict school failure and conduct disorder with greater accuracy than any single member of the aggregate.

Formal Similarities

Similar mathematical descriptions for a set of phenomena is the usual way this criterion is met. The fact that the same mathematics will explain the concave surface of water in a pail whether the pail or the universe is rotating defines the physicist's concept of equivalence.

Scholars devising neural networks rely on formal criteria. If a particular program intended to simulate a psychological or physiological event predicted the empirical data, the investigator would be tempted to regard the empirical event and the simulation as belonging to the same category. The increased interest in computational neuroscience guarantees that this criterion will become more prevalent.

Combining Criteria

A lesson to be taken from the history of disciplines more mature than psychology is that progress often occurs when several bases for categorization are used. The biological concept of species utilizes similarity in contemporary features and evolutionary history. The classification of neurotransmitters relies on similarity in chemical structure as well as immediate consequences in the central nervous system. The concept of the visual area in the brain is based on both similarity in neuronal structure and immediate consequences following stimulation or lesion.

Future progress in psychology will follow the increased use of multiple criteria. For example, the classification of emotions should be based, at a minimum, on behavioral and physiological features, as well as the incentive that provoked the changes in both systems. Cognitive scientists are adding the nature of the incentive (the specific information the subject is manipulating) to the nature of the response (whether a perceptual judgment, a retrieved memory, or an inference) in classifying cognitive functions. The time when textbooks will discuss memory in the abstract is over (Tulving, 1995).

Some Examples An empirical example of the utility of combining features is found in data from a large longitudinal sample of middle-class white children Nancy Snidman, Doreen Arcus, and I have been studying since they were 4 months old. We recently observed groups of $4\frac{1}{2}$-year-old children as they interacted with trios of children of the same age and sex (N = 123). The three children, who were unfamiliar to one another, first played together for 25 minutes in a large room with their mothers present. The mothers then left for 5 minutes, and after they returned, a single attractive toy was brought into the room for 3 minutes and then removed. Finally, an adult dressed in a gorilla costume entered and invited the children to approach.

This protocol permitted a classification of each child as shy/timid, sociable/bold, or belonging to neither of these extremes. The 22% of the group who were classified as shy/timid appeared very similar in their behavior with the other two children. However, the earlier longitudinal data available on these children permitted us to parse this shy/timid group into two very different subgroups.

When these children were 14 months old, they encountered, in a laboratory setting, a series of unfamiliar objects, people, and situations. Some children were fearful (they showed clear behavioral signs of fear to three or more episodes); some were less fearful (fear to fewer than three episodes). In addition, each child had been classified at 4 months as high- or low-reactive to stimulation, based on the amount of vigorous motor activity and crying to auditory, visual, and olfactory stimulation. High-reactive infants—about 20% of the sample—showed vigorous motor behavior and frequent distress. Low-reactives—about 40% of the sample—showed minimal motor activity and no distress.

These early data, collected at 4 and 14 months, permitted a division of the twenty-seven $4\frac{1}{2}$-year-olds who had been classified as shy/timid with same-sex peers into a small group (22% of the shy/timid children) who had been low-reactive at 4 months and minimally fearful at 14 months. Shyness

Table 12.1
Relation of behavior with peers at $4\frac{1}{2}$ years of age to four different early classification

	Peer Play Category		
Early History	Sociable/Bold (n = 59)	Shy/Timid (n = 27)	Neither (n = 37)
4 mo.–14 mo.			
High-reactive–high fear	6 (10%)	17 (64%)	12 (32%)
High-reactive–low fear	3 (6%)	2 (7%)	5 (14%)
Low-reactive–high fear	9 (15%)	2 (7%)	6 (16%)
Low-reactive–low fear	41 (69%)	6 (22%)	14 (38%)

with peers is an unexpected outcome for children with this early temperament. The second, larger group (69% of the shy/timid children) had been high-reactive and very fearful earlier (table 12.1). These children are psychologically different from the small group of shy/timid children who had been low-reactive and minimally fearful earlier in life. Similarly, the large group of sociable/bold children who had been low-reactive and minimally fearful (69%)—the expected outcome—were different from the 10% who had been high-reactive and fearful and should be assigned to a different classification.

A second example of the usefulness of past history is found in an analysis of the frequency of spontaneous comments and smiles while these same 4-year-old children interacted with an unfamiliar female examiner. Thirty percent of the children talked and smiled frequently with the female examiner (values greater than the median of 40 comments and 20 smiles); 28% were quiet and emotionally subdued (fewer than 40 comments and 20 smiles). As expected, 67% of the highly talkative and smiling children had been low-reactive at 4 months and minimally fearful at 14 months. Although only 11% of the affectively exuberant children had been high-reactive and fearful, their earlier behavior implies that they should be placed in a different category. One distinctive quality of the high-reactive infants who became affectively exuberant was an extreme garrulousness—they talked continually and asked the examiner many questions. This quality was not present among the talkative children who had been low-reactive and minimally fearful.

Extremes   Discussion of this sample of children is relevant to the relatively certain prediction that psychologists in the future will become critical of the contemporary premise that most qualities are continua. As a result, they will more often assume nonlinear rather than linear relations between variables. One result of this new attitude will be the study of individuals who have extreme scores.

One of the $4\frac{1}{2}$-year-old children in our longitudinal sample displayed 95 smiles—the highest score—during the 1-hour interaction with the female examiner. This girl was very different from the two girls with the next largest smile scores and, of course, different from the majority of the sample. This high-smiling girl displayed far less motor arousal, but many more smiles, during the battery administered at 4 months of age.

Many other examples of nonlinear relations between variables that form continuous distributions could be cited. It is a common finding in most natural domains that different profiles of mechanisms produce very different magnitudes on the measurements of interest. That is why hurricanes are regarded as qualitatively discrete events. As the next cohort of psychologists who study human personality appreciate this fact, they will begin to consider the possibility that individuals with extreme values may represent a special category. That decision g will affect not only the statistical treatment of data but, more important, the conceptualization of behavior.

Weighting Features

The absence of consensus regarding the weights to assign to varied features—present or past—remains an obstacle to theoretical progress. Biologists enjoy the advantages of greater agreement on the assignment of weights; for example, evolutionary biologists weight the features that have implications for reproduction. Indeed, Linnaeus's major insight was to rely on characteristics involved in mating when he classified animal forms. The anatomist, believing that function follows structure, gives weight to location as well as structural similarity of cells in charting the brain. Because alleviation of a patient's symptoms is a desired goal, physicians award greater weight to similar therapeutic outcomes than to presumed site of action or sometimes even chemical structure.

Behavioral scientists, by contrast, enjoy less consensus on the assignment of weights. Some developmental psychologists emphasize the cognitive capacities of the child; others focus on emotional experience; still others award significance to the child's future adaptation. The first group awards emphasis to language, memory, and reasoning; the second to anxiety, fear, and anger, while the third weights familial social class and biological risk early in life. A premature child born to indifferent parents who, at age 3, has retarded language skills and is quiet, shy, and withdrawn could be classified as (1) developmentally delayed, (2) insecurely attached, or (3) at risk for later social problems.

Scientists who study fear in animals do not always agree on the significant defining characteristics. Neuroscientists award weight to the brain circuits that mediate conditioned freezing or autonomic reactivity, while psychologists are more likely to emphasize the incentive conditions. Thus, LeDoux (1989) and Davis (1992) award significance to the neural elements that make up the fear circuit, especially the thalamus, amygdala, hypothalamus, striatum, and central gray substance. Fanselow (1994) and Treit et al. (1993a,b) emphasize the specific incentive conditions (whether a conditioned stimulus paired with shock, an intruder, or an open, brightly lighted arm of an elevated maze), and the specific behavioral response (freezing, defensive aggression, burying, or avoidance of a probe that delivered shock).

Social scientists interested in human behavior are divided between those who award significance to the individual's goals and feeling states and those who regard the harmony of the larger social context as more significant. The former group note that most individuals in Western society have motives for wealth, power, recognition, friendships, sensory pleasure, actualization of talents, and a feeling of virtue. Hence, similarity in the hierarchy of these goal states, within a person, should be a theoretically useful basis for categorizing individuals.

Scholars concerned with the social context in which agents act (e.g., political scientists or sociologists) more often rely on criteria that lead, or do not lead, to a more civil, harmonious society. That choice yields a different set of classifications. The categories "delinquent" and "psychopath" reflect the community's worry over its safety, rather than a A concern with the psychological state of the adolescent or adult criminal. By contrast, the category "anxiety disorder" takes the emotional state of the patient as its focal concern. Thus, psychologists and psychiatrists confound two different criteria in their current classification schemes. All anxious patients are unhappy with their conscious state. Many delinquents, however, are not unhappy with their conscious state; they just do not want to be incarcerated.

There is nothing wrong with using different classification schemes, but it can be theoretically awkward to use different criteria in a single scheme. Such a strategy is similar to classifying cows as mammals, commodities, and a source of protein in the same conceptual system.

Many scientists might reply to this argument by claiming that the logical coherence and predictive power of the network of concepts are the only criteria to apply in classification. For example, the frequency, rather than the intensity, of light striking a surface is the salient feature of the photoelectric effect. Similarly, the mass of an object, not its shape or substance, is the critical feature that allows prediction of its acceleration when a force is applied. These insights had to be learned through experimentation and could not be decided, a priori, by philosophical analysis.

But biological systems, unlike photons and stones, are malleable to changing environmental circumstances. Thus, psychologists will become more self-conscious about the choice they have with respect to the ethical status and amenability to intervention of varied outcomes. Consider, as an example, the controversy created by *The Bell Curve* (Herrnstein & Murray, 1994). Hunt (1995) has noted that the associations between social class, IQ, and parental education are low among individuals with high IQ scores. It is primarily persons with IQs less than 85 who have a substantial probability of encountering problems in our society. Thus, scholars interested in this area of inquiry have a choice of weighting the economic status of the family, the education of the parents, or the IQ of the child in predicting the latter's future profile. Each choice has different theoretical implications and it is not obvious that one solution is better than another. Unlike the concept of equivalence in physics, it does make a difference if the psychologist assumes that low family income, poor parental education, or a child's intellectual ability is the critical feature in predicting the child's future. Indeed, it is precisely because the future state of the person (or the society) is of such concern that the choice of features will become an explicit rather than an implicit issue for psychologists.

Finally, the division between neuroscientists and psychologists in choice of features will grow larger because the former wish to explain contemporary brain states while the latter remain preoccupied with future behavioral and emotional states of the individual. Hence, the two groups will necessarily focus on different aspects of nature. Psychologists who study fearful monkeys emphasize contemporary behavior or pedigree, or both (Suomi, 1991). Scientists who study susceptibility to conditioned fear in rats focus on neuronal and receptor reactivities in specific brain circuits. But developmental psychologists studying fear award special weight to behavioral qualities like avoidance of unfamiliar events and self-reports of fear.

These substantial differences in the features chosen to define an abstract state will become more apparent in the future. Hence, a concept like fear eventually will have such different meanings that new words will be invented to distinguish the different sources of evidence that serve as the foundation for each concept. This prediction has a salutary aspect, however. Currently, neuroscientists have borrowed, temporarily, the words that psychologists have used for a long time to refer to human emotional and cognitive states—fear, remember, perceive, and comprehend are some examples. As we discover that these psychological events are emergent from, but not isomorphic with, the underlying physiology, the error contained in a simple form of biological reductionism will become evident and a cooperative attitude between the two groups will replace the occasional competitive one.

Summary

This chapter has tried to make the following points. First, the invention of new methods will produce major changes in theory. One of the most significant will be an ability to measure acute and chronic emotional states with sensitivity. That advantage will challenge the currently popular view that some early experiences create permanent changes in the affective life of the person.

Second, the return of temperamental concepts will motivate psychologists to look for interactions between temperament and experience, rather than test only for the main effect of an environment. Finally, psychologists will recognize the utility of adding biological features as well as past history to contemporary behaviors in creating the next set of theoretically useful categories. Although there is a natural tendency for psychologists to focus on the future in classifying behavioral events, that preference requires choosing among different outcomes. The neural state of the brain, the emotional state of the person, and the harmony of the community are three different criteria; favoring one over another leads to a distinct set of weights and, ultimately, to different theories. The recognition that each set of criteria is legitimate and none is more fundamental than another will be one of the happy victories of the next century.

Acknowledgment

Preparation of this paper was supported in part by grants from the John D. and Catherine T. MacArthur Foundation and the W. T. Grant Foundation.

References

Ainsworth, M. D. S., Blehar, M. C., Waters, E., & Wall, S. (1978). *Patterns of attachment*. Hillsdale, NJ: Erlbaum.

Caspi, A., & Silva, P. A. (1995). Temperamental qualities at age three predict personality traits in young adulthood. *Child Development, 66*, 486–498.

Davidson, R. J. (1994). Asymmetric brain function, affective style, and psychopathology. *Development and Psychopathology, 6*, 741–758.

Davis M. (1992). The role of the amygdala in conditioned fear. In J. P. Aggleton (Ed.), *The amygdala* (pp. 255–306). New York: Wiley.

Ekman, P., 1980. Biological and cultural contributions to body and facial movement in the expression of emotions. In A. O. Rorty (Ed.), *Explaining emotions* (pp. 73–102). Berkeley: University of California Press.

Fanselow, M. S. (1994). Neural organization of the defensive behavior system responsible for fear. *Psychonomic Bulletin and Review, 1*, 429–438.

Fox, N. A., Calkins, S. D., & Bell, M. A. (1994). Neural plasticity and development in the first two years of life. *Development and Psychopathology, 6*, 677–696.

Goosens, F. A., & van IJzendoorn, M. H. (1990). Quality of infants' attachment to professional caregivers. *Child Development, 64*, 832–837.

Greenough, W. T. (1987). Experience effects on the developing and the mature brain. In N. A. Krasnegor, E. M. Blass, M. A. Hofer, & W. P. Smotherman (Eds.), *Perinatal development* (pp. 195–223). New York: Academic Press.

Gunnar, M. R. (1994). Psychoendocrine studies of temperament and stress in early childhood. In J. Bates & T. Wachs (Eds.), *Temperament. Individual differences at the interface of biology and behavior.* Washington, DC: American Psychiatric Association Press.

Herrnstein, R., & Murray, C. (1994). *The bell curve.* Chicago: Free Press.

Hunt, E. (1995). The role of intelligence in modern society. *American Scientist, 83,* 356–368.

Izard, C. E. (1977). *Human emotions.* New York: Plenum Press.

Kagan, J. (1994). *Galen's prophecy.* New York: Basic Books.

Kagan, J. (1995). Reactions to difference. Presented at the meeting of the American Psychological Association. August 1995.

LeDoux J. E. (1989). Cognitive-emotion interactions in the brain. *Cognition and Emotion, 3,* 267–289.

Magnusson, D. (1989). *Individual development from an interactional perspective: A longitudinal study.* Hillsdale, NJ: Erlbaum.

McRae, R. R., & Costa, P. C. (1987). Validation of the five factor model of personality across instruments and observers. *Journal of Personality and Social Psychology, 52,* 81–90.

Penman, S. (1995). Rethinking cell structure. *Proceedings of the National Academy of Sciences of the United States of America, 92,* 5251–5257.

Porges, S. W. (1992). Vagal tone. *Pediatrics, 90,* 498–504.

Rigden, J. S. (1987). *Rabi.* New York: Basic Books.

Schacter, D. L. (1987). Implicit memory. *Journal of Experimental Psychology: Learning Memory and Cognition, 3,* 501–518.

Suomi, S. (1991). Early stress and adult emotional reactivity in rhesus monkeys. In *Childhood environment and adult disease* (pp. 171–188). CIBA Symposium 156. Chichester: Wiley.

Treit, D., Pesold, C., & Rotzinger, S. (1993a). Dissociating the anti-fear effects of septal and amygdaloid lesions using two pharmacologically validated models of rat anxiety. *Behavioral Neuroscience, 107*, 770–785.

Treit, D., Pesold, C., & Rotzinger, S. (1993b). Noninteractive effects of diazepam and amygdaloid lesions in two animal models of anxiety. *Behavioral Neuroscience, 107*, 1099–1105.

Tulving, E. (1995). Organization of memory: Quo vadis? In M. S. Gazzaniga (Ed.), *The cognitive neurosciences* (pp. 839–850). Cambridge, MA: MIT Press.

Weiner, H. (1992). *Perturbing the organism.* Chicago: University of Chicago Press.

Werner, E. E. (1993). Risk, resilience, and recovery. *Development and Psychopathology, 5*, 503–515.

Whitehead, A. N. (1928). *Science and the modern world.* New York: Macmillan.

13 The Goal of Theory in Experimental Psychology

GEORGE SPERLING

Aesthetics and Utility in Science

When we evaluate a scientific theory in terms of its utility for a particular task, there is little problem in deciding whether a theory is good or bad. The question becomes simply: Is the theory useful or not? For example, when electromagnetic theory is used to design a generator for producing electricity, or a psychological testing theory is used to design a better test for predicting an individual's success in a particular training program, the theories are evaluated according to how well they meet their goals. There also are secondary practical goals for theories, such as serving as mnemonic aids to facilitate the recall of experimental facts. We do not consider these separately.

Much of science is not directly practical. It serves, rather, to satisfy our curiosity about ourselves and our universe. For example, while it is fascinating to have learned that the present universe originated in a big bang 17 or so billion years ago, such knowledge does not have any immediate practical applications. This is an example of the purely aesthetic pursuit of science. Of course, some of such knowledge may ultimately prove useful, so we can regard the aesthetic pursuit of science as being merely one extreme on the continuum that runs from immediate to infinitely deferred utility.

For brevity, I will designate as aesthetic the pursuit of problems where there is no immediate practical application by which to evaluate a theory. While it is difficult to estimate precisely what fraction of research in experimental psychology has been aesthetically motivated, I suspect that it is large—

This article is an elaboration of Sperling, G. (1978). The goal of theory in experimental psychology. *Bell Laboratories Technical Memorandum TM-78-1221-12*, July 26, 1978. Murray Hill, NJ: AT&T Bell Labs.

larger than most psychologists would care to admit. Therefore it is reasonable to explicitly consider aesthetic goals for theories, and also, incidentally, for theoretical enterprises in general, for example, choice of problems, style of presentation, and so on. What precisely is the goal of theory in the realms of deferred utility and pure aesthetics? I propose that the goal of theory is to provide the best description of a phenomenon (or class of phenomena) at a particular desired level of complexity. Experiments and careful observation provide the critical phenomena to be described.

Lest the reader's hopes be prematurely raised, be warned hereby that the terms "phenomenon," "theory," and "complexity" will not be defined here—they are assumed to have their ordinary meanings. The aim is not to make fine distinctions but to call attention to very general characteristics of psychological research that might be interesting and perhaps useful to readers regardless of the particular, idiosyncratic meanings these words may have for them. Nor is the problem of criteria to evaluate the "goodness" of theories treated here. The purpose of this chapter is not to rank existing theories but to expose implicit assumptions and to suggest profitable new directions for theorizing by psychologists.

Theories in Classical Physics

We begin by observing that psychology and biology are fundamentally different from a discipline such as classical physics which all too often has been inappropriately used as a model for science as a whole. In classical physics, complex properties are predicted from elementary principles because the principles are relatively exhaustive for a particular situation. Classical thermodynamics is a noted example. The various relations between the mass, temperature, pressure, volume, and specific heat of a gas are derivable as consequences from relatively simple assumptions about the masses and movements of the molecules of which the gas is composed. On the basis of these principles, precise prediction about the behavior of gases is possible. These marvelous predictions are restricted, however, to gases. Prediction about the change of state from gas to liquid requires radically new principles.

Gravity is perhaps the most famous example of classical physics. Newton's law states that the force F of gravimetric attraction between two objects is proportional to the product of their masses ($m_1 m_2$) and inversely proportional to the square of the distance d between them: $F = m_1 m_2 / d^2$. It is simple and incredibly accurate. When there are several objects in motion and they interact via gravity, the motions can be very complex. By working out the consequences of Newton's equation in great depth, one can predict to the nearest second eclipses that will occur hundreds of years in the future. Complex properties derived from simple principles occur throughout classical physics: the simple relations between electricity and magnetism ultimately govern the design of complex electrical circuits; the simple principles of optics govern the design of exceedingly sophisticated multicomponent lenses; and there are many other examples. In these cases, physicists start with a few assumptions and soon are involved in incredibly complex consequences. Insofar as physicists persevere and are able to calculate the consequences, they find that their predictions are quite accurate because no important new principles come into play. The original assumptions were relatively exhaustive. In these cases, classical physics has achieved theoretical simplicity at the cost of computational complexity.

The Discovery vs. the Invention of Theories

Physicists say they are discovering fundamental laws of nature—as though there were laws, like Easter eggs, lying in hiding, just waiting to be discovered. Scientists invent elegant computations that accurately describe nature. The laws exist only in the physicists' minds and writings, not in nature. To illustrate the problem, consider the question: Is light best described as particles or waves? Then consider the analogous question about a newly discovered mini-animal called a "mouse." We wish to describe the mouse in terms of previously known animals no smaller than dogs or rabbits. We observe that a mouse has some rabbitlike behavior. It is very fearful, it is momentarily motionless when threatened, and it lives in holes in the ground. On the other hand, when it comes to food, the mouse has doglike preferences. So for some behaviors, the rabbit model of the mouse works best; for others, the dog model. But the mouse is not a mixture of rabbit and dog—it is a mouse! The rabbitlike and doglike descriptions are invented to aid the human conceptualization of a new entity. And the same is true of the phenomena of particle physics. These phenomena are given names, and described by analogy to more familiar concepts, with equations developed in other contexts. But a phenomenon such as light is neither a wave nor a particle, it is *light*. The descriptions or laws that have been invented to describe it have been invented by, and for the convenience of, the human mind.

What to Measure?

Another aspect of theory—one that is overlooked in physics but is critical in psychology—is that the theory must tell us what measurements to make and how. For example, in classical thermodynamics, measurements are of volume, temperature, and pressure. In gravitation, we measure mass and position (as a function of time). In psychology, the measurement problem often is so critical and difficult that a measurement "solution" is considered to be an essential ingredient of the theory. For example, in a theory that proposes that success in school is some joint function of ability and motivation, the crux is the measurement of ability and motivation rather then the precise specification of the functional relation between them.

Theories in Psychology

Like physics, psychology, too, has powerful principles: for example, reinforcement. If a behavior produces a favorable outcome, the behavior is more likely than before to occur again. But as a student of cognitive psychology, I have observed over and over again that close examination of any particular phenomenon in cognitive psychology reveals that a simple principle accounts for only part of the, explanation. The attempt to improve the precision does not require better computation—it requires additional principles for every special case, and every case is special. As we gain more knowledge, the new knowledge does not yield an aesthetically pleasing theory. On the contrary, new knowledge usually causes psychologists to reject simpler, aesthetically more pleasing theories in favor of more complex, aesthetically less pleasing theories. For example, in aptitude testing it used to be thought that one factor, IQ (intelligence quotient) or g (general ability factor), was the main predictor of academic performance. Now we recognize that there are many independent and partially independent specific abilities that determine components of particular performances, not to mention other important, multidimensional factors such as ambition and prior training. In practical applications, the trend clearly is—as it should be—toward more complex, specialized tests rather than toward simpler, general tests. In fact, in studying almost any behavior, at first glance only a few variables seem to be important; later we discover that practically everything matters a little.

SUPERFICIAL DIFFERENCES BETWEEN PHYSICAL AND PSYCHOLOGICAL THEORIES

Despite the apparent difference in the structure of physical and of psychological theories, it has often been suggested that there is no essential difference between them. It is simply that physicists and engineers surround themselves only with those systems they understand; therefore, their theories appear to be more potent. If physicists had to deal with naturally occurring problems, such as smashing a particular martini cocktail on the kitchen floor and predicting precisely the shapes of the broken glass and of the puddles, and the location of the olive, physicists would be as unspecific as psychologists—claiming an understanding of the general mechanisms involved but unable to generate precise predictions for the individual case.

THE IMPORTANCE OF EVOLUTION AND LEARNING FOR PSYCHOLOGICAL THEORIES

While there undoubtedly is a kernel of truth to these "choice-of-problem" and "individual-case" hypotheses, I believe there is a profound difference between classical physics and the biological sciences that lies even deeper. I suggest that there is a twofold reason for the complexity of psychology and biology. Darwinian evolution has provided organisms with complex, interacting, innate mechanisms; and learning makes the current state of a complex organism (such as a human) an incredibly complex function of its history.

Consider first evolution: Organisms evolved to deal successfully with their environment. As a new environmental problem arose, a new biological adaptation evolved. But, while the first adaptation was solving part of the problem, it probably uncovered new, second-order unsolved problems. Thus adaptation follows upon adaptation. The result, ultimately, is a piling up of corrections, modifications, and adaptations upon each other. Moreover, an optimal solution balances many considerations related to survival of the individual and of the species. For example, there is only a limited amount of genetic code that can be devoted to solutions for any particular environmental problem, only a limited amount of space and energy within the organism for mechanisms subserving a single function, and only a limited amount of time to be allocated for but one purpose. The solution to one environmental problem cannot operate in isolation. We, and the other survivors of this evolutionary process, are the beneficiaries of an incredibly large number of interdependent, interacting mechanisms. And interacting mechanisms are inherently more difficult to analyze than the independent processes that classical physics concerns itself with.

Second, even if we were to understand all the mechanisms that evolved to facilitate the performance of some particular psychological function, through learning these mechanisms will have been modified and new ones acquired. Because of learning, any psychological theory with a pretense of precision must have a method for either (1) dealing with the entire history of the organism (so that its present state can be computed) or (2) precisely measuring its present state, where measurements of the present psychological state are quite a few orders of magnitude more complex than measurements of physical state, such as temperature or position.

THE COMPLEXITY OF A "SIMPLE" PSYCHOLOGICAL TASK

To illustrate what this complexity means for cognitive psychology, consider perhaps the simplest psychological experiment: the measurement of visual reaction time. The subject is told "Press the button as soon as you see the light. Get ready." The measured reaction time, from light flash (stimulus) to button press (response), depends on numerous factors, among which are:

• The intensity, size, shape, color, temporal wave form, and retinal location of the stimulus (to list just a few stimulus variables)

• The sequence of previously presented stimuli and knowledge of the set of alternative stimuli

• The particular foreperiod (from warning "get ready" to light onset)

• The distribution of prior foreperiods

• Previous reaction times

• Attention and expectancies

• Overall alertness, physiological state

- The explicit and implicit systems of payoffs and penalties for quick reactions and for false reactions

- Previous practice

- Phase of the stimulus relative to the brain's electrical alpha rhythm

- Individual differences (in age, body type, past training, motivation, interpretation of instructions, values of rewards, etc.)

A choice reaction time, in which the subject makes a different response depending on which of two or more stimuli occur, is enormously more complicated, as are tasks that involve the use of linguistic stimuli, such as words or sentences. Even in simplest reaction time experiments, many of the relevant factors interact, that is, the effect of one factor depends on the values of the others, so factors cannot be studied in isolation.

THE INDIRECT USE OF PRECISE THEORIES

In the past century, an enormous amount has been learned about many of the factors that control reaction times (and many other behavior tasks). There has been a gradual acceptance of the inherent complexity of even simple behavioral tasks, and the development of experimental paradigms and conceptual tools to deal with these complexities. It is fortunate that there is no urgent demand for a really precise theory of simple reaction times; we are satisfied to know the distribution of reaction times over a large number of trials, and we do not require prediction of the individual trial. Indeed, at this time, most of the interest in refinement of experimental theories is aesthetic. The thrust of research that attempts precision has been mainly to establish evidence for some particular proposed theory (relative to others) rather than to describe the observations themselves very precisely. To build a modern airplane or an electronic computer, numerous precise physical theories are required. We do not need the same precision to merely "further understanding," though precise prediction is taken by some as evidence that we do indeed "understand." For example, suppose it were to be demonstrated that the entire variation of reaction time with light intensity could be attributed entirely to the transducer properties of the retina. It would greatly further understanding but would not, in and of itself, improve the accuracy of a reaction-time theory one bit. That would require a theory of the retina.

Theories Are Inherently Incomplete or Imprecise

Not surprisingly, the quest for precision in psychological theories has thus far been futile. Every psychological theory that purports to deal with significant behavior is either wrong when examined in critical detail, or the theory is so imprecise that it makes no sense to examine it in detail.

For example, consider again the reinforcement theory. It seems so simple it could hardly be wrong, but the lack of precision is damaging. Reinforcement theory assumes we know what particular response has been reinforced. And that implicitly assumes there is only one internal, reinforceable motor program that can generate the response we observe. To choose an extreme counterexample, suppose the animal (or person) is testing a hypothesis and the hypothesis functions as a reinforceable response (e.g., "If I push button A once and button B twice I will get the reward"). If the theorist guesses wrongly about precisely which particular hypothesis is operable at the moment, his theory cannot predict individual responses, though it may be quite accurate in a statistical sense when averaged over many subjects and trials. A similar argument holds with respect to the discriminative stimulus that is provided. Perhaps the organism was paying attention to something else on that particular trial. These examples illustrate the problem if one does not have complete knowledge of the organism's internal state.

If the theorist's concern is just with the average behavior of a large number of animals or of one animal over a large number of trials, ignorance about precisely what aspect of the stimulus was conditioned to precisely which particular response may be unimportant—these fine details disappear in the averages. However, as soon as we examine behavior microscopically in individual cases, these fluctuations in conditioning will be revealed as significant departures from a theory that assumes a particular stimulus and a particular response to be conditioned and does not treat individual and trial-to-trial variations.

The Futility of Statistical Tests

Because theories are inherently incomplete or imprecise, there is no ready solution for the evaluation of theories—not even that favorite of psychologists, comparing predictions of a theory with data from an experiment by means of a statistical test. The aim of statistical tests is to determine whether or not the predictions of the theory and the observed experimental data agree as well as would be expected if the theory were true. Unfortunately, as statisticians perpetually remind us, the "acceptance of a fit" does not mean the theory is either good or true—it only means the data are even "worse" than the theory. Better or more accurate data would always have rejected the theory because mechanisms (sources of variance) extraneous to the current theory would have been discriminated and revealed as significant departures. Statistics is most useful when it is used not to make absolute judgments of quality but to describe quantitatively the magnitude of the failure of a theory or to facilitate comparison of two theories that have different numbers of parameters.

Faced with the fact that every theory is only partially specified and only partially correct, we need other criteria to evaluate the goodness of a theory. Even when the number of parameters in two competitive theories is the same, accuracy of prediction as measured by a statistical test is only one of many criteria that might be used; other criteria are the generality of the theory, its consistency with other theories, and so forth.

A Criterion for Evaluating Theories

A general approach to the problem of "which theory" is to consider the best theory at each level of complexity. The sense of "best" and of "complexity" are matters of judgment, and will change in time as the scientific vocabulary and context change. We may improve the precision of any theory by making it more complex, but that does not necessarily make it preferable.

Consider the following example of theoretical difficulties that arise in answering the question, What is the function of the retina? This question also makes clear the essential confusion between yesterday's theory and today's fact (i.e., well-established theory). Hundreds of years ago, the avant-garde theorist might have proposed what today we regard as a fact, that the retina transduces light to provide neural input to the brain for further processing.

At a more complex level of theory, we may propose that the retina reduces the dynamic range of visual signals, that it emphasizes information near the fovea relative to the periphery, and that it reduces dimensionality of color information. Still further specification of retinal function might involve writing equations for different spatial-frequency channels of retinal output, and specifying interactions and connectivity within the retina.

Unfortunately for theory, but fortunately for vision, the retina is an exceedingly complex organ. It contains dozens of different kinds and sizes of neurons; their relative distribution varies from place to place; and they have evolved to satisfy many different purposes. The complete description of the retina is an enumeration of the properties of these neurons and their connections. Eventually we expect to have this ultimate description of the retina, that is, to be able to specify the properties of every class of neurons and to list their connections to all other neurons. Insofar as such a specification (presumably recorded in a computer larger and faster than today's models) would enable us to calculate the output of the retina for every conceivable input, it answers the question of What does the retina do? (It is an example of perfect reductionism—deriving the properties of the retina from more elementary knowledge.) But the level of complexity is too high. Studying the computer program is hardly better than studying the retina directly. This complete answer may not help us to discover elegant, useful, and partially correct answers at much simpler levels—the sort of answers readers of this chapter might desire.

The Necessity of Theory

In the United States, during the second quarter of the 20th century, in revulsion against the overblown theories of the turn-of the century mentalists, several movements arose that abjured formal theory. Most notable was *behaviorism* which originated with John B. Watson and persisted though B. F. Skinner. In parallel, there was a movement toward an eclectic style of research that has been dubbed "dustbowl empiricism." In both approaches, there was an implicit notion that one could simply enumerate and catalog the useful stimulus-response relationships that characterize human and animal behavior with requiring any formal theory.

The difficulty of a reliance on enumeration of stimulus-response relationships is illustrated by a simple, low-resolution computer screen. For example, a primitive screen consisting of 256 pixels, each with eight levels of intensity resolution, can produce 8^{256} different displays. This is a much larger number than the number of elementary particles in the universe. Without theories to reduce the input space, there would not be enough matter in the universe to record the stimulus-response relationships for even this static computer display. And this is an incredibly reduced situation compared to the dynamic real world in which experimental psychology operates. On the other hand, relatively simple theories of sensory processing can predict quite well which of these displays could be discriminated from a blank screen, from one another, and so on, although psychology is still a long way from a comprehensive theory of visual processing. The take-home message is that theories are necessary for progress. A second principle is that natural processes of Darwinian selection permit some theories to survive longer than others; the next section considers the bases of longevity among theories.

Looking Ahead

It is interesting to contrast the views of their discipline of physicists and psychologists. Classical physicists were able to simultaneously achieve theoretical simplicity, precision, and generality—at the price of derivational complexity. Some physicists still believe that new physical theories will encompass an increasingly greater range of phenomena and be even more precise than their predecessors. Possibly, the new theories may even have simple axioms, succeeding in maintaining simple axioms at the cost of ever more complex derivations and computations.

Today, in psychology, the most general theories also are simple, but they are of limited practical utility because either the theories are incomplete or imprecise or the quantities in the theory cannot be measured precisely. Increases in precision are wrought at a double cost: loss of generality and loss of simplicity. This I believe reflects the essential nature of psychology, and it represents an essential difference between psychology and classical physics.

What is a theoretical psychologist to do—theorize in greater detail about less and less until he achieves perfect mastery of almost nothing at all? A psychologist working on a practical problem works until he achieves cost-effective precision and the generality required to solve that problem. Better solutions are possible but not worth the effort. A psychologist seeking basic understanding also confronts the certainty that there is no final answer to any interesting question; there always will be new, unforeseen complications. But if a theorist can discover the best answer to a problem, at a given level of complexity, then this is a permanent contribution that cannot be improved.

My view is that science is like the Great Wall of China, and that a lasting scientific contribution is like the placement of one stone in that wall. The best theory at a given level of complexity is such a stone because, at that level of complexity, it cannot be improved. Of course it would be better if a scientist who proposed such a theory also provided us with a proof, or at least a compelling argument, that the proposed theory was indeed "best." But these arguments usually require a higher level of information, information that is not available when the theory is proposed. And notions of utility, of aesthetic desirability, and of complexity change. Methods that seemed complex yesterday are routine today.

Insofar as there is a central, unchanging core of meaning to the concepts of complexity and accuracy, a good, partially correct theory conceived today can look forward to immortality. This is the most favorable outlook of any scientific endeavor. Scientists, particularly psychologists, who seek the aesthetic experience of "understanding" should strive not only for more precise theories but also for simpler and more general ones at a given level of precision, and seek the best possible theory at a given level of complexity.

Acknowledgment

Supported by the Air Force Office of Scientific Research, Life Sciences Directorate, Visual Information Processing Program.

14 How to Prepare for Our Future of Totally Unexpected Opportunities

Neal E. Miller

My crystal ball is cloudy about the future, but looking at the past, it shows me things I couldn't possibly have anticipated when I entered psychology as a graduate student in 1931. At that time, the psychology department at Stanford University had hand-cranked calculators. You entered the larger of the numbers you wanted to multiply in the keyboard and then turned the crank at the top the correct number of times for the right-hand digit of the multiplier. Then you moved the top register over one space and turned the crank the correct number of times for the next unit of the multiplier. In the early 1940s, the first computer, the ENIAC, was 3 ft deep, 10 ft high, and a 100 ft long. Now I have a desktop one approximately 100 times more powerful.

While I was a student, physiological psychologists like Lashley were studying the behavioral effects of cutting out large parts of an animal's brain; now they study the factors that affect the flow of calcium or other ions through channels in specific single neurons as a result of specific types of stimulation and how these processes influence the long-term firing of these neurons. In my early days at Yale we made most of our own apparatus. It was a happy day when the police confiscated a pinball machine that we could take apart to get a bonanza of relays and solenoids.

I could not have predicted the many practical results that experimental psychologists produced in such a variety of applied settings when they were yanked out of their ivory towers by World War II. Their successes led to enormous increases in the demand for clinical, industrial, and other applied psychologists and to vastly increased support for basic research. More recently, entirely new areas, such as behavioral medicine and psychoneuroimmunology, have emerged, to mention only ones with which I am most familiar. One result of these changes is that in the 60 years since I entered graduate school the American Psychological Association (APA) has grown from a membership of 1267 with cozy meetings that could easily be held on a college campus to a membership of 72,202, with meetings that require hotels in the cities with the largest convention centers. Another result is that an increasingly important function of the APA is to facilitate communication among its diverging specialties, each of which has valuable contributions to make to the others and to our common goal of understanding human behavior.

Since I could not have predicted these foregoing and many other astonishing changes, how can I predict the future with any confidence, except to say that huge and unexpected changes almost certainly will occur. But perhaps by looking at the past, I can say something about how we can prepare current students of psychology to successfully take advantage of the unexpected opportunities that will occur.

In dealing with unexpected opportunities in new situations, the secret weapon of psychology has been training in the understanding of the scientific method and its application to complex behavioral problems. Let me give some of the examples with which I am most familiar. The first years of World War II had established the great value of the Air Force, a new and woefully neglected element of the conservative armed forces. Thus, when the United States entered the war there was a great need for the rapid expansion of the Army Air Force, making it necessary to rapidly train unprecedentedly large numbers of pilots. Many young men were eager to volunteer for this glamorous service, and since many of these failed the rigorous, expensive, and accelerated pilot training, there was an urgent need to select those most likely to succeed. Traditionally, such selection was entirely in the hands of flight surgeons. Most of these in the expanding Air Force were young psychiatrists pulled out of their clinics into this novel situation. There they simply applied the same interviewing techniques they had been trained to use with their patients without any serious attempt to use scientific methods to evaluate and improve their procedures.

The psychologists pulled out of their universities were given permission to try to develop a classification battery of tests to select for pilot and other forms of training. There they used scientific test-development techniques including item analysis and the correlation of different tests with one another and with the criterion of pass/fail in primary flying training. They developed and refined a battery of objective tests that was empirically validated.

The scores on this battery, called stanines, were made available to the psychiatrists. But most of them ridiculed or ignored these test scores. They picked out a few individuals, extreme cases like someone who had wet his bed until the age of 9 but got high scores on our tests of perceptual and motor skills, in contrast to someone who was president of his senior class in high school, captain of the football team, and engaged to the girl selected as the beauty queen but got a low score with us.

Confronted with this problem, the psychologists applied a simple, scientific research method. They checked up on the success of more than a thousand cases in which the psychiatrist/flight surgeons had neglected unacceptably low scores on our battery of tests and sent the low-scoring candidates to flight training. The result was the occurrence of the high percentage of failures that our test had predicted; the unvalidated clinical judgment of the psychiatrist/flight surgeons had not added a thing. Presented with this fact, headquarters issued a statement that, while the flight surgeons could disqualify some applicants who scored high on our tests, they could not qualify any who scored below the criterion we set.

As a result of massive amounts of data conclusively proving the savings introduced by using the pilot selection tests, psychologists were given opportunities to work on problems in other areas of the Air Force. There, by applying their scientific training to situations in which science had not previously been applied, psychologists proved that they could be useful. For example, at the school where gunners for defending bombers were trained, psychologists first showed that, while giving gunners practice at firing at targets towed behind planes flying parallel to the bombers yielded distributions with some scores being high and others being low, those scores were meaningless because those on odd-numbered missions had no correlation with those on even-numbered ones and because the scores at the end of training were no better than those at the beginning. Apparently the practice with delayed knowledge of results, because the targets could not be scored until after the end of the mission, was not teaching the gunners to fire a proper distance ahead of the target.

Analysis with the help of mathematicians showed that the lack of any learning was a good thing. If they had learned, it would have been to aim at the wrong place. Attacking fighter planes with fixed guns that can only fire straight ahead can't hit bombers by flying parallel to them like the towed target that the gunner must aim somewhat ahead of in order to hit the place where the target will be by the time the bullets arrive. In order to keep their guns aimed at the bomber, the fighters must come in on a pursuit curve, in which case the correct thing is to aim slightly behind the fighter, which will curve into the path of the defensive bullets.

An ingenious application of analysis of variance was used to determine which of the many factors involved in a navigator's performance contributed the most to how near he came to his destination. This showed that by far the most important source of error was the accuracy of calibrating the compass before the mission started. This result produced an important change in the emphasis on training in that critical procedure.

These and many other examples of proven, practical contributions by psychologists who applied their training in research to different activities in World War II contributed to the inclusion of psychology as a science to be supported by the National Science Foundation (NSF) and the National Institutes of Health (NIH).

In the more recent development in the field of behavioral medicine, the same value of training in basic behavioral principles and in the application of the scientific method to behavioral problems has been a valuable source of professional advances. In fact, one of the early ways in which psychologists have proved themselves useful to physicians in physical medicine has been in serving as consultants on experimental design and statistical procedures.

But principles cannot be applied in a vacuum. In addition to knowledge of them, be they ones of scientific method or behavioral laws, one must know the conditions to which they are applied. In the gunnery example it was necessary to know that fighter planes with guns fixed to fire straight ahead have to fly in a pursuit curve in order to hit the bomber as a target. In behavioral medicine it has been necessary for psychologists to learn a good deal about the vocabulary, traditions, procedures, needs, opportunities, limitation, and other specific conditions of the medical specialties in which they are working. The same will be true for the future novel applications the nature of which we cannot now imagine. This brings me to my most important point. In order to adapt to the new conditions and exploit effectively the radical advances in psychological knowledge and techniques that are very likely to occur during the future 10, 20, 30, 40, or 50 years of their professional careers, it will be highly desirable for psychologists, particularly the pioneering ones on the cutting edge, to be educated for a lifetime of continued learning.

One key element of preparation for a lifetime of continued learning of unanticipated new things is the basic understanding of the scientific method that I have been discussing here and elsewhere (Miller, 1985, 1992). Of course an understanding of the fundamental principles and basic facts of psychology and other behavioral sciences is a desirable foundation, but these should be selected carefully rather than crowding in unessential details that can be filled in when needed. Another important element is learning to judge the quality of research. This is important for a career in research, but it is also important for the practitioner who wants to be able to judge and take advantage of the best new research and theory and not be misled by faulty interpretations or exaggerated claims for inadequately evaluated techniques. As I have said before (Miller, 1987), students should be repeatedly exposed in widely different complex contexts to common sources of artifacts, such as selection errors, regression to the mean, halo and placebo effects, the effects of motivations and expectations on perception that contribute to scoring errors and thus the need for "blind" procedures. Sometimes they should be assigned articles containing such errors, ideally made by prestigious individuals, to test their ability to spot the error. Reviewing a variety of current articles in the critical atmosphere of a journal club can also be a means of giving such training. But the atmosphere also should be critical of the student's failure to see the germ of a fruitful idea in a flawed study as well as of failure to detect technical flaws; it should not be nihilistic.

In different courses that the students take, case histories of scientific developments should be prepared to illustrate how blind alleys can be entered, discovered, and abandoned; how unexpected or accidental findings can lead to radical new advances; how commonly accepted explanations can sometimes be turned upside down; how in a new and little understood area, unsuspected confounding factors can cause different experiments to produce apparently contradictory results; how controversies are ultimately resolved. It is important for our students and also for future citizens to be taught in introductory courses an *understanding* of the *process* by which basic research leads to new knowledge that sometimes can lead, often unpredictably, to extremely valuable applications. They should also get an understanding of the ingenuity and effort that may be required to develop these applications. Such understanding should be one of the most important goals of the case histories.

The most important factor, however, in training students to learn something completely new by themselves is to require them to do it in one or more areas in which they are completely unfamiliar. They should learn to start with a good summary and then read in the original some of the key articles from which they may find that the summary is inaccurate or inadequate in certain respects. Similarly they should be required to learn a new technique by themselves. Success in such practice can give them the confidence and motivation to learn the new things that they will need to learn in their future careers. They may not learn as many facts in this way as they would if comprehensively force-fed, but what they do learn about teaching themselves will be far more valuable than most facts. In a rapidly changing world one of the most important things that we can give to our students is an education for a lifetime of continued learning.

References

Miller, N. E. (1985). Prologue. In P. G. Zimbardo, *Psychology and life* (11th ed., pp. i–vii). Glenview, IL: Scott, Foresman.

Miller, N. E. (1987). Education for a lifetime of learning. In G. C. Stone, S. M. Weiss, J. D. Matarazzo, N. E. Miller, J. Rodin, C. D. Belar, M. J. Follick, & J. E. Singer (Eds.), *Health psychology: A discipline and a profession*. Chicago: University of Chicago Press.

Miller, N. E. (1992). Introducing and teaching much-needed understanding of the scientific process. *American Psychologist, 47*(7), 848–850.

15 The Future of Psychology

Hans J. Eysenck

The Scientific Revolution

The best way of telling where a man is going is to find out where he has come from. The best way of telling how he will behave in the future is to see how he has behaved in the past. So perhaps to determine the future of psychology it may be useful to try and understand its past—how it came to become a science, how it developed, and where it stands now. I think it is helpful to realize that the birth and growth of a scientific psychology can be looked upon as part of a much greater developmental process—what has been called the scientific revolution (Briggs, 1969; Bullough, 1970; Busalla, 1968; Cohen, 1994; Hall, 1954). This revolution marks the true beginning of science, as we understand it, and it is now usually placed in the 17th century, in spite of some efforts to place its beginning much earlier (Duhem, 1906, 1909, 1913).

This revolution embraced the *physical* sciences; chemistry came later, biology later still, and psychology last of all. This sequence is interesting: it recapitulates the sequence of the age at which scientists do their best work (Simonton, 1984). Mathematicians and physicists do their best work when young; chemists are somewhat older, biologists older still, with psychologists and other social scientists bringing up the rear. Psychology has usually been regarded as the last of the sciences to be born in the great scientific revolution, but its birth closely resembles that of the other sciences as recorded and interpreted by historians of science (Cohen, 1994). We have a developmental, pre-paradigmatic phase, with predecessors like Fechner, Weber, Helmholtz, and the like, presaging the form of arrival of a new science we now conveniently identify with Wundt's founding of the Leipzig laboratory. There is the combination of *experimentation* and *mathematization* which characterized the work of Galileo, Kepler, Descartes, Huygens, and Newton, and there is also the *specialization* and the growth of a separate scientific language so characteristic of the 17th-century revolution.

I do not want here to pursue this idea in any detail; our interest is in the future rather than the past. But recalling what happened in the 17th century may alert us to similar developments likely to happen in psychology in the future—and indeed already beginning to happen. Readers interested in the scientific revolution should consult the great names associated with the writing of its history—Burtt (1972), Butterfield (1957), Dijksterhuis (1961), Hooykaas (1973), Koyré (1966), and Maier, (1982); they will find much in these books to align with the development of modern psychology, and use in the prediction of its future. I shall next take up one of these developmental strands, and try to use it to predict one important development in psychology.

Before doing so, I would like to point out that this general point of view is an extension of an idea put forward originally by Kurt Lewin (1931) in his very influential paper, "The Conflict Between Aristotelian and Galileian Modes of Thought in Contemporary Psychology." Typically Aristotelian, according to Lewin, are his extremely anthropomorphic modes of thought, with their evaluative distinctions. Some causes are "good," emanating from a body's tendency toward perfection—hence the movements of the planets are circular around the earth, because the circle is the most perfect figure. Others are "bad"—disturbances due to change and the opposing forces of other bodies. "Like the distinction between earthly and heavenly, the no less valuative distinction between 'normal' and 'pathological' has for a long time sharply differentiated two fields of psychological fact and thus separated the phenomena which are fundamentally most nearly related" (p. 143). Lewin's paper was a highly original, pathbreaking attempt to characterize the scientific revolution in psychology and help it along; historical findings by historians of science since then have greatly advanced our understanding of just what characterized the great scientific revolution in which somewhat belatedly psychology is taking part (Cohen, 1994).

Ordeal by Quackery

Physical science did not spring suddenly out of nothing, like Athena from the head of Zeus; it was preceded by preparadigmatic, Aristotelian notions from which it had to liberate itself, a rejection popularly identified with Galileo and his battle with the Inquisition. Psychology in a similar manner had to battle (and still has to battle) with a commonsense psychology that is based, partly on experience, partly on literature. To many people Shakespeare, Dickens, and Shaw are more reliable guides to emotion and other psychological concepts than any modern psychologist. Newton, in his *Principia*, warns that the sense in which he uses the term "mass" is different from the sense in which this term is used by the hoi-polloi, but adds that we should pay no attention to them. In the same way the psychological meaning of "intelligence" is similar to, but not identical with, that given by the man in the street, and if he doesn't like it he'll just have to lump it! The development of a specialized scientific language is a necessity in a developing science, and perhaps the use of g instead of "intelligence" will reduce confusions otherwise inevitable.

Science also, from its beginning, had to battle with a tradition of quackery. Astronomy had to rid itself of its connections with astrology. Chemistry had to cut out its connection with alchemy. The battle was bitter and protracted. Newton was devoted to alchemy, and did much work in that field (Westfall, 1980); needless to say it did not produce any new knowledge. Kepler was employed as court astrologer (Caspar, 1959) and his astronomical labors were secondary. Not until the time of Dalton did chemistry rid itself of this incubus (Greenaway, 1966). The relation was not of course quite so one-sided as it may seem—the mystical notion of the alchemist often harbored important anticipation of chemical reality. Thus Paracelsus founded his "spagyric art of chemistry" on the *tria prima* of sulfur, mercury, and salt; the first two, of course, represent the fundamental duality of metals and non-metals, now known to be due to a shortage or excess of atoms, with salt being characterized by the exchanges taking place between the metal and non-metal ions. But the occasional factual content in astrology and alchemy did not make either a science, and their magical argumentation had to go to make possible the emergence of proper scientific thinking (Thorndike, 1923–1958; Webster, 1982; Yates, 1972). The *hermetic tradition* in the end was simply not compatible with a scientific development (Yates, 1964).

In psychology, too, there is such a battle between science and quackery, with such doctrines as those of existentialism, "humanistic" psychology, hermeneutics, and above all psychoanalysis constituting the nonscientific part (Eysenck, 1985). Psychoanalysts in particular have consistently disputed the point; humanistic and hermeneutic psychologists usually admit that their theories lie outside the scientific field and do not admit of the usual type of "proof." Many experts have made the point, in considerable detail, that whatever the Freudian opus may be adjudged to be, it bears no relation to what is ordinarily understood by "science" (Ellenberger, 1970; Esterson, 1993; Eysenck, 1985; Gruenbaum, 1984; Pohlen & Bautz-Holzherr, 1991; Prokop et al., 1990; Rachman, 1963; Scharnberg, 1993; Sulloway, 1979; Thornton, 1983; Zilbergeld, 1983; Zimmer, 1986; and Zwang, 1985). Other authors making the same point are quoted by Eysenck (1985). There are two major reasons for this growing disbelief in Freud's scientific pretensions.

In the first place there is much evidence that the confident prediction that psychotherapy based on "dynamic" foundations would produce cures of neurotic conditions, and that no other "symptom-oriented" therapy could do so, has been amply discounted. Eysenck (1952) analyzed all available studies comparing the effects of Freudian analysis with the effects of doing nothing at all (no treatment), and found no difference. This finding, and the suggestion that there was no scientific evidence for the effectiveness of Freudian psychotherapy, was fiercely criticized, although none of the critics brought forward any positive evidence to show that psychoanalysis did actually have any such positive effects. What is the position now (Eysenck, 1994d)?

The best evidence offered is a meta-analysis of 19 clinically relevant comparative outcome studies published from 1978 to 1988 in which short-term psychodynamic psychotherapy (STPP) was evaluated as to overall effects, differential effects, and moderating effects as against no treatment controls (NT), and alternative psychotherapies (AP) respectively (Swartberg & Stiles, 1991). STPP showed a very small superiority against NT immediately post treatment, but at 6 months' and 12 months' follow-up there were no differences. Thus on this vital point, these 1991 results bear out my 1952 conclusion. It was also found that STPP was inferior to AP at post treatment, at 6 months' follow-up, and considerably so at 12 months' follow-up. Thus Freud's theory is completely contradicted in both its major parts: psychoanalysis does *not* have any positive effect on neurotic disorders and other methods succeed very much better. Indeed, there is now a vast literature that shows that behavior therapy outperforms psychoanalytic and generally dynamic therapy in relation to almost every type of mental disorder (Grawe et al., 1994). A very detailed examination of the whole matter is given by Giles (1993), who comes co the same conclusion.

It is sometimes suggested that Freudian theory might be correct even if the effects of psychotherapy are disappointing. Many experimental studies have attempted to find evidence for various aspects of Freudian theories, but with very little success (Eysenck & Wilson, 1973; Kline, 1982; Eysenck, 1994c). Even the apparently most successful studies, such as those of Silverman (1983) are deeply flawed and have been extensively criticized (Eysenck, 1994c). The extensive study of the validity of Freud's observations leaves little doubt that in his writings what is true is not new, and what is new is not true (Eysenck, 1985). All this has led to a dramatic fall in the esteem in which Freudian theories are held, and a recognition on the part of psychoanalysts that psychoanalysis is indeed "a theory in crisis" (Edelson, 1988).

Is it too strong to speak of "quackery" in connection with psycho-analysis? Consider the absolute refusal on the part of psychoanalysts to give up their pretense of preaching a *true* doctrine, and of being able to *cure* neurotic patients. Indeed, they still demand that all who treat such patients should undergo several years of psychoanalytic treatment themselves (perhaps "brain-washing" would be a better term), and continue to administer a very expensive and time-consuming treatment in the face of a vast body of evidence showing that such treatment is utterly useless, and may often be counterproductive (Mays & Franks, 1985). What would orthodox medicine say about someone who produced a drug, based on a certain theory, which was meant to be a cure, indeed the only cure, for a given disease, but which was shown in 19 trials to be completely useless? What would medicine say if this person continued to make outrageous claims for both theory and drug, even though experimental tests of the theory gave almost completely negative results? Quackery is the word that inevitably comes to mind, and the history of medicine gives us many examples.

My conclusion would be that we must separate ourselves from such nonscientific and indeed antiscientific modes of thinking, theorizing, and practicing, if we are to have a psychology that can be regarded as *scientific*. Just as astronomy had to cut the cord that bound it to astrology, and just as chemistry had to separate from alchemy, so psychology will have to renounce its romance with psychoanalysis and obtain a proper divorce if it wishes to be taken seriously. One hundred years is surely sufficient time to give to psycho-analysis to provide some evidence, however slender, of its value. Its failure to do so must surely now convince even the most credulous that psychoanalysis does not and cannot make any realistic contribution to a scientific psychology, and does not form part and parcel of our science. Like most divorces this may require a hard decision to make, and leave us with many sorrowful reminders of past happiness, but we cannot continue half-science and half-superstition.

There is only one way to cut the Gordian knot, and the longer we hesitate, the greater the trauma. The next century should see us start with a clean sheet as far as mental alchemy is concerned.

The Mind-Body Continuum

Descartes taught us to regard body and mind as two entirely separate entities, and this belief has haunted us for over 300 years, and has produced endless philosophical speculations. The evidence is now conclusive that these speculations are quite irrelevant to the actualities we have to deal with. Just as physicists used to believe in the duality of space and time, but had to learn that we are dealing with a space-time continuum, so we will have to learn that we have to deal with a mind-body continuum. Physical events can influence mental events, and mental events can influence physical events; indeed, there is a kind of double aspect element about this interaction. Spinoza already suggested in his identity theory that body and mind were *una eademque res sed duobus modis expressa*—two aspects or dimensions of a single reality. It is of course still possible to maintain philosophical notions of predetermination—that some god laid down a parallelism of mental and physical activity that gives the impression of interaction, but this is the kind of argument that would justify solipsism—impossible to refute because no testable consequences follow from it, and hence quite unscientific.

What sort of evidence is there for a double aspect theory that would not flow from an *idealist* (only mind exists) or a *realist* (only matter exists) viewpoint? Consider the work of Jacobson (1938), and later studies summarized by McGuigan (1978, 1994). Using thee electromyograph (EMG), Jacobson found that minuscule (covert) muscular contraction patterns are present whenever we *imagine* a bodily movement, and these contractions, and the electrical messages preceding and initiating them, are identical with those producing the actual movements imagined. Thus when we imagine hitting a tennis ball, or sweeping the floor, we initiate subconsciously and covertly the very movements that would occur on a much larger scale were we to *actually* hit a tennis ball, or sweep the room. Thought is reflected in EEG activity (disruption of the alpha rhythm). The electrocardiograph (ECG) indicates special heart responses when cognition indicates certain emotional patterns, such as fear. The electro-oculograph (EOG) shows eye movements being especially active during thought, and during visualization. Visceral activity, too, is intrinsically involved in emotional processes. The list is endless and suggests that there is *no mental activity without a physical complement* (McGuigan, 1994).

The major scientific and practical impact of this general law has been in relation to the so-called psychosomatic diseases. I will here confine myself to a brief consideration of recent work on the cancer-prone and the coronary heart disease–prone personality (Eysenck, 1991). Even as early as 2000 years ago, Greek physicians argued for the existence of a cancer-prone personality, and recent work has given much support for such a view (Eysenck, 1994b). The main characteristics of the cancer-prone personality were (1) inability to express emotions like fear, anger, and anxiety, and (2) inability to cope adequately with stress, leading to feelings of hopelessness, helplessness, and finally depression. Much research has shown that cancer patients do indeed show these traits reliably more often than controls, and prospective studies have shown that the likelihood of contracting cancer can be predicted successfully in healthy people over a 10-year period. The same is true of coronary heart disease, where the predisposing characteristics are anger, hostility, and aggression.

Figure 15.1 shows some results from such a prospective study, using a random sample of healthy men and women with an average age of 50. On the basis of questionnaire responses these were divided into four types: (1) cancer-prone; (2) coronary heart disease–prone; (3) hysterical personality; and (4) healthy, autonomous personality. Ten years later, mortality as shown on death certificates was established. It will be clear that type 1 persons show a high incidence of cancer mortality, as expected, while type 2 persons show a high incidence of heart disease mortality. Types 3 and 4, as expected, show very little mortality (Eysenck, 1991). Several other studies have successfully replicated this demonstration (Eysenck, 1994a).

The importance of a healthy personality (type 4) can be illustrated in another study, using a 105-item questionnaire measuring *self-regulation*, that is, autonomy *from* neurotic and other emotional factors preventing a person from acting to maximize his or her own potentials and needs. The questionnaire was administered to a large group of healthy men and women, who were followed for a period of 15 years, when mortality from cancer, CHD, and other causes was ascertained. The results are shown in figures 15.2 and 15.3; clearly, personality was strongly related to mortality (Eysenck, 1994b). These data provide good support for a statement made in 1906 by Sir William Osler, often called the father of British medicine: "It is very often much more important what person has the disease, than what disease the person has" (Osler, 1906).

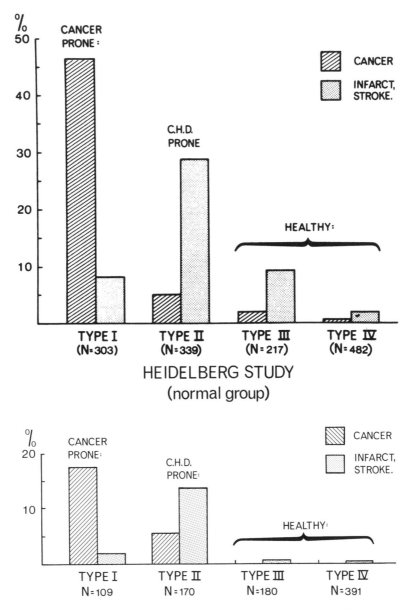

Figure 15.1   Mortality from cancer and coronary heart disease (*CHD*) of cancer-prone, CHD-prone, and psychologically healthy people after 10-year follow-up. (Eysenck, 1991.)

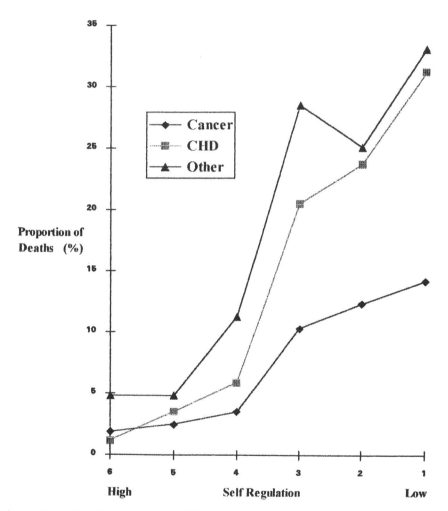

Figure 15.2   Death from cancer, CHD, and other causes in males high and low in degree of self-regulation. (Eysenck, 1994b.)

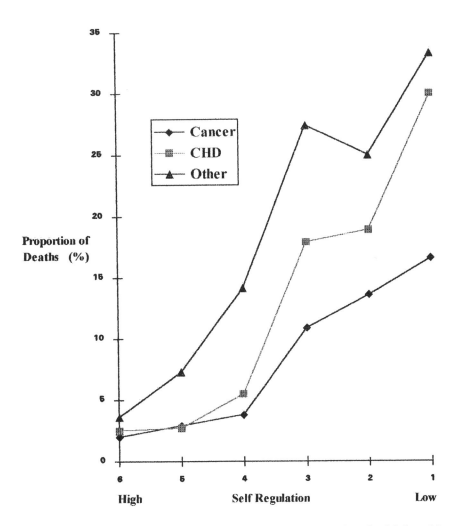

Figure 15.3   Death from cancer, CHD, and other causes in females high and low in degree of self-regulation. (Eysenck, 1994b.)

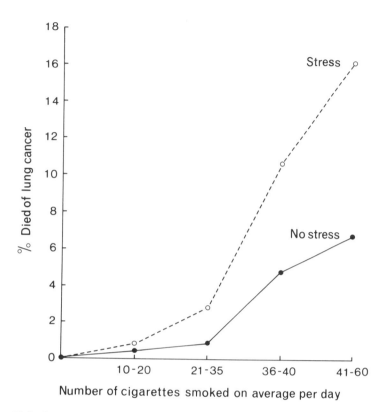

Figure 15.4 Lung cancer mortality of smokers depending on degree of stress. (Eysenck, 1991.)

Of course, psychological risk factors interact with physical risk factors (Eysenck, 1994e). Figure 15.4 shows the interaction of smoking with the personality/stress combination as measured by the type 1 questionnaire (Eysenck, 1991). Again we are concerned with a prospective study, and the dependent variable concerned is lung cancer. There clearly is a monotonic relation between smoking and lung cancer, but at each level of smoking stress clearly interacts with smoking, so that mortality is much greater when both risk factors appear in combination (Eysenck, 1991). The effects of psychosocial factors are much easier to undo than are those of smoking; not only is there little evidence that giving up smoking reduces mortality from smoking (Eysenck, 1991) but also changing type 1 personality, or type 2 personality, in a more healthy direction has proved quite feasible, and successful in reducing the incidence and mortality of cancer and CHD (Eysenck & Grossarth-Maticek, 1991). Such findings suggest that the hypothesis of a mind-body continuum has far-reaching effects, and may be worthy of serious consideration.

Some of the consequences of this type of work may lead to a closer co-operation between psychology and the medical profession. Medical doctors have shown a remarkable resistance to abandoning their reductionist and materialist philosophy, however contrary to well-established facts this may be. It seems obvious that *prevention* is better than *cure*, and of course there is little prospect of *cure* as far as cancer is concerned. When in 1971 President Nixon declared war on cancer, it was confidently hoped and anticipated that death from cancer would be halved by the year 2000. Twenty-four *billion* dollars were spent on this crusade. What was the effect? The death rate from cancer *increased* by 7% between 1975 and 1990 (figures controlled for population growth and death from other diseases)!

By contrast, psychological research in this field, holding out much better prospects of *preventing* cancer, has received only derisory support, amounting to less than 0.1% of that offered to the medical profession. It is to be hoped that in the next millenium reason will prevail, and psychology will be much more involved in both research and therapy. Even for terminal cancer it has been shown that psychological treatment can prolong life and improve its quality, to an extent at least as great as do chemotherapy and allied medical remedies, and can do so without the serious side effects so tragically charac-teristic of medical intervention (Eysenck, 1991). It has also been found that *interaction* between medical and psychological treatment is *synergistic*—the two together do significantly better than would be expected if we simply added together their individual effects (Eysenck & Grossarth-Maticek, 1991).

It may be worth adding that there is now a good theory, amply con-firmed by dozens of laboratory experiments, to show how *mental* events, like coping and depression, can influence *physical* diseases like cancer. It has fre-quently been shown that the depressive reactions to failure to cope result in high cortisol concentrations; these are also known to have a deleterious effect on the immune system, which in turn controls and eliminates the ever-growing cancer cells in the body. Depression and the resulting cortisol increase have been shown to be responsive to psychological therapy. Much of course remains to be done, but the outlines of a causal theory are well established (Lewis et al., 1994).

Man Is a Biosocial Animal: Genetics

It would be difficult to find anyone who seriously doubts the truth of the statement that man is driven by both biological and social forces, yet this realization has had little effect on psychological research and theorizing during the past 50 years. Social factors have been emphasized out of all proportion, and biological factors have been dismissed almost contemptuously. There have been two major reasons for this. In the first place the great victory of *behaviorism*, over all other competing systems, led to the adoption of the views of Watson and Skinner which eliminated, for all purposes, biological factors and gave exclusive eminence to behavioral factors, such as reinforcement. Skinner explicitly rejected all of psychophysiology, relating brain processes to a "black box" in the brain, and declared concepts like cognition, personality, intelligence, and many others to be relics of ancient beliefs of no concern to a scientific psychology. He completely disregarded the obvious fact that even in his system concern with individual differences is essential because clearly reinforcers differ from person to person—a point not perhaps obvious if you confine your studies to hungry pigeons in a Skinner box!

In the second place, these years experienced the growth of *political correctness*, an ideological system of beliefs concerned with the absolute rejection of biological causes of human behavior, however factually incorrect such rejection might be. The combination of behaviorism and political correctness proved invincible, however odd an assortment of bedfellows they might seem to be. Advocates of biological approaches to psychological problems found little financial support, little academic encouragement, and few outlets in psychological publications. The more daring were harassed, persecuted, and often even attacked bodily (Pearson, 1991). It was a shameful period for what purports to be a scientific discipline and a democratic community, and the introduction of *political* dogma into scientific debates will continue to make rational discourse difficult.

Much of the argument has been concerned with the alleged controversy between "hereditarians" and "environmentalists." Hereditarians, in the sense of psychologists or geneticists asserting that behavior was 100% controlled by heredity, never existed of course; no one ever doubted that environment had a considerable effect on behavior. There were indeed 100% environmentalists, but they were few in number, and their case was so obviously absurd that few joined their ranks in any official way. But what prevailed was a much more insidious environmentalism, stressing exclusively environmental causes, while publicly not disagreeing with the official doctrine that the problem was never one of heredity *or* environment, but rather a quantitative one, of how much of each, under what circumstances, and in what sort of interaction. This realistic attitude was completely abandoned when research was carried out or interpretations made of research findings. Thus in the literature on social attitudes it was simply *assumed* that genetic factors were completely absent, and research planning paid no attention to the fact that this was an unjustified a priori assumption. The demonstration by Eaves and Eysenck (1974) that genetic factors accounted for at least half the variance of attitudes related to religion, politics, criminality, etc., failed to disturb this axiomatic belief, but the publication of our book *Genes, Culture and Personality* (Eaves, Eysenck, & Martin, 1989) and other recent studies may do something to remove this iron curtain. Clearly no research can give meaningful results that does not take into account genetic factors in the planning.

Interpretation of studies in personality, intelligence, or social attitudes nearly always refused to consider the possibility of genetic interpretations. If behavior X on the part of the parents was found to be correlated with behavior Y on the part of the child, the conclusion was nearly always made that X *caused* Y—parents who beat their children cause the children to be aggressive and sadistic. But of course equally possible is the alternative view that the children have inherited aggressive and sadistic genes from aggressive and sadistic parents. The finding of a *correlation* between X and Y does not allow us to make a causal interpretation of the finding. But throughout the past 50 years such impermissible interpretations were made, and passed by peer reviewers and editors alike, to produce a body of literature that had no rational basis for its conclusions.

All this might have been forgiven if Newman and colleagues (1937) had been correct in their conclusion from their own studies that there was little if any genetic variance in personality differences. Unfortunately, their study was deeply flawed both methodologically and statistically (Eysenck, 1967), and in two pioneering studies, I have shown that genetic factors accounted for over half the variance in two major personality factors, neuroticism and extroversion (Eysenck & Prell, 1952; Eysenck, 1956). The statistical treatment may appear primitive from a perspective 40 years later, but much more sophisticated studies, carried out on a much larger scale, have since amply confirmed my earlier conclusions (Eaves et al., 1989). These modern studies, encompassing 15,000, 12,000, and 8000 twins respectively, establish the major facts in this field without any question: Heredity is much the most important factor in accounting for differences in personality.

It is sometimes said that geneticists are only interested in establishing the degree of heritability of a given trait or ability, and that this is of little interest because if something is inherited, there is no way of changing it. Nothing could be further from the truth. Let us consider the first point. Heritability is best understood in terms of the components of variance that enter into it: $h^2 = V_G/V_P$, where V_G is the genetic variance, and V_P is the phenotypic (total) variance. Genetic variance has four components:

$$V_G = V_A + V_D + V_{EP} + V_{AM},$$

where V_A is additive genetic variance, V_D nonadditive genetic variance due to dominance at the same gene loci V_{EP} is nonadditive genetic variance due to interaction between different gene loci (epistasis), and V_{AM} is genetic variance due to assortative mating (like marrying like). The phenotypic variance is made up of five components:

$$V_P = V_G + V_E + V_{GE} + \text{Cov GE} + V_e,$$

where V_E is additive environmental variance independent of the genotype, V_{GE} is variance due to interaction of genotype and environment, Cov GE is covariance of genotypes and environments, and V_e is error variance due to unreliability of measurement.

This simple enumeration will indicate two things. In the first place, heritability is only one aspect of the total architecture of genetics; others may be equally or more important, and must certainly be considered. In the second place the general formula contains environmental factors and interactions, as well as genetic ones; in other words, it encompasses the *total* variance of phenotypic behavior patterns. It would be wrong to characterize this approach as hereditarian; it deals with *all* the causal factors that may be instrumental in producing individual differences, and attempts to quantify their respective contributions and interactions. It indicates that we cannot meaningfully omit V_G and simply concentrate on V_E, as has been the custom over the past 50 years; to do so is scientifically meaningless. Ignorance of these simple facts has given rise to numerous failures to appreciate just what is implied by statements that genetic factors account for $X\%$ of the variance; I shall list some of these presently. Before doing so I want to make one further point.

Geneticists divide V_E (the environmental variance) into V_{EB} and V_{EW}, that is, environmental variance between families, or *shared* environmental variance, and environmental variance *within* families, that is, arising from accidental happenings that produce differences in personality or ability between children in the same family. Until the present, practically all psychological theories of personality have focused on V_{EB}, that is, differential upbringing of children in different families, as being responsible for personality differences, paying particular attention to the first 5 years of life. Recent work has shown conclusively that this emphasis is wrong; V_{EW} accounts for practically the total environmental variance in personality differences (Eaves et al., 1989). This fact alone would be sufficient to indicate that genetic analysis does far more than simply assess heritability. It results in findings that are absolutely *fundamental* to understanding the genesis of individual differences, and can demonstrate the falsity of firmly embedded personality theories.

Nor is it true that because something is genetically determined, there is nothing that can be done about it. Nothing could be more mistaken. One example may serve to make this point. There is a well-known disease called phenylketonuria, which affects about 1 child in 40,000 in England. This disorder causes mental defects, and it has been found that about 1 in every 100 patients in hospitals for severely mentally handicapped children suffer from phenylketonuria. This disorder is known to be inherited and it is, in fact, due to a single recessive gene. It was first recognized by a Norwegian physician, Foelling, in 1934. The great majority of children suffering from it have a level of mental performance that is usually found in children half their age. These children can be distinguished from other mentally handicapped or from normal children by testing their urine, which yields a green-colored reaction with a solution of ferric chloride, due to the presence of derivatives of phenylalanine. Here we have a perfect example of a disorder produced entirely by hereditary causes, where the cause is simple and well understood, and where the presence of the disorder can be determined with accuracy.

Is there reason to believe that "therapeutic nihilism" is called for? Definitely not. However, we must go on to demonstrate in what way the gene actually produces the mental defect. It has been shown that children affected by phenylketonuria are unable to convert phenylalanine into tyrosine; they can only break it down to a limited extent. It is not clear why this should produce mental deficiency but it seems probable that some of the incomplete breakdown products of phenylalanine are poisonous to the nervous system. Phenylalanine, fortunately, is not an essential part of the diet, provided that tyrosine is present in the diet. It is possible to maintain those children on a diet that is almost free of phenylalanine, thus eliminating the danger of poisoning to the nervous system. It has been found that when this method of treatment is begun in the first few months of life, there is a very good chance that the child will grow up without the mental handicap he or she would otherwise have encountered. In other words, by understanding the precise way in which heredity works, and by understanding precisely what it does to the organism, we can arrange a rational method of therapy which will make use of the forces of nature, rather than trying to counteract them.

Now for some other misunderstandings of the meaning of "genetic determination." (1) Heritability is a population statistic; it characterizes a special group, and may vary from one group to another. Nor does it apply to individuals; if the heritability of intelligence in native white American adults is 80%, that does *not* mean that any particular American white adult has his or her IQ determined to the extent of 80% by heredity. And the figure of 80% might have been different 200 years ago, and it might be different now for adult native-born Indians, or Chinese. (2) Genetic determinism does not mean that we are condemned to a caste system, with the children of dull parents always dull, and those of bright parents always bright. Figure 15.5 illustrates this erroneous belief, while figure 15.6 illustrates the correct version: *Regression to the mean* assures social mobility as actually found. Some geniuses like Newton and Gauss have come from very undistinguished soil; some illustrious parents have very dull children. The segregation of genes constitutes a vitally important lottery of life!

It is very much to be hoped that in the next century all students of psychology will receive an adequate instruction in behavior genetics, including methodology, statistics, and results. Without such an education in biological reality there is little hope of achieving a proper scientific understanding of personality theory and the development of mental abilities. Neither would it be possible, in the absence of such teaching, to research and understand the contribution of environmental factors. Nature and nurture are two sides of one and the same coin, and cannot be treated separately; their effects and interactions must always be studied jointly (Plomin & McCleary, 1993).

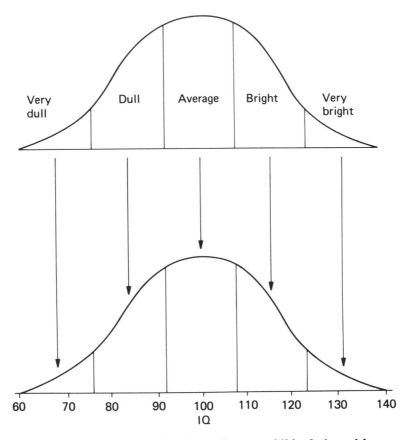

Figure 15.5 Erroneous but popular view of parent-child relation with respect to the inheritance of IQ. (Eysenck, 1982.)

The Biological Basis of Personality and Intellect

If heredity is so powerful in determining differences in personality and intelligence, then it must surely follow that there are *biological intermediaries* between DNA and behavior. Different allele forms of a gene are due to different sequences of the bases in the DNA, which result in different sequences of amino acids in the protein, which might, as a consequence, alter functional properties. Thus genes influence the proteins that are critical to the functioning of the organ systems that determine behavior—but clearly they cannot do

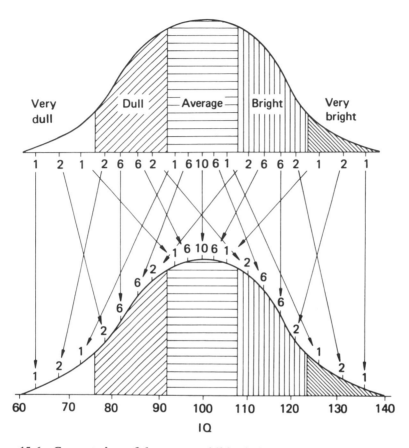

Figure 15.6   Correct view of the parent-child relation with respect to inheritance of IQ. (Eysenck, 1982.)

that directly; there must be hormonal, physiological, and neurological intermediaries. Until recently there was little interest in these matters, probably because of the widely shared disregard for genetic and biological factors, but recently the climate has changed dramatically, and now there are numerous experimental studies, and also a number of summaries of research results, often with theoretical interpretations (Eysenck, 1990, 1993, 1994a; Gale & Eysenck, 1992; Mangan, 1982; Stemmler, 1992; Strelau & Eysenck, 1987; Strelau et al., 1985, Thayer, 1989; Vernon, 1993, 1994; Zuckerman, 1991). All this work should be seen against the background of biological psychology (McGuigan,

1994; Birbaumer & Schmidt, 1990), which is beginning to fill in the gap in our textbooks produced by the "black box" approach of old-style behaviorism.

I tried to indicate the way the psychometric study of individual differences could be integrated with our present-day knowledge of psychobiology and psychophysiology in *The Biological Basis of Personality* (Eysenck, 1967), and much of the research summarized in the books and papers mentioned in the last paragraph has (largely) confirmed and (to a lesser extent) altered the theories there advanced (Eysenck, 1981), while my book *A Model for Intelligence* tried to do the same for intelligence (Eysenck, 1982). It is noteworthy that through such individual differences constructs as have been employed in this field, psychopathology has also involved other fields, such as criminality (Raine, 1993) where previously a strictly environmental-sociological approach reigned serene.

The importance of these new developments can best be seen in the context of Cronbach's (1957) famous presidential address to the American Psychological Association (APA), in which he pointed out the existence of two disciplines of scientific psychology—the experimental and the correlational—and suggested that only by unifying and combining them would psychology ever become a proper science. I have always believed that this is both a *true* and a *vitally important*—consideration and have tried to combine these two traditions. A good example of the odd way in which these two disciplines completely disregard the contribution of each other is *memory*. Ever since the days of Ebbinghaus, experimentalists have tried to disentangle iconic, short-term and long-term memory, with the aim of achieving a better understanding of the mechanisms and processes involved. At the same time psychologists interested in individual differences have constructed memory tests without paying any attention to the results of the experimental studies, just as the experimentalists paid no attention to the outcomes of correlational studies! This surely is absurd and nonscientific. I have tried, in one particular instance, to show how the two can be combined, and to the great advantage of both, so that we could achieve a better understanding of both the processes involved, and the relation of the phenomena to personality (Eysenck & Frith, 1977). It is my most urgent hope that this unification of the experimental and correlational aspects of psychology will proceed apace in the coming century, together with a better integration of psychophysiological advances.

One example may indicate the advantages of using an integrated approach to achieve a better understanding of concepts and processes. Consider intelligence. There are three major ways of looking at intelligence, as illustrated in figure 15.7. Genetic analyses have suggested a strong heredity component, and as argued above, this suggests an intermediary psychophysiological link between DNA and behavior, as measured by means of psychometric devices (IQ). Much recent research has tried to identify this biological intelligence, and demonstrate its relation to IQ, and beyond it with social or practical intelligence.

The history of this research and the theories involved have been recorded elsewhere (Eysenck, 1993; Deary & Caryl, 1993). Very briefly, we look at *evoked potentials*, that is, EEG recordings of our subjects where a sudden stimulus is introduced (at point B in figure 15.8) during an EEG recording of the resting subject. The resulting waves are then studied to discover differences between high- and low-IQ subjects. Typical recordings for a bright, an average, and a dull child are shown in figure 15.9. Differences are noted in *latency* (waves follow each other more quickly for brighter children) and in *complexity* (brighter children have more complex wave forms). These differences can be explained in terms of speed of nervous transmission of information through the cortex (mental speed), and of error-free transmission—if errors occur they wipe out the smaller, complex features of the trace, leaving only the large sinusoidal wave forms. This is not the place to discuss all the details of this process; the argument gets exceedingly complex. It is merely intended to suggest how the integration of psychometric procedures, and experimental and psychophysiological experimentation, can give rise to important new findings (Barrett & Eysenck, 1992, 1994).

Conclusions

The changes I hope to see in the next century are in a very real sense extrapolations of advances already taking place (Matarazzo, 1992). Many psychologists are determined to make psychology more scientific, and the recent breakaway of the American Psychological Society from the APA, following upon a similar earlier breakaway of the Experimental Society from the British Psychological Society, illustrates the impatience of science-oriented experimentalists with bread-and-butter clinicians and other applied groups. If we want to prevent the breakup of psychology as a single science we had better heed this dissatisfaction with the inclusion of obviously (and often vocally) non- and antiscientific groups in our councils.

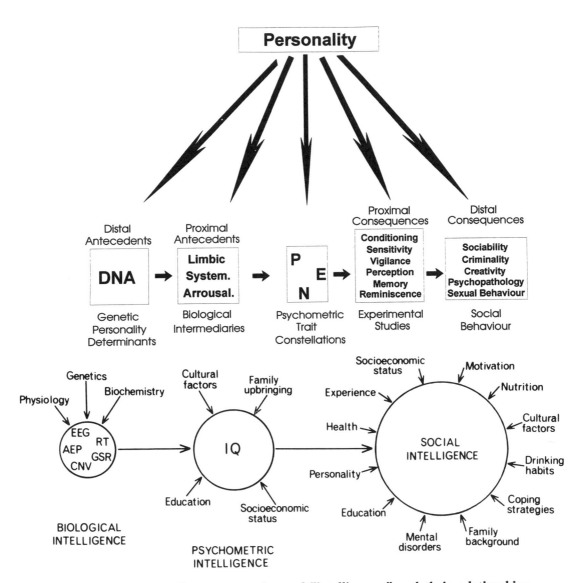

Figure 15.7 Different conceptions of "intelligence," and their relationships. *EEG*, electroencephalogram; *AEP*, average evoked potential; *CNV*, contingent negative variation; *GSR*, Galvanic skin response; *RT*, Reaction time. (Eysenck, 1994a.)

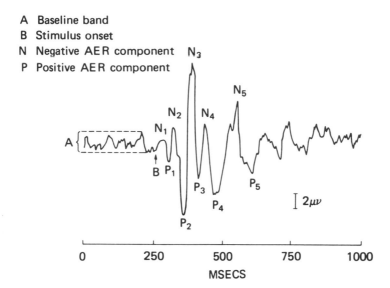

Figure 15.8   Nature of the average and evoked potential. *AER,* **average evoked response.**

The growing impact of biological factors, whether in the form of *genetic* implications or hormonal psychophysiological intermediaries between DNA and behavior, can hardly be doubted, and the advances already made will undoubtedly continue. We are close to finding genetic marker variables for personality traits and cognitive abilities, and the discovery of the position of relevant genes on the genome is only a matter of time—perhaps 10 or 20 years. Similarly, our understanding of the biological roots of our behavior is growing by leaps and bounds, constrained only by lack of funds. These are all growing points, and slowly we are leaving behind the absurdities of a science constructed by political ideologists, subservient to political correctness, and following the dictates of old-fashioned behaviorism.

Together with this very active experimental program we have theoretical advances, along the lines of sociobiology, that are likely to reinstate the notion of man as a *biosocial* animal, a notion that should never have been permitted to be given up by radical behaviorists disregarding both cognitive and biological variables. Not all behaviorists fell into this trap, of course; Hull made special provision for personality variables in his system, and Kenneth and Janet Spence

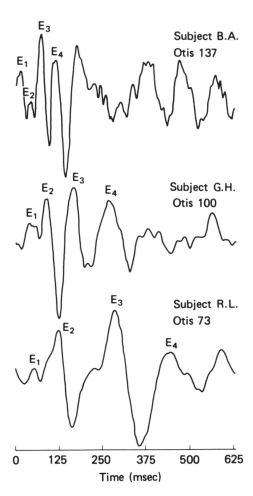

Figure 15.9 Typical evoked potentials of a bright, an average, and a dull child.

demonstrated how this could be done by treating anxiety as a drive variable, making and testing many quite specific predictions that showed the power of this procedure (Eysenck, 1973). Perhaps the next century will see a return to their brave and scientifically necessary attempt to create a unified system of explanation for behavior, based on the quantitative relation between a few properly defined variables.

It also seems likely that the abandonment of Cartesian ways of thinking will see a growth in the scientific understanding of psychosomatic diseases, and a desire on the part of society to use this knowledge for the prevention of such scourges as cancer and coronary heart disease. Again, promising beginnings have been made, and the path seems clear. Psychology has the potential to make a great and important contribution to social and individual well-being. All that is holding us back is the presence of well-organized and powerful antiscientific groups, like the psychoanalysts, and of an equally well-organized and powerful behaviorist group, protecting their ancient environmentalist dogmas. If only we could free ourselves of the shades of Freud and Skinner, Jung and Watson, what a flowing of psychological knowledge there would be! Only the next generation of psychologists will be able to put all this into operation, and to reap the rewards, given that my extrapolations are not too far from the truth!

References

Barrett, P., & Eysenck, H. J. (1992). Brain electrical potentials and intelligence. In A. Gale & M. W. Eysenck (Eds.), *Handbook of individual differences: Biological perspectives* (pp. 255–285). London: Wiley.

Barrett, P., & Eysenck, H. J. (1994). The relationship between evoked potential component analysis, latency, contour length, variability, zero-crossings, and psychometric intelligence. *Personality and Individual Differences, 16,* 3–32.

Birbaumer, N., & Schmidt, P. (1990). *Biologische Psychologie.* New York: Springer-Verlag.

Briggs, R. (1969). *The scientific revolution of the seventeenth century.* London: Longmans.

Bullough, V. (Ed.) (1970). *The scientific revolution.* Huntington, NY: Krieger.

Burtt, E. (1972). *The metaphysical foundation of modern physical science*. London: Routledge & Kegan Paul.

Busalla, G. (Ed.) (1968). *The rise of modern science*. Lexington, MA: Heath.

Butterfield, H. (1957). *The origins of modern science, 1300–1800*. London: Bell.

Caspar, M. (1959). *Kepler*. London: Abelard-Schuman.

Cohen, H. F. (1994). *The scientific revolution*. Chicago: The University of Chicago Press.

Cronbach, L. J. (1957). The two disciplines of scientific psychology. *American Psychologist, 12*, 671–684.

Deary, I., & Caryl, P. (1993). Intelligence, EEG, and evoked potentials. In P. A. Vernon (Ed.), *Biological approaches to the study of human intelligence* (pp. 259–316). Norwood, NJ: Ablex.

Dijksterhuis, E. (1961). *The mechanization of the world picture*. Oxford: Oxford University Press.

Duhem, P. (1906, 1909, 1913). *Etudes sur Leonard de Vinci: Ceux qu'il a lus ceux qui l'ont lu* (3 vols.). Paris: Hermans.

Eaves, L., & Eysenck, H. J. (1974). Genetics and the development of social attitudes. *Nature, 249*, 288–289.

Eaves, L., Eysenck, H., & Martin, N. (1989). *Genes, Culture and Personality*. London: Academic Press.

Edelson, M. (1988). *Psychoanalysis: A theory in crisis*. Chicago: University of Chicago Press.

Ellenberger, H. (1970). *The discovery of the unconscious*. London: Allen Lane.

Esterson, A. (1993). *Seductive mirage*. Chicago: Open Court.

Eysenck, H. J. (1952). The effects of psychotherapy: An evaluation. *Journal of Consulting Psychology, 16*, 319–324.

Eysenck, H. J. (1956). The evaluation of extraversion-introversion. *Acta Psychologia*, *12*, 95–110.

Eysenck, H. J. (1967). *The biological basis of personality*. Springfield, IL: Thomas.

Eysenck, H. J. (1973). Personality, learning, and "anxiety." In H. J. Eysenck (Ed.), *Handbook of abnormal psychology* (pp. 390–418). London: Pitman.

Eysenck, H. J. (Ed.) (1981). *A model for personality*. New York: Springer-Verlag.

Eysenck, H. J. (Ed.) (1982). *A model for intelligence*. New York: Springer-Verlag.

Eysenck, H. J. (1985). *Decline and fall of the Freudian empire*. London: Viking.

Eysenck, H. J. (1990). Biological dimensions of personality. In L. A. Pervin (Ed.), *Handbook of personality* (pp. 244–272). New York: Guilford.

Eysenck, H. J. (1991). *Smoking, personality and stress: Psychosocial factors in the prevention of cancer and coronary heart disease*. New York: Springer-Verlag.

Eysenck, H. J., (1993). The biological basis of intelligence. In P. A. Vernon (Ed.)., *Biological approaches to the study of human intelligence* (pp. 1–32). Norwood, NJ: Ablex.

Eysenck, H. J. (1994a). Personality: Biological foundations. In P. A. Vernon (Ed.), *The neuropsychology of individual differences* (pp. 11–207). New York: Academic Press.

Eysenck, H. J. (1994b). Cancer, personality and stress: Prediction and prevention. *Advances in Behaviour Research and Therapy*, *16*, 167–215.

Eysenck, H. J. (1994c). Psicoanalisis y terapia de conducta: El error Freudiant. *Psicologia Conductual*, *2*, 149–164.

Eysenck, H. J. (1994d). The outcome problem in psychotherapy: What have we learned? *Behaviour Research and Therapy*, *32*, 477–495.

Eysenck, H. J. (1994e). Synergistic interaction between psychosocial and physical factors in the causation of lung cancer. In C. Lewis, C. O'Sullivan, & J. Barraclough (Eds.), *The psychoimmunology of cancer* (pp. 163–178). Oxford: Oxford University Press.

Eysenck, H. J., & Frith, C. D. (1977). *Reminiscence, motivation and personality*. New York: Plenum Press.

Eysenck, H. J., & Grossarth-Maticek, R. (1991). Creative novation behaviour therapy as a prophylactic treatment for cancer and coronary heart disease: II. Effects of treatment. *Behaviour Research and Therapy, 29*, 17–31.

Eysenck, H. J., & Prell, D. (1952). The inheritance of neuroticism: An experimental study. *Journal of Mental Science, 97*, 441–465.

Eysenck, H. J. & Wilson, G. (1973). *The experimental study of Freudian theories*. London: Methuen.

Gale, A., & Eysenck, M. W. (1992). *Handbook of individual differences: Biological perspectives*. London: Wiley.

Giles, I. (1993). *Handbook of effective psychotherapy*. New York: Plenum Press.

Grawe, K., Donati, P., & Bernaner, F. (1994). *Psychotherapie im Wandel*. Heidelberg: Hogrefe.

Greenaway, F. (1966). *John Dalton and the atom*. London: Heinemann.

Gruenbaum, A. (1984). *The foundations of psychoanalysis*. Berkeley: University of California Press.

Hall, A. R. (1954). *The Scientific Revolution, 1500–1800*. London: Longmans.

Hooykaas, R. (1973). *Religion and the rise of modern science*. Edinburgh: Scottish Academic Press.

Jacobson, E. (1938). *Progressive relaxation*. Chicago: University of Chicago Press.

Kline, P. (1982). *Fact and fantasy in Freudian theory*. London: Methuen.

Koyré, A. (1966). *Etudes Galileens*. Paris: Hermann.

Lewin, K. (1931). The conflict between Aristotelian and Galileian modes of thought in contemporary psychology. *Journal of General Psychology, 5*, 141–177.

Lewis, C., O'Sullivan, C., & Barraclogh, J. (1994). *The psychoimmunology of cancer: Mind and body in the fight for survival.* Oxford: Oxford University Press.

Maier, A. (1982). *On the threshold of exact science.* Philadelphia: University of Pennsylvania Press.

Mangan, G. (1982). *The biology of human conduct.* Oxford: Pergamon Press.

Matarazzo, J. (1992). Psychological testing and assessment in the 21st century. *American Psychologist, 47,* 1007–1018.

Mays, D., & Franks, C. (1985). *Negative outcome in psychotherapy and what to do about it.* New York: Springer-Verlag.

McGuigan, J. (1978). *Cognitive psychophysiology: Principles of covert behaviour.* Hillsdale, NJ: Erlbaum.

McGuigan J. (1994). *Biological psychology.* Englewood Cliffs, NJ: Prentice Hall.

Newman, H., Freeman, F., & Holzinger, K. (1937). *Twins.* Chicago: University of Chicago Press.

Osler, W. (1906). *Aequanimitas.* New York: McGraw-Hill.

Pearson, R. (1991). *Race, intelligence and bias in academe.* Washington, DC: Scott-Townsend.

Plomin, R., & McCleary, G. (1993). *Nature, nurture and psychology.* Washington, DC: American Psychological Association.

Pohlen, M., & Bautz-Holzherr, M. (1991). *Eine andere Aufklärung: Das Freudsche Subjekt in der Analyse.* Frankfurt: Suhrkamp.

Prokop, L., Prokop, O., & Prokop, H. (1990). *Grenzen der Toleranz in der Medizin.* Berlin: Verlag Gesundheit.

Rachman, S. (1963) (Ed.). *Critical essays on psychoanalysis.* Oxford: Pergamon.

Raine, A. (1993). *The psychopathology of crime.* New York: Academic Press.

Scharnberg, M. (1993). *The non-authentic nature of Freud's observation.* (2 vols). Uppsala, Sweden: University Press.

Silverman, L. H. (1983). The subliminal psychodynamic activation studies. *Journal of Abnormal Psychology, 91,* 126–130.

Simoton, D. K. (1984). *Genius, creativity and leadership.* Cambridge, MA: Harvard University Press.

Stemmler, G. (1992). *Differential psychophysiology: Persons in situations.* New York: Springer-Verlag.

Strelau, J., & Eysenck, H. J. (Eds.) (1987). *Personality dimensions and arousal.* New York: Plenum Press.

Strelau, J., Farley, F., & Gale, A. (Eds.) (1985). *The biological basis of personality and behaviour* (2 vols.). Washington, DC: Hemisphere.

Sulloway, F. J. (1979). *Freud: Biologist of the mind.* New York: Basic Books.

Swartberg, M., & Stiles, T. (1991). Comparative effects of short-term psychodynamic psychotherapy: A meta-analysis. *Journal of Consulting and Clinical Psychology, 59,* 704–714.

Thayer, R. (1989). *The biophysiology of mood and arousal.* Oxford: Oxford University Press.

Thorndike, L. (1923/1958). *History of magic and experimental science.* Cambridge, England: Cambridge University Press.

Thornton, E. M. (1983). *Freud and cocaine.* London: Blond & Briggs.

Vernon, P. A. (Ed.) (1993). *Biological approaches to the study of human intelligence.* Norwood, NJ: Ablex.

Vernon, P. A. (Ed.) (1994). *The neuropsychology of individual differences.* New York: Academic Press.

Webster, C. (1982). *From Paracelsus to Newton.* Cambridge: Cambridge University Press.

Westfall, R. (1980). *Never at rest: A biography of Newton*. Cambridge: Cambridge University Press.

Yates, F. (1964). *Giordano Bruno and the Hermetic tradition*. Chicago: University of Chicago Press.

Yates, F. (1972). *The Rosicrucian enlightenment*. Routledge & Kegan Paul.

Zilbergeld, B. (1983). *The Shrinking of America*. Toronto: Little, Brown.

Zimmer, D. (1986). *Tiefenschwindel*. Hamburg: Rowohlt.

Zuckerman, M. (1991). *Psychobiology of personality*. Cambridge: Cambridge University Press.

Zwang, G. (1985). *La statue de Freud*. Paris: Laffont.

IV   THE SCIENCE OF THE MIND

16   Mind Sciences and the 21st Century

Robert L. Solso

The previous authors have presented an absorbing mélange of ideas about the future of mind sciences worthy of your careful reading. As provocative as these chapters are to current readers, one may speculate that they may be even more fascinating to readers throughout the 21st century.

In this final chapter I have the enviable responsibility of giving an overview of the book, identifying some common and distinctive themes, commenting on the contents, and adding a few words that express my own views on the science of the mind as it might be played out in the 21st century. While some readers may rush to read this chapter first (such is the impetuous temperament of our generation) hoping to find a "reader's digest" of the contents—a kind of *Cliff Notes* for *Mind and Brain Sciences in the 21st Century*—I recommend you read the original contents, which you hold in your hand. It is not modesty that motivates my recommendation, but the literary competence and intellectual quality of these essays is of such a nature that to deny yourself the pleasure and stimulation of reading the original works would be to miss the essence of this book.

This analysis is loosely organized around three hypotheses regarding the fate of future developments in mind sciences: the vector extrapolation hypothesis, the contrarian reaction, and the multiple influence model, which were introduced in the previous volume (Solso, 1995; See also Solso, 1996). Briefly, the vector extrapolation hypothesis (VEH) is based on the idea that once a trend, or vector, is reliably established; further developments are likely to continue. The accuracy of the predicted tendency of any VEH is contingent on the strength of the vector, the distance of the prediction into the future, and the perspicacity of the prophet. (The last is, admittedly, a vague concept whose validity may be established only after a predicted event has occurred or not occurred. For example, the validity of predicting that positron emission tomography research will yield secrets about the role of the hippocampus and memory in the next 10 years may be only measured, in fact, after 10 years.) The contrarian reaction (CR) is the notion that once a trend has been reliably identified, the future of that trend will be the reverse of the initial trend or in some meaningful way modified. The idea that PET research will uncover secrets about memory in the future, as mentioned above, might, in a contrarian's mind, be just the reverse. That is, the CR view would be that PET research would not continue to yield meaningful data on memory but, perhaps, become replaced by another, yet undiscovered, research instrument. Arrows shot into the air fall to earth, according to the CRers. The multiple influence model (MIM), on the other hand, purports to examine a wide range of critical variables, such as sociological, scientific, ethical, political, and natural variables, in predicting the eventual resolution of scientific expectations. Thus, an arrow shot into the air might continue to soar (VEH), fall to earth (CR), or wiggle-waggle (MIM).

The Most Humanly Important Topic of All: Consciousness

We begin with consciousness and the 21st century—a central topic during the beginning of the 20th century and one that continues to excite interest, debate, and experimentation during its final decade. When the followers of John B. Watson thought the topic had been discarded in the wastebin of nonobjective science (along with a dozen or more healthy ideas and special environments) consciousness again emerges not only as a meritorious object of experimental analysis but, in the mind of many cognitive scientists, and a whole host of splendidly idealistic metaphysicians, as *the* primary topic with which psychologists should be concerned. And lest current-day behaviorists become ill at the thought of Watson's will being undone, a careful reading of his classic 1913 article in *Psychological Review* (as pointed out by Richard Thompson; see chapter 3) shows that the first guru of behaviorism believed consciousness to be a phenomenon that cannot be measured directly, but indirectly, by measuring behavior, as, one might add, in implicit memory experiments, currently the rage in experimental psychology, as measured through priming techniques. By effectively banning research on consciousness, did post-Watsonian behaviorists misinterpret his words? This we do know: the study of consciousness by experimental psychologists was anathema throughout most of the 20th century.

Like Hydra, the multiheaded water serpent, when one head of consciousness was cut off two new ones appeared. Toward the end of the 20th century, experimental psychology is on the verge of hyperconsciousness. Endel Tulving pointed out there are over 10,000 entries related to consciousness in MEDLINE between 1970 and 1995 and 18,000 entries in PsycLIT between 1970 and 1995. As Tulving so aptly states, "The richness of the literature is largely attributable to the fact that just about anything that has something to do with the behavior of organisms and cognitive phenomena of human beings has been seen to be related to consciousness." Nevertheless, consciousness remains a slippery concept at the end of the 20th century.

Slippery or not, some of the leading scholars of the 20th century, Bernard Baars, Carl Sagan and Ann Druyan, Richard Thompson, Endel Tulving, Michael Posner and Daniel Levitin, and Karl Pribram agree that the topic is central to the understanding of psychology. Further, many believe that issues and ambiguities are likely to be cleared up in the next century. The trend, in VEH terms, seems to be on the ascendancy, and modern scholars (like their 19th-century counterparts) seem to believe that "truth" is just around the corner. Beyond that, the authors in this book differ markedly in the way they approach the problem and, as such, provide a microcosmic laboratory for the synoptic view of the state of psychology as we close the century.

Bernard Baars has spent much of his professional life studying consciousness, organizing conferences, editing papers, and conducting experiments on consciousness. Because people's "inner worlds" are personally important, so too, argues Baars, should our science focus on these matters. Furthermore, with the emergence of sophisticated brain imaging technology, precise experimental methods, and improved methods for modeling neural nets and cognitive architectures, the time to "turn the powerful lens of science inward" is at hand. Lest these technologies drive our research programs on consciousness, Baars opines that we need *think* about the topic with great clarity. The way he thinks about consciousness is as what he calls a "variable," in the same way that immediate memory, selective attention, and the like are variables. Solid progress toward understanding consciousness is just around the corner. While most reasonable scientists would find little to argue with in Baars's analysis, some are still troubled by the fact that finding reliable data on one's "inner" speech may still be an elusive experimental problem and subject to contamination because of unavoidable individual differences. But then, that is the challenge we face, not a poison pill to be swallowed. Science should never be content to solve only easy problems.

Baars approaches consciousness from the standpoint of scientific psychology in which technology and experimental design play a central role in achieving enlightenment on a topic he believes is central to our understanding of ourselves and others. At the same time, there is an unmistakable humanistic current that flows through this chapter in which consciousness is not only a "variable" but is sentient. It is *the* defining property of humankind.

In Carl Sagan and Ann Druyan's chapter, "What Thin Partitions . . . ," the grand idea of who we are is sought by examining the lives of other creatures. Consider the life of a humble moth, who repeatedly flies into a glass window never learning that some transparent objects are impenetrable. They never seem to learn, and for good neurological reasons. While even the highest forms of human life, heads of state, baseball players, movie actors, and esteemed professors, for example, have also been known to bash into glass doors, the latter group rarely repeat the blunder, at least not immediately, and also for good neurological reasons. The idea of "insects as robots" and "humans as smart robots" comes to mind and in the following passage by Sagan and Druyan the idea of comparative consciousness is addressed: "So here's a bejeweled insect, elegantly architectured, prancing among the dust grains in the noonday sun. Does it have any emotions, any consciousness? Or is it only a subtle robot made of organic matter, a carbon-based automaton packed with sensors and actuators, programs and subroutines, all ultimately manufactured according to the DNA instructions? . . . We might be willing to grant the proposition that insects are robots. . . ." Yet, if we see ourselves as others do (a tricky matter of extraconsciousness), then might we also conclude that humans behave mostly automatically? Mostly unconsciously? What are the differences between species? Such musings bring to mind Blake's contemplative poem that begins, "Tiger, Tiger, burning bright, in the forests of the night; What immortal hand or eye could frame thy fearful symmetry . . . " and ends, "Did He smile his work to see; Did He who made the lamb make thee?" Did the hand that created the insect create consciousness only in humans? If so, why?

From a discussion of the distinction between consciousness in humans and other animals we turn to Richard Thompson's thoughtful essay on "Will the Mind Become the Brain in the 21st Century?" Thompson, one of the world's leading neuroscientists, was hard iron forged in the crucible of the

"dustbowl of empiricism" at the University of Wisconsin by the hands of
Harry Harlow, Wulf Brogden, and David Grant, who were shaped in turn by
the hand of Watson. So it is consistent with his background that Thompson
would introduce behaviorism, the yoke cognitive psychologists thought they
had successfully disposed of several decades ago, by quoting Watson's surprisingly reasonable, albeit entirely internally consistent notion that phenomena
like "consciousness" and "mind" might be measurable even though, presently,
they can only be observed indirectly by (you guessed it) measuring *behavior.*

How might the "secret thoughts" of consciousness—such thoughts as
a young man or woman might have while on a first date—be behaviorally
measured outside of introspection, which when vocalized is "behavior?"
Thompson's view on the matter is that they might be measured by "recording
the electrical/mechanical activity of the vocal apparatus" which is a consequence of the neuronal process that "is" thoughts. Thompson expands the
range of behaviorism by pointing out that the "important advances made in
cognitive psychology are all due entirely to careful measures of behavior." And
who could argue with that point? How else could the inner workings of the
mind be observed? Yet, there is an inner voice in me that whispers, No one
can ever tell (or measure) your conscious thoughts, not even Alan Gevins's
home EEG machine. It would seem that Watsonian "behaviorism" and "cognitive psychologists" share some common features and, as Smith implies, during the innocent early days of cognitive psychology, measurements of memory
were based on performance, not the underlying neural function.

Thompson also deals with the theme of "thin partitions" in considering
consciousness and phylogenetic order. While many neuroscientists opine that
other primates and sea mammals have some degree of consciousness, it seems
to stretch the meaning of the term to ascribe consciousness to flies, worms, and
moths (see Sagan and Druyan): Perhaps birds do it, bees do it, and even educated fleas do it, but if they do, they do it considerably less.

Cognitive psychologists have devoted a remarkable amount of energy
and funds to the investigation of attention, a topic closely related to consciousness. Thompson recounts these studies and adds his own careful critique.
Finally, Thompson concludes his chapter by returning to his opening theme of
the measurement of behavior and concludes that mind and consciousness may
never be more directly measured than with behavioral (including verbal)
reports and sees in the future that "As we learn more about brain processes, the
links between patterns of brain activity and behavioral reports will grow even

closer, to the point where there is no longer any need to postulate intervening variables such as 'mind' or 'awareness'" and that these advances will come from the development of "artificial" minds and "the increasing characterization of brain substrates of verbal and other aspects of behavior."

There are few areas of cognitive psychology that have not been changed by Endel Tulving during the last part of this century. His influence has been so profound that he is a latter-day Hermann Ebbinghaus, William James, and (with this chapter) Henry James rolled into one person. Fortunately, for we readers of "FACT: The First Axiom of Consciousness and Thought," Tulving was visited by a person who was an emissary of a committee on brain-mind sciences from the year 2096 who allowed E. T. to read the compendium of the Condensed History (CH) of C-Sci or what 20th-century scientists might call Consciousness-Science. One trouble, however, was that E. T. could use only his memory to record the events from CH, which, although very good, is, nonetheless, fallible.

While the conventional wisdom throughout humankind suggests that consciousness is mostly a human attribute, E. T. found that throughout the 21st century even lifeless machines were "conscious"—an even more radical view than that proposed by Sagan and Druyan and Thompson (who implied that moths and other animals may possess this trait). Thin partitions, indeed! But then, in the next century, all terms related to consciousness, such as awareness, attention, and grespy, and even arousal and alertness were subsumed under the C label. And, as is the case with 20th-century psychology, scientists in the 21st century fell into two camps: those who chose to experience consciousness and write about it, eschewing data, tables, graphs, and measurements, and those who studied consciousness in the more traditional experimental tradition. The study of consciousness took a change of direction—a Significant Historical Happening (SHH)—with the virtually assembled international telecongress which convened in 2018. C seemed to hit the fan when delegates debated the topic of machine consciousness only to be "saved" by a scholar, whose initials are G.O.D., who through clever (if not totally precise) use of Aristotelian reasoning, arrived at the First Axiom of Consciousness and Thought (FACT), *viz.* "If a thing is not alive, it cannot be conscious, nor can it think." All people who are alive and conscious and thinking will be more alive, more conscious, and certainly thinking deeper after reading Tulving.

Looking at Brains in the 21st Century

Driven by the need to know and spectacular technological developments (e.g., PET, fMRI, and EEG), the study of the human brain during the closing moments of the 20th century has shown what has long been suspected about the brain and cognition: each cognitive act, from thinking about a chess solution, to reading, to doing mental arithmetic, to listening to music, to imagining a face, busies a distinctive network of the human brain. It is apparent to all brain scientists that imaging technology and cognitive science are just beginning to make inroads into the science of the mind (and the results, so far, are impressive). The next century will certainly see the arrow of imaging technology reach new heights with increasingly more powerful and precise techniques and the applications of those techniques will likely be compelling. In spite of what promises to be an illustrious chapter in the history of brain sciences, those who are doing the pioneering work in this exciting field as we close the 20th century seem to express the view that it's a good time to be alive and working on important issues.

The first chapter in this section, by Edward Smith, traces the emergence of cognitive psychology, its reaction against behaviorism, its initial aversion to neuroscience, and finally the wedding of cognitive science to the neurosciences. The convergence of these disciplines during the last few years of this century are due to three reasons, according to Smith: biologically oriented investigations can alter cognitive theories; neuroimaging techniques may provide more directly interpretable information than behavioral measures (see Thompson for a discussion of the utility and purpose of behavioral measures in psychology); and cognitive neuroscience may suggest new ways of organizing the field of cognition. These points are appropriately illustrated through an experiment conducted by Smith and his collaborator John Jonides in which PET imaging technology is applied to working memory. Here we see the use of neurotechnology to corroborate some ideas about the nature of memory which have been around for the past 100 years; namely, the idea of a dual-memory system as suggested by William James and which was behaviorally confirmed between 1950 and 1980 by experiments largely based on verbal material. Smith shows us some beautiful data and schematic drawings (based on PET images) in which a regional analysis of the results of cerebral blood flow show a type of two-component architecture in which there is strong evidence for verbal and spatial working memories. Thus, the way cognitive theorists parse the brain and mind might be based on spatial and object information and, in humans at least, around visual vs. verbal distinctions.

The feast cognition enjoyed throughout the latter part of this century may, according to Smith, be ready to be carved differently in the next century because of more exacting brain imaging techniques. We wish, along with Ed Smith, that the division of human cognition takes place at its joints.

Imagining the imaging of the future is the theme of the chapter by Michael Posner and Daniel Levitin who with unabashed exuberance declare that "it still amazes us that we can see pictures of our own minds at work." Similar remarks might have been made by Louis Daguerre (inventor of the daguerreotype) and Wilhelm Roentgen (discoverer of x-ray technology) during the last century and, unless I am terribly wrong, someone in the next century will also exclaim, "I see wonderful things!" It's a great time to be alive, but not the only great time in science.

Posner and Levitin's crystal ball is clear as they predict that new ways of imaging brain activity will be invented and even if no new methods come along, the current methods will show greater detail and spatial resolution. Lest the passion for making even finer-grained maps of the brain become the dominant force in neurocognition, we are reminded that we need to use this information to seek principles of how cognitive activity is distributed in brain regions. While speculating about the future of the neurosciences, Posner and Levitin also present a concise tutorial on the important findings made thus far in this exciting field.

Among the problems for future generations to ponder and decipher is how the anatomy, circuitry, and plasticity of the brain are involved in high-level cognitive tasks, such as chess playing, learning a second language, and relearning patterns of activities following a stroke or other closed head injury. The authors give us a glimpse of the future of the perennial problem child of the 20th century—consciousness—with the more philosophical than scientific question, Is consciousness a function or a process and Where is it? (We are teased with an answer to the second question and that is to look in the anterior cingulate, but also elsewhere.) In closing, Posner and Levitin express the hope that the work of future neuroscientists will break down the barriers that have separated those who study mental events and those who study physical events and that the increased knowledge of the brain's anatomy will lead to better models of the mind.

In his chapter, Alan Gevins asks, What to do with your own personal brain scanner? But before he gives his answers, you are required to learn something about his laboratory, the history of the EEG laboratory at Mayo Clinic, communicating with the dead, Zen philosophy, Beavis and Butthead ("Let's say you are working at a computer, writing a term paper analyzing Bevis and Butthead from the point of view of Bakunin's theory of anarchy." Sure.), and a few other serious topics. All of this is good reading and researchers, students, and even observers of the progress of science will understand and be amused by the history of brain research as seen through the uncorrected lenses of one who has fought the battles of budgets, bureaucracies, and bunglers.

There is another subtle message in this chapter which we have not seen since Hilgard's Foreword and that is Gevins's reminder that we have traveled far in the 20th century—as far as Dr. Yeager traveled with his wife in the Model T Ford (study figure 7.1, please). Retrospective observations (as made by Hilgard, Roediger, and Miller) serve as poignant reminders of how far science has come in just the last two thirds of the century. Had Gevins shown us the way people got around at the beginning of the century he would have depicted a horse and buggy. The century that brought advancements in transportation (which changed a civilization) also created a technological revolution which will probably (at least in my crystal ball) form the basis for a new wave of scientific achievements initiated not so much by model building and theoretical representations of observations but by the development, improvement, and invention of systems, equipment, and hardware and software that will allow us to run faster, jump higher, and cover more ground. I'm not too sure that we will understand all of what we see, however. (See closing remarks.)

Gevins sees the trend in computers and EEG machines (which is "just a computer with some wires touching the head and a little amplifier") continuing along the same line as in the past—"It's a sure bet that computers will continue to get smaller-faster-cheaper" (s-f-c) and that "traffic and parking in the city will get worse, that the stock market will go up and down and then up again, and that the length of skirts will increase and decrease." Things will change; some VEHs, some MIMs, and some Contrarian predictions may be found in his chapter. The bit about computers is (perhaps) the most important for Gevins's work with EEG machines. Like computers, which are integral components of EEG machines, brainwave machines will get s-f-c. In a short time, with miniaturization of such devices, they will be unobtrusively built into a baseball cap with the electrical activity of the brain being transmitted by telemetry to some central computing system—a kind of one-way modem in which brain activities are sent through cyberspace. Are such devices practical? You bet! And Gevins presents eight things you can do with your own Personal Brain Scanner (PBS). Read the chapter; buy the machine; get a dorky baseball hat; and get a life.

Karl Pribram brings a unique perspective to this section in the respect that his basic education is in medicine (he received an M. D. degree from the University of Chicago). For most of his professional life he has actively pursued topics such as brain and behavioral research, always with a strong dose of philosophy mixed in. His writings have combined technically sophisticated ideas with deeper inquiries as to the profound meaning of his ideas. Readers of his chapter "The Deep and Surface Structure of Memory and Conscious Learning: Toward a 21st Century Model" will not be disappointed as this renowned brain scientist presents an intellectual tour de force in which two worlds of memory are considered. The theme of this chapter is based on "deep and surface"[1] structures of memory and conscious learning. (Once again, as psychologists and neuroscientists approach the close of this century, talk of consciousness, once an imprecation to serious behavioral psychologists, resurfaces.) At a fundamental level, the deep structure of memory is posited to be located in the connective web of brain tissue (what Pribram identifies as the "synapotodendritic" level of processing) while the surface structure involves specific neural circuits implicated in encoding and decoding experiences, the coding of experienced episodes of events, and the organization of skills and practice, or what could be called the what, when and whence, and how of experience. As one glides through this carefully crafted chapter, the sheer elegance of words, images, and biochemical processes mingle freely with a grand theory of memory and consciousness that considers both the experiential level and the molecular level, where memories and consciousness reside, not sequestered in some inscrutable structure, but as clearly identifiable matters of physics laid out in graceful symmetry. While some readers may want to fetch their reference book on brain sciences, the author makes it all worthwhile and does include brief tutorials throughout the chapter for those who have forgotten what axonic depolarization at the presynaptic site might look like.

To simplify some of the notions mentioned above (and cast them in another context), it seems that Karl Pribram's theories and expectations for the future of brain sciences represent a strong VEH in the respect that we will probe more deeply into the brain in pursuit of both where and how memories are stored at a microscopic level and, perhaps more important, will understand how these fundamental synaptic processes and structures function as we go through life perceiving, remembering, and acting on environmental signals.

If you always wanted to know what brains were for but were too bashful to ask, then the chapter by Michael Gazzaniga is not to be overlooked. Sex. That is the simple purpose of the brain. The fact that brains do other things besides enjoy reproductive success is sometimes interpreted as the purpose of brains and is, alas, just an epiphenomenon. While some may be ecstatic over this revelation, others may be disappointed that their oeuvre has been spent chasing shadows. While Pribram borrows Chomsky's title, Gazzaniga borrows his linguistic theory as an example of a complex variant interpretation of a more or less simple biological phenomenon. From language development, to drug abuse, to hemispheric processes, to normal memory functioning, to the neuron as a computational unit, to ants building huge mounds in the tropics (thin partitions?), to brain-imaging techniques, the reader is taken through an Indiana Jones roller-coaster of imaginative ideas, flowing rhetoric, and serious speculation on the meaning of brain sciences.

The future of these investigations seems to be on two levels—one technical and the other philosophical. Here Gazzaniga and Pribram, both eminent brain scientists, seems to share the same concern that though technical knowledge will likely continue to vector deeper and deeper into the cortex and surrounding areas—like astronomers of the future, we will see deeper and clearer—still, questions of much more profound interest disturb thinking scholars in the remaining seconds of this millennium. Some of those questions are, curiously, questions raised toward the end of the last century by Charles Darwin (see *Origin of Species*, 1859, and *Descent of Man*, 1871) in considering the way the brain responds to environmental changes. Perhaps even philosophy and the deep thinking of scientists and artists will be identified. Can change be far behind?

Psychology ±100 Years

The third section deals with conventional topics of standard psychology as practiced throughout the 20th century, *viz.* memory, psychological theory, categorization, psychological organizations, and empirical methodology in psychology, by the leading authorities in these areas: Henry Roediger, George Sperling, Gay Snodgrass, Jerry Kagan, Neal Miller, and Hans Eysenck.

The section begins with an engaging chapter by Henry L. Roediger III, a leading contemporary specialist in the field of memory and a student of Endel Tulving. Roediger turns the table on the notion of predicting the future by *starting* 1000 years ago—testing the hypothesis that hindsight is 20/20—and working forward to today. As Roddy so effectively points out, the prediction game as practiced by our intellectual ancestors has been played poorly. Even if we turn the clock back a quarter century, to roughly 1975, when professor Roediger (and several of the current writers and the editor) were beginning their careers, the burning issues in memory laboratories were sensory memories (iconic "memory"; see George Sperling), imagery (see Bower, *The Science of the Mind: 2001 and Beyond*), dualistic memory, serial recall (see Murdock, *The Science of the Mind: 2001 and Beyond*), transfer effects, retrieval effects (see Tulving) with structural knowledge, attention (see Posner), and short-term memory recognition (à la The Sternberg Paradigm) just coming into focus. All of these topics enjoyed about 15 years of fame, which is much more than Andy Warhol allocated, but nevertheless have faded, as "hot" topics, like the memory of an old stroll through the park. What Roediger finds interesting is the rise of topics we never heard of, or imagined, when we began our careers. Such things as the levels-of-processing approach to memory, the rise of neuroscientific studies, implicit memory research, and metacognition. And, if we follow the vector of past histories (a VEH), we might assume that these topics, so burning in today's laboratories, will become passé with the next generation. Perhaps, but some topics, because they are driven by inevitable technological improvements, seen to have a long run ahead, such as neurological imaging methodology which is certain to give us fresh information as to how the brain works and processes information as well as lead to new theories of the mind.

Roediger ends his chapter with 11 (more or less specific) predictions about the future of psychology, including the first (Contrarian) prediction that "most of the specific predictions in this volume will be wrong," in which "most" is operationalized as "80%." A one-in-five hit rate seems awfully low, but then, perhaps, one of the misses may be that prognostication. Let's read Professor Roediger's time capsule in 2025 (should we all live so long.)

Gay Snodgrass thinks that we might not only live so long but also might be so ravished by Alzheimer's dementia that the significance of Roediger's prediction will fall on mindless creatures. Professor Snodgrass, thinly disguised as Joy Smoothlawn, gives an address in the year 2050 (25 years after we reread Roediger) and gives an impressive overview of 20th-century memory topics, including dualistic models, short-term memory capacity (à la George Miller), picture and visual memory (à la Paivio, Sperling, and Snodgrass), semantic memory (Collins and Loftus), mental rotation (see Shepard, *The Science of the Mind: 2001 and Beyond*), "memory" as event information and meaning information (see Tulving), implicit and explicit memory (à la Squire), "connectionism" (Rumelhart and McClelland), and "levels of processing" (à la Craik), as well as other topics. Now, if your memory is still intact, you will recognize that her list is similar to the one mentioned in the previous chapter. At least, contemporary memory experts agree on their past, if not their future.

The future of memory research, as seen by Snodgrass, is a Contrarian's view. The halcyon days of "rich" government grants for basic scientific research will have dried up, leaving a dusty trail for scientist to trod. Many cognitive scientists may be unemployed and yet there will be an increased need for the services of memory experts, especially in evaluating memory abilities and providing programs for the enhancement of memory among the increased number of elderly people (including those of us who live to 2050). We are reminded that a logical consequence (a VEH) of extended lives, overpopulation, and limited resources is a presuicide agreement in which cogent people resolve that if their mental and physical condition deteriorates beyond a certain level, that they finally will be relieved of their pain and suffering—a type of proactive "living will" common today. Professor Snodgrass has taken an important theme and used it as a vehicle for understanding memory research, as well as the personal and social problems that all of us must ultimately face.

Professor Jerome Kagan's chapter on the future of psychological categories begins with "Anyone reading the most respected psychological texts written 100 years ago would realize that accurate prediction of the future is impossible ... " Some might remark (after reading Roediger's chapter) that that statement is "like déjà vu all over again." Kagan goes on to explain, however, that it is impossible to predict the future because "even the most prescient prophets cannot anticipate the new machines, historical conditions, and theoretical conceptions that are presently unformed." And how true that observation is: Freud, Jung, Titchener, Wundt, and a dozen other characters could not have foreseen the invention of fMRI, PET scans, the transistor, or high-speed personal computers—all of which have not only changed our lives in profound ways but also the way we view the mind. If Kagan's optimism about future developments is correct, and the trend of technology continues to ascend, then future generations are in for a world much different from ours.

Only three main predictions are made (with many subcomponets embedded in each): technical discoveries will be made that will permit psychologists to study phenomena more precisely; "infant determinism" (the immutable formation of personality during a child's early years) will end; and advances in neurosciences and developmental psychology will allow for more discrete and different patterns of classification of psychological phenomena.

Kagan makes a critical observation many overlook: the way the mind organizes information about itself largely determines human psychology. This somewhat narcissistic trait is uniquely characteristic of the human species—no other animal ponders the question of "Little lamb who made thee?" What other creature contemplates questions of self-identity, the source of knowledge, and teleological questions which are simply summed in the basic questions of Who am I? Where did I come from? and What is my destiny? Could it be that in Kagan's chapter profound answers are provided? What is splendidly sagacious in this brief essay is that one gets the sense that the truth about the meaning of life is as much in the journey as in the attainment. Is it better to search than to find? Deep questions are riddles not to be answered but to be examined and this chapter provides a rich backdrop for the understanding of the technical developments that will undeniably follow.

As "our" century is about to end, it is a good time to look at the goal of theories in experimental psychology, which is the theme of the chapter by George Sperling. The development of psychological theories in psychology was frequently a matter of model building, itself based on classical physics. Yet, psychology and biology are fundamentally different from theoretical physics and those differences are clearly illustrated in this chapter. Throughout our century, psychologists have tried earnestly to fashion theories or models of behavior that will precisely account for even simple behavioral principles, such as a theory of reinforcement which will reliably account for the relationship between action and consequence. However, as one part of the puzzle is described by the model, other features appear which require modification, expansion, and revision of a once simple, elegant, and precise model.

Are theories in psychology desirable or even necessary? As we opened the century there was a profusion of theories introduced by mentalists who were rebuffed by the "antitheorists;" notably such characters as Watson and B. F. Skinner and the "dustbowl empiricists"[2] who believe that psychological science progresses without any theories at all or, in the case of dustbowl empiricism, only after exhaustive testing of hypotheses. Sperling points out that sometimes it is impossible to enumerate all of the events, such as all of the stimulus-response connections, that make up simple actions. We must rely on theories to reduce the input load. The future of scientific discoveries in psychology is something like the building of a great wall, such as the Great Wall of China, according to Sperling. Here, lasting scientific contributions are like the addition of one stone to the structure and the best theory at a given level of complexity is such a block because it cannot be improved. May all theories of psychology in the 21st century achieve such immortality.

The final two chapters in this section are written by two of the best-know psychologists of the 20th century—Neal E. Miller and Hans J. Eysenck.

Miller suggests that looking back over the growth of psychological organizations, one could not have foreseen the changes we have undergone in the 20th century. So, reasons Miller, we should be vigilant in changing and dealing with unexpected opportunities that new situations afford. He cites one example of the situation that arose during World War II in which psychologists were recruited from their universities to develop a battery of classification tests. (The classification of human attributes, as noted by both Miller and Kagan, is a fundamental aspect of human psychology as practiced during the 20th century and, for Kagan, connotes deeper philosophical implications for the human species.) Miller reminds us that scientific psychology developed during our current century and that an understanding of the fundamental principles and basic facts of psychology is a desirable basis for future developments. We are left with the challenge to learn something entirely new as a preparation for "unexpected opportunities."

A fitting conclusion to this section and the book is found in Eysenck's "The Future of Psychology." Psychology is treated as a science, as most contemporary scholars would like to believe, and cast in the larger framework of the scientific revolution which swept through the academies of the 17th century, continuing until today. This is a stirring chapter both from the standpoint of its eloquence and Eysenck's penetrating critique of the odious pressures within psychology that have detracted us from the scientific study of the human species. Science, including the Johnny-come-lately psychology, is in a life-and-death battle with quackery and charlatans. As astronomy fought astrology, and chemistry, alchemy, psychology has a whole closet full of demons to be exorcised, not the least of which are Freudian psychoanalysis and behaviorism, against which Professor Eysenck has waged a lifelong campaign.

The main message here is that psychoanalytic theory, which was a dominant theory of the mind during the early part of the 20th century and still attracts numerous followers (see Kosslyn's chapter "Freud Returns?" in the first volume of this series), fails when one tries to find experimental evidence for its various components. Eysenck even contends that those published experiments that verify Freudian theories are flawed. Personality theories, as well as other theories in psychology, must be verified empirically through sound, data-based experimentation which leads to reproducible findings and justifiable conclusions. The determinants of behavior are multiple and the relative balance of causes is a vexing scientific problem. Eysenck seems to feel, however, that psychology, including scientific psychology, has underestimated the importance of biological factors involved in its formulas.

The Future of Mind Sciences

Many authors present a consistent view of the history of 20th-century psychology—important characters, techniques, findings, experiments, and even the interpretation of results. Also, there are many similar predictions in the preceding chapters. The agreement among many authors as to the significance of historical issues, especially during the past century, which has seen bitter debate over such topics as psychoanalysis, behaviorism, internal representations, imagery, and consciousness, to name but a few items, may seem odd. Lest the reader deep into the next century believe that these issues do not still arouse sharp debate among psychologists as we close this century, I would point out that the contributing authors do not represent a stratified sample of psychologists, but a selected group who (more or less) agree on the basic tenets of experimental psychology. However, even within this (more or less) homogeneous group we find disagreements regarding such themes as behaviorism, which many cognitive psychologists thought was dead and buried and chose to simply disregard. Consider the positions of Thompson and Roediger who envision a return to "behaviorism." And the position of Eysenck and, to some degree, Baars, who believe the dragon has not yet been slain. I believe it is important to put a fine point on these arguments. The reason modern cognitive scientists rejected behaviorism was not on the basis of the measurement of behavior, or the utility of shaping behavior, or even the formation of societies based on positive reinforcement techniques, but on the political clout—dare I call it "mind control"—exercised by behaviorists toward scientists who elected to study the things the brain does, such as memory, imagery, consciousness, and so on. A pretty good science can be built on these topics using overt, objective measures of behavior. See George Sperling's chapter for an analysis of psychological theories vis-à-vis behaviorism. The fine point is that, while the study of behavior will (out of necessity) be with us for the foreseeable future, the narrow version of "Behaviorism" (the dogma) will not return.

There is one theme that runs throughout almost every chapter in this book and that is, we will know more about the mind/brain in the next century than we do now. Arguably, each century since the Renaissance has seen progress in scientific knowledge and with exciting new tools (high-speed computers with awesome memories, PET, fMRI, EEG, and other equipment in the pipeline) we should be able to see farther, clearer, and wider. Will we know what we see? A few of the authors address this deeper question, including Baars, Pribram, Gazzaniga, and Sperling, but even these authors are more or less inattentive to the multiple influence of the probable historical consequences of present actions (a MIM).

In general, the contributors to this volume do not discuss the impact of extrascientific vectors on the future of mind sciences—an understandable omission, as the authors were instructed to write on the topic of mind sciences, not the effect of the environment on mind sciences. However, as no man is an island, no science happens in a vacuum. The fact that many authors disregard the impact of other ingredients in their views of the future of psychology may be because many Western scientists[3] have lived in nonthreatening surroundings in which stable economic and political circumstances are assumed. Yet, the reasonably stable platform enjoyed through most of this century (and others) could fall apart abruptly with cataclysmic effects on scientific activity. Consider the doomsday list[4]: the creation of a pernicious virus impervious to antidotes; life extension to an average age of 120 (see Snodgrass); irreparable damage to the atmosphere (today's headline warns that Microscopic Particles of Pollution May Cause 64,000 Deaths in 1996, and 1995 was the warmest year on record); depletion of the earth's essential natural resources; terrorism and social chaos; a decomposition of the natural chain of life (one fifth of freshwater fish species have become extinct or endangered in recent years); wars; nuclear bomb proliferation and use; a growing number of disenfranchised people (27.4 million people were considered "refugees" at the beginning of 1995), and unchecked population growth—the world's population is 5.7 billion (in 1995, an increase of 87 million over the previous year). Furthermore, social progress (as conventionally defined) has had the effect of removing people from their environment to the point where counterfeit experiences are prized more than natural ones.[5] The sad list is much longer.[6] The idea is that scientific "progress" is a fragile flower whose growth rests as much on forces outside of itself as within itself.

The future of the science of the mind and other sciences (and all sorts of scholarship) will be influenced greatly by what I believe will be a fundamental change in the way scholarship will be performed as well as its application. The reformation of scientific activities will transfigure science so markedly that future historians will call it a "paradigm shift." This "Third Millennium Science" will usher in radical new techniques, operation modes, and communication networks, which will change the way we see ourselves and the universe, and have profound social and environmental impact. This envisioned paradigm change will (must) include forces from several different areas (MIM): the spread of information through worldwide networks which will allow all scientists working on common problems to be in contact with one another and the vast collection of relevant data (a related effect is that the location of laboratories and workstations will change, affecting city and community planning in profound ways); the invention and use of elegant techniques (imaging techniques and chemical techniques) for studying the brain will lead to better measurements and more reliable conclusions; the development of global governance, which will affect all scientific and cultural activities; and issues related to the environment and population. Other forces that will contribute to a paradigm shift include scientific and artistic validation by nonhuman objective techniques; genetic engineering in which human neurology and body functioning are fundamentally changed; the development of organic computers that interface with human brains; and contact with extraterrestrials.

I start with a nondeterministic assumption. The future of mind sciences is to be done by us. Of course, some may be passive observers and let the future happen with little advance planning, and others may consider the multiple forces that shape a science, a civilization. However, because it is reasonable to believe that we can design the future (or more specifically the potential futures), I predict that serious planning for the future will become a major new area of scholarship. Precious little is known of this field, which has been plagued with fortune tellers, palm readers, and soothsayers. The science of forecasting is a serious affair and it is likely (at least in my view) that it will become an enterprise in and of itself, not because of its predictive nature, but because of its planning nature. Can scientists do this, or is it the nature of science to do one experiment based on previous work and to meander through the stars without compass or course?

Magnificent things in the future aside, we will still be trying to understand it all with a brain born and bred in the Pleistocene whose function is to mate, eat, and smell the roses. Will we be able to comprehend what we have wrought, or will we revert to the pursuit of more bucolic pleasures?

As the arrows glide along their inquisitive paths, we know not their final destination. However, if only a few of these predictions are realized, the 21st century will appear on the surface to be profoundly different from the one we are about to depart but basic human psychology will be essentially the same.

Notes

1. Pribram borrows the terms "deep" and "surface" from Noam Chomsky, but his theory bears little in common with linguistic theory.

2. Sperling uses the term "dustbowl empiricism," which most people associate with Midwestern schools of psychology who, in the 1940s and 1950s, insisted on hard data and clear empirical measures of psychological phenomena. It is noted that Richard Thompson calls it the "dustbowl *of* empiricism" and mentions in his chapter that Harry Harlow had that inscribed on a chamber pot in his office.

3. Here I refer to Western scientists in general, not contributing authors to this book, some of whom have suffered through violent social upheaval, including wars.

4. Data based on *Vital Signs: 1996* by Lester R. Brown. Washington DC: Worldwatch Institute.

5. I am both amused and upset when I see a huge stretch limousine barreling along the roadway next to beautiful Lake Tahoe with a television set turned on for its passengers.

6. See Solso (1995) for more on this topic.

References

Solso, R. L. (1995). Turning the corner. In R. L. Solso & D. W. Massaro (Eds.) *The Science of the Mind: 2001 and Beyond* (pp. 3–16). New York: Oxford.

Solso, R. L. (1996). Psychology in the 21st century: Beyond the 6th decimal point. *Russian Journal of Psychology*,

About the Authors

Bernard J. Baars received his Ph.D. in Cognitive Psychology from UCLA in 1977. Since then he has held research positions at the University of California at San Diego, State University of New York, the University of California at San Francisco, and the Wright Institute, where he has worked since 1986. He is Founding President of the Association for Scientific Study of Consciousness and is Founding Co-Editor of *Consciousness and Cognition: An International Journal*. Dr. Baars is the author of *Consciousness Discovered: A Walk Through the Theater of the Mind* as well as numerous book chapters and journal articles relating to consciousness and cognition.

Hans J. Eysenck moved from Berlin to England in 1934 in order to escape the Hitler regime. From 1942–45 he was Experimental Psychologist at the Mill Hill Emergency Hospital. In 1946 he founded and became Director of the Department of Psychology in the newly formed Institute of Psychiatry and was Professor of Psychology in the University of London until his retirement in 1983. He is founder and editor of the journal *Personality and Individual Differences*, and founder and past editor of *Behaviour and Research Therapy*. Dr. Eysenck is now Professor Emeritus of Psychology and currently is actively participating in research into personality and individual differences, the psychophysiology of intelligence, and the genetics of personality and intelligence, as well as studying psychosocial factors in the prevention of cancer and coronary heart disease. He was awarded the Distinguished Scientist Award of the American Psychological Association in 1988 and became a William James Fellow of the American Psychological Society in 1994. He is the author of 77 books and has written or contributed to over 1,050 scientific papers.

Michael S. Gazzaniga earned his Ph.D. in psychobiology from the California Institute of Technology in 1964. He has been a professor at the University of California at Santa Barbara, New York University Graduate School, the State University of New York, Cornell University Medical College, the University of California at Davis and Dartmouth Medical School. He is Fellow of the American Association for the Advancement of Science (1980), the American Neurological Association (1981), the Society of Experimental Psychologists (1982), and the American Psychological Association (1982). He is Editor-in-Chief of the *Journal of Cognitive Neuroscience*, Associate Editor of *Cerebral Cortex*, and edited *The Cognitive Neurosciences*. Dr. Gazzaniga, as much as any other researcher, has helped to bring together the research of neurology and psychology, blazing the path for cognitive neuroscience in the 21st century.

Alan Gevins received a B.S. from the Massachusetts Institute of Technology in 1967 and qualified for a Ph.D. in Cognitive Science from the California Institute of Asian Studies in 1971. In 1972, he joined the EEG Laboratory of the Langley Porter Neuropsychiatric Institute at the University of California School of Medicine in San

Francisco as a Senior Operations Research Analyst and became Director of the laboratory in 1974. He is the author of more than 100 scientific publications and 11 patents and is internationally known for both engineering research in neuroelectric signal processing and for basic science studies of human cognitive brain function. His research is currently supported by grants from the National Institute of Mental Health, the Air Force Office of Scientific Research, NASA, the Air Force Armstrong Laboratory, the National Institute of Neurological Diseases and Strokes, the National Science Foundation, the National Institute of Occupational Health and Safety, and the National Institute of Alcohol and Alcohol Abuse.

Ernest R. Hilgard began an unprecedented career in psychology following his Ph.D. from Yale University in 1930. Three years later he accepted a position at Stanford, where he has spent the rest of his career. He is perhaps best known for his work at the Laboratory of Hypnosis Research at Stanford, where he served as Director from 1957 to 1979. In addition to serving as President of the American Psychological Association (APA), Dr. Hilgard is a member of the National Academies of Education and Sciences. His numerous awards include the Warren Medal in Experimental Psychology, the APA's Distinguished Scientific Contribution Award, and the APA Certificate for Distinguished Lifetime Contributions to Psychology. His classic textbooks include *Conditioning and Learning*, *Theories of Learning*, and *Introduction to Psychology*. In addition to his distinguished career in academia, Dr. Hilgard has a remarkable public service record which includes a U.S. Education Mission to Japan; a Consultant on Education to James B. Conant, West Berlin; and a Consultant on Education to Hebrew University, Jerusalem.

Jerome Kagan received his Ph.D. in Psychology from Yale University in 1954. Since then, he has held the position of Instructor in Psychology at The Ohio State University, Senior Research Associate and Chairman of the Department of Psychology at the Fels Research Institute, and Professor of Psychology at Harvard University (where he has remained since 1964). He is Fellow of the American Association for the Advancement of Science and the American Academy of Arts and Sciences; a recipient of the Distinguished Scientist Award of the Society for Research in Child Development, the William James Award and G. Stanley Hall Award of the American Psychological Association, and the Distinguished Scientist Award of the American Psychological Society; and is Head of Section J of the American Association for the Advancement of Science. His hundreds of publications, including contributions to 12 textbooks, deal primarily with his multifaceted approach to developmental psychology.

Daniel J. Levitin is currently working as a graduate student with Michael Posner at the University of Oregon, with a Ph.D. expected in 1996. Mr. Levitin has published extensively in the fields of music and sound engineering and has produced a number of award-winning musical pieces. His research in cognitive psychology includes work on memory for music and its evolutionary consequences.

Neal E. Miller has had a long and distinguished career in psychology, beginning with his Masters Degree from Stanford and Ph.D. from Yale in 1935. After 30 years of teaching and research at Yale, where he was James Rowland Angell Professor of Psychology, he moved to Rockefeller University, where he is emeritus professor. Dr. Miller was awarded the Citation for Outstanding Lifetime Contribution to Psychology as well as the National Medal of Science. He has served as President of the American Psychological Association, the Society for Neuroscience, and the Academy of Behavioral Medicine Research, and is a member of the National Academy of Science. He is the recipient of numerous honorary degrees from the University of Pennsylvania and the University of Michigan as well as an honorary degree in celebration of the 500th anniversary of the University of Uppsala, Sweden.

With nearly 200 publications in the past 35 years, **Michael I. Posner** has been one of the more prolific researchers in the field of cognitive science. Along with his Ph.D. in psychology from the University of Michigan, Dr. Posner's strong background in the natural sciences (he has a bachelor's degree in physics) has made him a perfect candidate to help bridge the narrowing gap between neuroscience and psychology. He is perhaps most noted for his seminal work in attention and cognitive psychology and most recently with PET scan research, particularly in isolating the neurological bases of attention. He currently is Professor of Psychology at the University of Oregon, where he has worked since 1965. Professor Posner is the recipient of numerous awards including the Ersted Award for distinguished teaching and the APA Distinguished Scientific Contribution Award; he was elected to membership in the National Academy of Sciences and a Fellow in the American Academy of Arts and Sciences. He recently was acknowledged as Scientist of the Year from the Oregon Academy of Sciences (1995).

Karl H. Pribram received both his B.S. and M.D. degrees at the University of Chicago and went on to become certified in the specialties of neurological surgery and behavioral psychotherapy. Over the past three decades Dr. Pribram has devoted himself to brain/behavioral research at the Yerkes Laboratories of Primate Biology while Karl Lashley was Director; at Yale University where he taught neurophysiology and physiological psychology; and for 30 years at Stanford University, where he received a lifetime research career award from the National Institute of Health as Professor of Neuroscience in the departments of psychology and of psychiatry and behavioral sciences. In 1958 Professor Pribram co-wrote *Plans and the Structure of Behavior* with George Miller and Eugene Galanter, which was immediately recognized as an outstanding work that changed the direction of psychology. Upon becoming Emeritus at Stanford, Dr. Pribram accepted the position of James P. and Anna King Distinguished Professor at Radford University, where he is supported by the Virginia Commonwealth Eminent Scholar Program. In 1992, he received an honorary doctorate in psychology from the University of Montreal. Much of Dr. Pribram's current work involves gathering, analyzing, and reporting research results and writing reviews aimed at making these results relevant to mind/brain issues.

After earning a Ph.D. in psychology from Yale in 1973. **Henry L. Roediger III** began a 15-year teaching and research appointment at Purdue University. In 1988 he accepted the position of Lynette S. Autrey Professor of Psychology at Rice University, where he has since remained until recently accepting a position at Washington University in St. Louis. Dr. Roediger's honors include Fellow of the American Association for the Advancement of Science, the American Psychological Association, the American Psychological Society, and the Canadian Psychological Association, and a Guggenheim Fellowship for 1994–95. He was Chair of the Governing Board of the Psychonomic Society from 1989 to 1990 and was elected President of the Midwestern Psychological Association for 1992–93. He has, and currently holds, editorial positions for numerous psychological journals and references including the *Psychonomic Bulletin & Review*, the *Journal of Experimental Psychology: Learning, Memory, and Cognition*, and the *Encyclopedia of Psychology*. Dr. Roediger is known primarily for his research in many aspects of memory, including his noted recent work in the area of false memories.

Carl Sagan began his role in the American space program in the 1950s, when he served as consultant to NASA for a number of projects. He has since conducted seminal research in many areas of biology and astronomy. Through his work with numerous interest groups, astronomical societies, and journals, he has, perhaps more than anyone else of his time, helped to stimulate general interest in cosmology. His many awards and accolades include the NASA Medal for Exceptional Scientific Achievement and Distinguished Public Service, the NASA Apollo Achievement Award, the Public Welfare Medal (the highest award of the National Academy of Sciences), and a Pulitzer Prize for *Cosmos*, which became the most widely distributed science book published in the English language. He co-produced and co-wrote the Warner Brothers movie *Contact*, based on his novel.

Ann Druyan is an author, lecturer, and television producer whose work is largely concerned with the influence of science and technology on our civilization. Along with her husband, Carl Sagan, she co-wrote the television series COSMOS, and produced its updated and reformatted version. She is also co-writer and co-producer of *Contact*, the forthcoming film. Ms. Druyan is the author or co-author of several books, including *Comet*, which was on the *New York Times* best seller list for two months, and *Shadows of Forgotten Ancestors*. She is currently actively involved in a growing movement to inform and unite the world's political, scientific, and religious leaders in an effort to preserve the environment.

Edward E. Smith received his Ph.D. in Experimental Psychology from the University of Michigan in 1966. He has held teaching positions at the University of Wisconsin, Stanford University, Rockefeller University, Massachusetts Institute of Technology, and is currently Director of the Cognitive Science and Cognitive Neuroscience Program at the University of Michigan. Dr. Smith is member of the National Academy of Sciences, a Fellow of both the American Psychological Association and the American Psychological Society as well as a Guggenheim Fellow in 1992–93 and has served on the editorial board of nearly every major journal in cognitive psychology. Much of his recent research has been in the area of concept formation and categorization, although he has also worked extensively in the areas of induction and reasoning, organizational retrieval processes in memory, and the neuropsychology of memory.

Dr. Smith received a Guggenheim Fellowship, a member of the Society of Experimental Psychologists, and was elected into the American Academy of Arts and Sciences. Recently he has received the Distinguished Faculty Achievement Award from the University of Michigan.

After receiving her Ph.D. from the University of Pennsylvania, **J. Gay Snodgrass** began what has become a long and distinguished tenure at New York University. She is currently a Fellow of both the American Psychological Association and the American Psychological Society and is Director of the MA Program in Psychology at New York University. She has served as Consulting Editor for the *Journal of Experimental Psychology: General, Memory and Cognition*, and the *Journal of Psycholinguistic Research* and many other publications. Her research spans many key areas of cognitive psychology, including memory storage and retrieval, pattern recognition, and category formation.

Professor Snodgrass is the recipient of numerous awards and grants throughout her distinguished career including the World Who's Who of Women, Who's Who in Science and Engineering, and The International Authors and Writers Who's Who.

Robert L. Solso is the editor of "The Science of the Mind" series, a researcher, writer, and faculty member at the University of Nevada, Reno. After earning his doctorate from St. Louis University he taught at Loyola University of Chicago and then completed postdoctoral studies at Stanford University where he has taught on several occasions. In 1981 he was invited to Oxford University where he studied with the late Donald Broadbent. Dr. Solso has been interested in international psychology and is a board member of the European Society for the Study of Cognitive Systems. He was a senior Fulbright lecturer at Moscow State University and a visiting scholar at the Institute of Psychology in Moscow through support of the National Academy of Sciences. He has been a visiting scientist at the Institute of Perception in Eindhoven, The Netherlands. Dr. Solso is currently the president of the Western Psychological Association and Fellow in APS and APA. He is the author of *Cognitive Psychology*, *Cognition and the Visual Arts*, and editor of *The Science of the Mind: 2001 and Beyond* with Dominic Massaro.

George Sperling began what was to be a brilliant career by earning his Ph.D. at Harvard. Upon its publication in *Psychological Monographs*, his dissertation on the information available in brief visual presentations was recognized immediately as an important work. The phenomenon investigated, dubbed "iconic memory" by Ulric Neisser, not only was a new idea in cognitive psychology but also formed the basis for the development of cognitive psychology and information processing models that followed.

Sperling spent most of his career at New York University, where he continued to develop theories in visual cognition, mathematical models, and perception. He recently moved to the University of California, Irvine, where he continues to head a very active laboratory. Among his many awards is membership in the National Academy of Sciences and the Award for Distinguished Scientific Contributions from the American Psychological Association (1988).

Richard F. Thompson is Keck Professor of Psychology and Biological Sciences and Director of the Program in Neural, Informational and Behavioral Sciences at the University of Southern California. Prior to this he has held positions at Stanford University, where he served as Chair of the Human Biology Program from 1980 to 1985, the University of California at Irvine, Harvard University, and the University of Oregon Medical School. He received his Ph.D. in psychobiology at the University of Wisconsin. His area of research and scholarly interest is the broad field of psychobiology with a focus on the neurobiological substrates of learning and memory. He has written several texts, edited several books and published over 300 research papers. Dr. Thompson's honors include the Howard Crosby Warren Medal of the Society of Experimental Psychologists and the Distinguished Scientific Contribution Award of the American Psychological Association. He was elected Chair of the Psychonomic Society, President of Division 6 of the American Psychological Association, Chair of the Psychology Section (Section 52) of the Nat-ional Academy of Sciences, Chair of the Psychology Section (Section J) of the American Association for the Advancement of Science, and, recently, President of the Western Psychology Association and President of the American Psychological Society. Among his many editorial positions, he has served as Chief Editor of the journals *Physiological Psychology* and *Journal of Comparative and Physiological Psychology* and Chief Editor (and founder) of the journal *Behavioral Neurosciences* (1983–90).

Endel Tulving holds the Tanenbaum Chair in Cognitive Neuroscience at Rotman Research Institute of Baycrest Centre, University of Toronto, and is also a Distinguished Research Professor in Neuroscience and a Distinguished Professor of Psychology at University of California in Davis. He was born in Estonia in 1927 and came to Canada in 1949. He did his undergraduate work at the University of Toronto; his Ph.D. is from Harvard. He has studied human memory all of his professional life. He dared to use the word "consciousness" in writing about memory for the first time in 1970, and is now boldly predicting a bright future for "autonoesis," a higher form of consciousness that he has been writing about since 1985.

Professor Tulving's seminal work in memory and cognitive psychology has influenced nearly every corner of the field, and his recent work in neurocognition has opened up new vistas of research and the application of theoretical psychology to neurological studies of brain sciences. He has also had a significant effect through his students, who include Henry Roediger (this volume) and Robert Sternberg (*The Science of the Mind: 2001 and Beyond*); in a very real sense, all modern cognitive psychologists are students of Endel Tulving.

Name Index

Subject Index